Phenomenal Shakespeare

Blackwell Manifestos

In this new series major critics make timely interventions to address important concepts and subjects, including topics as diverse as, for example: Culture, Race, Religion, History, Society, Geography, Literature, Literary Theory, Shakespeare, Cinema, and Modernism. Written accessibly and with verve and spirit, these books follow no uniform prescription but set out to engage and challenge the broadest range of readers, from undergraduates to postgraduates, university teachers and general readers – all those, in short, interested in ongoing debates and controversies in the humanities and social sciences.

Already Published

The Idea of Culture	Terry Eagleton
The Future of Christianity	Alister E. McGrath
Reading After Theory	Valentine Cunningham
21st-Century Modernism	Marjorie Perloff
The Future of Theory	Jean-Michel Rabaté
True Religion	Graham Ward
Inventing Popular Culture	John Storey
Myths for the Masses	Hanno Hardt
The Future of War	Christopher Coker
The Rhetoric of RHETORIC	Wayne C. Booth
When Faiths Collide	Martin E. Marty
The Future of Environmental Criticism	Lawrence Buell
The Idea of Latin America	Walter D. Mignolo
The Future of Society	William Outhwaite
Provoking Democracy	Caroline Levine
Rescuing the Bible	Roland Boer
Our Victorian Education	Dinah Birch
The Idea of English Ethnicity	Robert Young
Living with Theory	Vincent B. Leitch
Uses of Literature	Rita Felski
Religion and the Human Future	David E. Klemm and William Schweiker
The State of the Novel	Dominic Head
In Defense of Reading	Daniel R. Schwarz
Why Victorian Literature Still Matters	Philip Davis
The Savage Text	Adrian Thatcher
The Myth of Popular Culture	Perry Meisel
Phenomenal Shakespeare	Bruce R. Smith

Phenomenal Shakespeare

Bruce R. Smith

WILEY-BLACKWELL

A John Wiley & Sons, Ltd., Publication

This edition first published 2010
© 2010 Bruce R. Smith

Blackwell Publishing was acquired by John Wiley & Sons in February 2007. Blackwell's publishing program has been merged with Wiley's global Scientific, Technical, and Medical business to form Wiley-Blackwell.

Registered Office
John Wiley & Sons Ltd, The Atrium, Southern Gate, Chichester, West Sussex, PO19 8SQ, United Kingdom

Editorial Offices
350 Main Street, Malden, MA 02148-5020, USA
9600 Garsington Road, Oxford, OX4 2DQ, UK
The Atrium, Southern Gate, Chichester, West Sussex, PO19 8SQ, UK

For details of our global editorial offices, for customer services, and for information about how to apply for permission to reuse the copyright material in this book please see our website at www.wiley.com/wiley-blackwell.

The right of Bruce R. Smith to be identified as the author of this work has been asserted in accordance with the UK Copyright, Designs and Patents Act 1988.

Library of Congress Cataloging-in-Publication Data

Smith, Bruce R., 1946–
    Phenomenal Shakespeare / Bruce R. Smith.
      p. cm. —(Blackwell manifestos)
    Includes bibliographical references and index.
      ISBN 978-0-6312-3548-4 (hardcover : alk. paper)—ISBN 978-0-6312-3549-1 (pbk. : alk. paper)
1. Shakespeare, William, 1564–1616–Criticism and interpretation. I. Title.

    PR2976.S49 2010
    822.3'3—dc22
                                              2009030169

A catalogue record for this book is available from the British Library.

Set in 11.5/13.5pt Bembo by SPi Publisher Services, Pondicherry, India
Printed and bound in Malaysia by Vivar Printing Sdn Bhd

1   2010

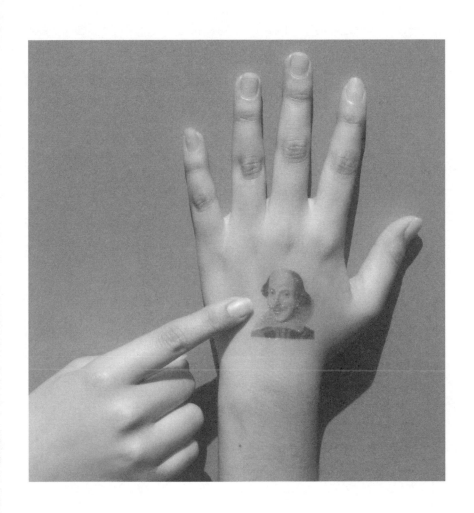

Contents

Acknowledgments   ix

Prologue: The Argument   xi

1   As It Likes You   1

2   How Should One Read a Shakespeare Sonnet?   38

3   Carnal Knowledge   82

4   Touching Moments   132

Epilogue: What Shakespeare Proves   177

Works Cited   187

Picture Credits   197

Index   199

Acknowledgments

The original inspiration for this book was a seminar called "Knowing Bodies: Towards an Historical Phenomenology" that I convened at the 1999 meeting of the Shakespeare Association of America in San Francisco. That 28 people signed up for the seminar, many of them graduate students, made me realize there was a tactic here worth pursuing. For that confirmation and for getting the conversation started in interesting directions I want to thank the participants in the inaugural seminar: Catherine Belling, Gina Bloom, Anston Bosman, Peter Cummings, Will Fisher, William Flesch, Susan Frye, Wes Folkerth, Skiles Howard, Daniel Kulmala, Joan Pong Linton, Cynthia Marshall, Gail Kern Paster, Marie A. Plasse, Martha Ronk, Lauren Shohet, James R. Siemon, Geraldo U. de Sousa, Scott Manning Stevens, Adriane L. Stewart, Ellen Summers, Jesse G. Swan, Joseph M. Tate, James Wells, Suzanne Wofford, Julian Yates, James J. Yoch, and Susan Zimmerman.

The ten years that have intervened between "Knowing Bodies" and *Phenomenal Shakespeare* have allowed me to try out the approach in classes and seminars at Georgetown University, the University of Southern California, and Middlebury College's Bread Loaf School of English. I am grateful to my students for their openness to ways of reading that initially seemed strange, and for their ingenuity, once they had made those ways their own, in prompting me to see, hear, and feel things I would have missed on my own. My ideas were given a hearing at a number of conferences, and I am grateful to the organizers in each case for inviting me: Peter Stallybrass ("Forms of Address," the English Institute, 2006), Lyn Tribble ("Embodying Shakespeare," the

Australia and New Zealand Shakespeare Association, 2008), Heidi Brayman Hackel and Heather James ("Literature Beyond Words," USC-Huntington Early Modern Studies Institute, 2009), Doug Trevor ("Shakespeare's Cruelty," Shakespeare Association of America, 2009), Ross Brown and Andy Lavender ("Theatre Noise," Central School for Speech and Drama, 2009), and Michael Witmore and Will West ("Phenomenal Performances: Getting a Feel for Shakespeare's Theater," Northwestern University, 2009). The generous encouragement, useful references, and difficult questions that I received from my auditors on these occasions are evident in almost every page of this book. A complete list of the people who made suggestions would be very long indeed. I am grateful to all of them.

Phenomenal Shakespeare is a more felicitous affair than it might have been thanks to readings of the penultimate draft by P. A. Skantze and Will West. As readers for the press, both of these individuals knew just where to put pressure (so to speak) on my arguments, and the book is the more robust for their efforts. I am indebted to both of these excitable but exacting readers.

Let me thank finally the people who literally lent me a hand—or two: Ana Karen Campos in the frontispiece, Crescenciano Garcia in Figures 2.1, 2.8, 2.9, 2.10, and 2.11, Rosalind Larry in Figure 3.1, and Joseph Roach in Figure 4.3. The hands in Figure 4.1 and the hand with the stylus in Figure 4.5 are my own.

It is the fashion in books like this one to end by thanking one's family for support over the long haul and to apologize for dishes not washed, hikes not taken, movies not seen. In my case it's not just slackness forgiven for which I am grateful but imagination nurtured. With deep thanks for the nurturing as well as the forgiveness I dedicate *Phenomenal Shakespeare* to my husband Gordon Davis.

B.R.S.
Santa Fe, New Mexico

Prologue: The Argument

That Shakespeare is *PHENOMENAL!* will hardly come as news. If you are reading this book, or only thinking about doing so, you already know that the infant baptized as "*Gulielmus filius Iohannes Shakspere*" in Holy Trinity Church, Stratford-upon-Avon, on April 26, 1564 (let's call him THWS, The Historical William Shakespeare) went on to write a corpus of plays and poems (CWWS, the Collected Works of William Shakespeare) that all foster the illusion of an author thoroughly in control (WSA, William Shakespeare as Author) and that have become a cultural institution (WSCI, William Shakespeare as Cultural Icon) from New York to Beijing and from Reykjavik to Johannesburg.[1] Shakespeare, we can safely say, is a phenomenon as we understand that term today.

[1] The record of THWS's baptism in the registers of Holy Trinity Church— "William, son of John Shakespeare"—is illustrated and discussed in Schoenbaum 1987: 24–6. I use "William Shakespeare as Author" (WSA) to refer to the supposed all-knowing all-controlling mind-in-charge that readers often assume is immanent in a text. WSA should not be confused with The Historical William Shakespeare, who may have entertained thoughts quite different from those registered in the Collected Works of William Shakespeare (CWWS), or with William Shakespeare as Cultural Icon (WSCI), whose identity has changed radically across four centuries. Nor should WSA be confused with the author in Roland Barthes' "Death of the Author" (1968), the author as a fiction that holds together the meanings from diverse sources that make up a text, or the "author function" in Michel Foucault's "What is an Author?" (1969), which exists as a structural principle but not as a guarantor of meaning outside the text. WSA is not a real person but a phenomenon, a by-product of reading a poem or watching a play.

As it happens, "phenomenon" was a word just coming into use during THWS's lifetime, but he was more likely to have read it in a book than to have heard anybody say it aloud. To judge from CWWS, the word did not figure in WSA's active vocabulary. Nonetheless, "phenomenon" was becoming a useful term, and the next-to-earliest instance recorded in the *Oxford English Dictionary* shows why. To say that the sun revolves around the earth, Francis Bacon observes in *The Advancement of Learning*, "is not repugnant to any of the *phenomena*" (Bacon 2000a: 93).[2] It is just repugnant to the demonstrations of geometry. "So the ordinary face and view of experience is many times satisfied by *several* theories and philosophies," Bacon concludes, "whereas to find *the real truth* requireth another manner of severity and attention" (Bacon 2000a: 94, emphases added). Ordinary experience, many theories, one truth: Bacon's three-step program is an inductive process in which theories do not exist apart from ordinary experience any more than truth exists apart from theories. However high he casts his gaze, Bacon's feet remain firmly on the ground. *The Advancement of Learning* was first published in 1605, about the same time WSA was looking towards the heavens in *King Lear*. Bacon, like other writers in English from the seventeenth and eighteenth centuries, reserves the word *phenomena* (always in the plural) specifically for appearances in the sky or the air, which was in fact the original meaning of the phrase τά φαινόμενα in Greek (*OED* 1989: "phenomenon," etymology and 1.b, with citations; Owen 1975: 113–26).[3] A word for these celestial appearances was needed by THWS and his contemporaries for a very good reason: science was increasingly undermining the veracity of what could be experienced firsthand

[2] In all cases, quotations from early modern sources are given in modern spelling and capitalization, but with original punctuation. I do this because most readers of this book will have encountered CWWS in modern spelling. To insist on original spelling for other authors—authors like Bacon, for example—is likely to make them seem quaint and far away.

[3] For elucidating this original usage of the word *phenomena* and for pointing me to Owen's article I am grateful to Lorraine Daston. On the epistemological challenges of "the new philosophy" see Watson 2006: 3–35.

(Watson 2006: 3–35). "The new philosophy," John Donne famously said, "calls all in doubt" (Donne 1978: 27).

In our own age of science and technology, that doubt hangs in the air more heavily than ever. Education in the early twenty-first century involves learning a great many things that you can't actually observe firsthand. From what I have read and been told, I can imagine electrons and neutrons, but I haven't actually seen any. Presumably I could remedy that situation by looking through a strong enough microscope, but even then the scale would be so different—the electrons and neutrons so small and I so large—that my experience would feel secondhand. According to Bacon, the same alienation effect extends to philosophy and the arts. In *The New Organon*, published in Latin 15 years after *The Advancement of Learning*, Bacon repeats his earlier remarks about how things appear in the sky, but he looks down and around to consider how things appear in the world of humankind. Bacon turns attention to the stories we tell ourselves about how things are—or rather about how they *seem* to be. Bacon calls these stories "idols of the theatre":

> For just as several accounts of the heavens can be fashioned from the *phenomena* of the air, so, and much more, various dogmas can be based and constructed upon the phenomena of philosophy. And the stories of this kind of *theatre* have something else in common with the dramatist's theatre, that narratives made up for the stage are neater and more elegant than true stories from history, and are the sort of thing people prefer. (Aphorism 1.62 in Bacon 2000b: 50, emphases original)

A bit later Bacon rephrases the distinction between "phenomena of the air" and "phenomena of philosophy" as a distinction between "nature" and "arts" (Aphorism 1.112 in Bacon 2000b: 87). Phenomena of *philosophy*? Phenomena of *arts*? What can Bacon mean by those terms? Although Bacon is remembered today as an advocate of the scientific method, his insistence on beginning with particulars, with observations, with hands-on experience extends to all forms of thinking. The trouble with "philosophers of the rational type," Bacon says, is that they leap too readily from how things *seem* to how things *are*—or rather to how they *presume* things are. Such hyper-rationalist thinkers "are diverted from experience by the variety of common phenomena, which have not been certainly understood or carefully examined and considered" (Aphorism 62 in Bacon 2000b: 51).

The trouble with theater, according to Bacon, is that the stories enacted there are too simple, too neat, too elegant. They are tidier than the "true stories" of history. (By "history" I take Bacon to mean not just the deeds of kings but human experience in general, human experience in all its teeming and tangled complexity.) Bacon's remedy—in philosophy, as presumably it would be in the theater—is to insist on particulars, even when the temptation is to move on quickly—too quickly—to what THWS, Bacon, and their contemporaries knew as "the argument." In early modern English "argument" could mean subject matter or theme (*OED* 1989: "argument," *n.*, †6) as well as a series of statements in support of a proposition (4) or, more generally, proof or manifestation (1). Arguably, the reason why the CWWS have continued to attract audiences and readers across four centuries is precisely because they are so attentive to particulars at the expense of argument. Take, for example, the shocking submission of Kate at the end of *The Taming of the Shrew*. Or the new Henry V's brusque rejection of Falstaff. Or Shylock's refusal to remain a comic stereotype. Or Isabella's wordless silence at the end of *Measure for Measure*. Or Macbeth's missing the point of his existential situation in his "Tomorrow and tomorrow and tomorrow" soliloquy. Or the way Cleopatra gets out of hand in a play whose argument, in the source, is all about Antony. Or Bertram's unbelievably lame last words in *All's Well That Ends Well*. Or the death of Cordelia. Or the conspicuous absence of contrition on the part of Antonio and Sebastian, the only two characters in *The Tempest* whom the audience actually sees trying to commit murder. These are not the fictions of an imagination too quickly prone to argument in the sense of support for a proposition.

Shakespeare's critics have not always read, watched, and listened in kind. Handed a subject or theme, many readers—perhaps most—want a proposition. If an obvious one doesn't seem to be there already, they supply it. Watchers and listeners in the theater may be more open-minded, but usually the director has chosen the proposition in advance.

Isabella doesn't have to stand there in silence when the Duke announces that he is going to marry her; she takes off her nun's habit and grasps his hand or she hesitates and gives her brother Claudio a significant look or she turns around and walks off the stage. Each of these directorial choices advances an argument: the details of the production have been lined up in support of a proposition, whether it be "*Pater* knows best" or "This play is really about incest" or "Shakespeare was a feminist." A production review or an academic article will be even more adamant in its demonstration of whatever proposition the author has decided to put forward. An argument, in its root sense of making something manifest, need not be so dogmatic. There are many possible reasons, plausible but contradictory, why Isabella should be scripted to say nothing. After so much talking on the part of the Duke, there may be something in the silence itself—or, more to the point, in the listeners' experience of that silence.

The argument in the pages to follow is "argument" in the most general sense of that word, argument as manifestation, evidence, token, proof. The first of these words begins the book; the fourth ends it. "Blackwell Manifestos": the series title and the description of the series as "timely interventions to address important concepts and subjects" may suggest a need for hammer, nails, and a cathedral door. One thinks of Wyndham Lewis's "Long Live the Vortex!" in issue one of *BLAST* (1914) or the Nicene Creed (CE 325) or Marx and Engels's *Manifest der Kommunistischen Partei* (1848) or Donna Haraway's "A Cyborg Manifesto" (1991) or the Declaration of the United Nations Conference on the Human Environment (1972) or Antonin Artaud's two "*Manifestes du Théâtre de la Cruauté*" (1931–2). To judge from all the titles listed at www.manifestos.net/, a need for manifestos has increased exponentially since the advent of the internet. So here is one more.

Just what is being manifested in these pages? Three things. First and most important are some particulars about CWWS that tend to get overlooked in the rush to propositions. I shall be paying attention, just as Bacon advises, to "the variety of common phenomena, which have not been certainly understood or carefully examined and considered." The emphasis will fall on common experiences: emotions, reading, watching and listening in the theater. Also to be made manifest are the goals, assumptions, and working methods of a new critical approach that has come to be known as "historical phenomenology." Inner gestures that inspire speech, the kinesthetic knowledge that comes with reading, and the pleasurable twinge of watching and hearing characters suffer on stage are difficult to talk about, not only because bodily sensations do not have a transparent relationship to language but because our keen awareness of cultural differences makes the project of talking about them look presumptuous if not impossible. Just because you or I find the thought of sex with animals distasteful (you *do*, don't you?) doesn't mean that THWS and his original readers did. *Phenomenal Shakespeare* offers evidence that subjective experience of poems and plays written 400 years ago can be approached from the outside in culturally specific and politically aware terms. *Approached.* We may not be able, in Bacon's terms, to understand such experience in the literal sense of standing under or within it, but we can at least carefully examine and consider it. In the process a third thing should be made manifest: why "Shakespeare"—THWS, CWWS, WSA, and WSCI, all four—remains phenomenal in our own time and place. By recovering the felt experience of "Shakespeare" in the past we may be able to recover the felt experience of "Shakespeare" that often goes missing in the here-and-now, at least in books like this one.

The plan of this book is simple: a how-to-do-it chapter is followed by three examples and a short conclusion. Chapter 1, "As It Likes You," lays out the principles and procedures of historical phenomenology as a way of reading and thinking, with an emphasis on the "likes." Three examples of such reading, thinking, and liking are put forward in the next three chapters, one on each of the genres in which THWS exercised his imagination. Chapter 2, "How Should One Read a Shakespeare Sonnet?" uses a single sonnet to explore two very different models of language and to argue (in sense number two) that the time has come to reconsider Saussure's model in light of William James's and Lev Vygotsky's model. Chapter 3, "Carnal Knowledge," returns *Venus and Adonis* to the ambient circumstances in which the narrative poem was originally read. In the process two kinds of sexual knowledge are contrasted: the law's outside-looking-in and the reader's inside-looking-out. Chapter 4, "Touching Moments," trains attention to the nexus between language and gesture in theatrical performance, with particular attention to scenes of cruelty in *King Lear*. A brief summation considers "What Shakespeare Proves."

In several senses, the book you are holding in your hands is a handbook. It provides a manual for how to do historical phenomenology. But it is also a book about hands. The human hand—with its carpus (wrist), metacarpus (palm), and digits (fingers)—figures in each of the book's chapters. The notion that there is such a thing as "the Renaissance hand" will come as no surprise to readers of Katherine Rowe's essay "God's handy worke" in *The Body in Parts* (Mazzio and Hillman 1997: 285–312) and of the essays in *Sensible Touch*, where the hand functions again and again as synecdoche not only for the sense of touch that pervades the entire human body but for human agency in doing things and saying things (Harvey 2003: 10–11, 242, 247–8). But the hand fits the task here in a more fundamental way. Aristotle's treatise "On the Soul" laid out for THWS and his contemporaries the ground plan of the psychology they used to explain what was happening when they sensed things outside their bodies, felt those things in their hearts, thought about those sensed and felt things with their minds, and acted upon those sensed, felt, and thought-about things with arms and hands. According to Aristotle, it is not just language that distinguishes humankind from other animals but an exquisite sense of touch. (Daniel Heller-Roazen's book *The Inner Touch: Archeology of a Sensation* narrates the afterlife of Aristotle's contention.) "While in respect of all the other senses we fall below many species of animals," Aristotle observes, "in respect of touch we far excel all other species in exactness of discrimination. That is why man is the most intelligent of all animals" (421a23–6 in Aristotle 1984: 1:670). A chapter on touch, in fact, concludes Aristotle's entire treatise, just as it concludes this handbook.

The argument of *Phenomenal Shakespeare* might better be posed as a question instead of a statement: what's so touching about "Shakespeare"? To get us started, take a second look at the frontispiece to this book. It illustrates a paradox that fascinated one of the twentieth century's great phenomenologists, Maurice Merleau-Ponty, in his last years. When you touch yourself, you trouble the usual distinction between subject (the toucher) and object (the touched). In Merleau-Ponty's words, "the touching is never exactly the touched" (quoted in Heller-Roazen 2007: 295). What comes in between the toucher and the touched remains a mystery to the rational mind—indeed, it defies the rational mind. Merleau-Ponty calls that something-in-between "the untouchable." Neither the rational mind nor the feeling body can get at it; neither the rational mind nor the feeling body can account for the whole, for the phenomenon. The situation is something like the familiar visual puzzle presented by the vase that can also be read as the profiles of two faces. Is that a vase I'm seeing there? Or is it two faces? The rational mind wants it to be one or the other, but "it" refuses to stay stable, now presenting itself to my mind as a vase, now as two faces. Such is the relationship between readers, audiences, and thinkers-about-things on the one hand and the poems and plays they read, watch, listen to, and think about on the other. What is the toucher and what is the touched? You. What is touching about "Shakespeare"? The in-between.

1

As It Likes You

If you're under the age of 40 (maybe even if you're older) you already *do* phenomenology when you tell a friend what a third party said. Consider how you might report what you heard Jaques say to the deer your friends had wounded in comparison with how the First and the Second Lord tell the story to Duke Senior in Act Two, scene one of *As You Like It*:

> DUKE SENIOR   But what said Jaques?
>   Did he not moralize this spectacle?
> FIRST LORD   O yes, into a thousand similes.
>   First, for his weeping into the needless stream;
>   "Poor deer," quoth he, "thou mak'st a testament
>   As worldlings do, giving thy sum of more
>   To that which had too much." Then being there alone,
>   Left and abandoned of his velvet friend,
>   "'Tis right," quoth he, "thus misery doth part
>   The flux of company."[1]

If the same scene were being performed in today's idiom, the First Lord's report might go more like this: "He was ... like, deer, you write

---

[1] *As You Like It*, 2.1.44–52. Unless otherwise indicated, all quotations from Shakespeare's plays and poems are taken from the Oxford Shakespeare, 2nd edn. (Shakespeare 2005), and are cited in the text by act, scene, and line numbers in the case of the plays, by sonnet number and line numbers in the case of the sonnets, and by line numbers in the case of the narrative poems.

your will just like people do" and "He was … like, right, misery takes care of too much company." "Like": apparently Jaques' thousand similes aren't enough. But "like" in these updated speeches is not a preposition like those you find in a simile. Instead, it functions as a "quotative" (Buchstaller 2003 and 2001), like the First Lord's "quoth."

The standard distinction between direct and indirect quotation fails to do justice to the range of situations in which people tell stories and quote other people. Instead of a binary (direct versus indirect quotation) we should imagine a continuum of performance possibilities, with mimesis (impersonation) at one end and diegesis (narration) at the other. Along this continuum Isabelle Buchstaller has ranged currently used quotatives according to how much scope they give for involvement on the part of the teller:

mimesis ⟵――――――――――――――――――⟶ diegesis
"said"　　　"went"　　　"was like"　　　"thought"

"Said" at one end of the continuum implies direct quotation, reportage of a speaker's actual words, while "thought" at the other end turns the reportage inward, to what the reporter felt when the other person was speaking. Somewhere in the middle are "went" and "was like." They bring the past event into visceral presence, inspiring sound effects and gestures that perform the reporter's feelings. In Buchstaller's summation,

> Using the new quotatives, speakers quote as if they were reproducing a real speech act but package it in a more expressive form, in sound and voice effects. This suggests that speakers take advantage of the full creative possibilities the language offers them in the new quotatives: a stream of consciousness-like displayal of inner states and attitudes realized in vivid, immediate speech. (Buchstaller 2001: 14)

"Like" affords these possibilities to today's speakers for the same reason it recommended itself to The Historical William Shakespeare (THWS) and the denizens of the Forest of Arden. "Like" does not purport to be or not to be: it compares and approximates, it blurs the boundary between inner and outer, it puts objects into subjects and subjects into objects.

In that respect, "like" is phenomenal. "Like" implicates *you* in *it*.

∶

Take the epilogue to *As You Like It*. The actor who has been playing Rosalind (in the original 1599 production the actor was a boy and sometimes these days is a man) moves freely back and forth, left and right along Buchstaller's continuum between mimesis and diegesis. Gender critics and queer critics in the late twentieth century have made this speech as famous as Hamlet's "To be or not to be" was in the nineteenth century. The blurring of distinctions with respect to gender, surely familiar already to readers of this book, also involves a blurring of distinctions with respect to pronouns, to what it pleases us to call "subject positions." "It is not the fashion to see the lady the epilogue," begins he/she/he (Ep. 1–2). So whom do we see speaking here—Rosalind as "the lady" or the actor who has played the role (which has included taking on the guise of Jupiter's sex toy Ganymede) or both? "What a case am I in then," exclaims the speaker, making some very nice puns on "case" as happenstance, state of affairs, body, suit of clothes, and (for the Latin-wise among the hearers) syntactical position as subject or object (*OED* 1989: "case," *n.*¹, I.†1.a, I.4.b; "case," *n.*², 3.a, †4.b; "case," *n.*¹, I.9.a).

"What a case am *I* in then": the confusion here is not just between *she* and *he*, between "Rosalind" and boy actor, but between *he/she/he* on the one hand and *I* on the other, between the character in the fiction being stashed away over there, in the space behind the speaker, and the person standing and speaking here toward the front of the stage. He/she/he solves this dilemma of first-person identity by turning to *you*, the people out there who are looking at *him/her/him* in third person, singular in *his/her/his* case and plural in *theirs*. "My way is to conjure you" (Ep. 10–11)—like, say, a judge administering an oath or a magician calling up the devil—and he/she/he begins with the women. "I charge you, O women, for the love you bear to men, to like as much of this play as please you" (Ep. 11–13)—a timely

3

reminder of the play's title. "And I charge you, O men, for the love you bear to women—as I perceive by your simpering none of you hates them—that between you and the women the play may please" (Ep. 13–16). The play on "play" was calculated to give apoplexy to the likes of Phillip Stubbes, who was sure that the main effect of play-watching was sexual arousal and that after the performance "every mate sorts to his mate, everyone brings another homeward of their way very friendly and in their secret conclaves (covertly) they play the sodomites, or worse" (Stubbes 1877–9: 22). With these verbal gestures directed toward *you*, the speaker breaks up the third-personhood of the play—*I* watching *them*, each speaking as an *I* to *me* and *us*—if that pure third-personhood ever really existed.

In the original production, as now, the epilogue's gestures cannot be only verbal. At the very least, the actor breaks away from the dancing cast ("Play, music," Duke Senior has commanded, "and you brides and bridegrooms all,/ With measure heaped in joy to th' measures fall" [5.4.176–7]) and moves toward the audience. If we take Duke Senior's reference to "rustic revelry" (5.4.175) at face value and imagine that the measures were hand-in-hand round-dances and not the bodily detached look-at-me dances favored at court (Howard 1998: 69–92), the actor would have to break hands with his fellows. What would he/she/he do with arms and hands then? Perhaps he/she/he would use them to sweep the house in a broad gesture of inclusion, but more certainly he/she/he would *point*, first to himself/herself/himself ("What a case am I in then …"), then to the women ("I charge you, O women …"), then to the men ("And I charge you, O men …").

Verbally at least, actor/Rosalind/Ganymede doesn't just point but comes up close, at least to the men in the audience, near enough to "kiss as many of you as had beards that pleased me, complexions that liked me, and breaths that I defied not" (Ep. 18–20). One would have thought such a thing impossible until the invention of the motion-picture camera and celluloid film. In movies, thanks to the camera with its close-up lens, we get much closer to actors' faces than we ever do to faces in real life except for whispering, kissing, and/or having sex. In moments like the epilogue to *As You Like It* we can get just as close to the actors as in films, not physically but psychologically. But there is an if-clause that doesn't apply to films: in the theater, we have to lend a hand. That is just what the epilogue, in the final lines, asks us to do: "And I am sure, as many as have good beards, or good faces, or sweet breaths will for my kind offer, when I make curtsy, bid me farewell" (Ep. 19–21). By clapping our hands we agree to be conjured. Indeed, we join in the conjuring. We join the round-dance. We revel in the phenomenon. We like *it*; it likes *us*.

:

Curiously, many academic critics since the 1970s have refused the epilogue's kind offer. They *don't* like it. They won't clap, much less kiss. I say "curiously," because *As You Like It* would seem to deconstruct norms of gender and sexuality in ways that are liberating for all concerned. At least I have thought so since seeing the National Theatre's all-male production, directed by Clifford Williams, at Wolf Trap Farm Park outside Washington, DC, in September 1974—this, despite *Time* magazine's assurance that what audiences witnessed in the original London production, seven years earlier, was "a remarkably chaste performance free of disturbing homoerotic overtones" (*Time* 1967). On the whole, though, academic critics since the 1970s have refused to be taken in by the sights and sounds of *As You Like It* in performance. Instead, as if acting on Bacon's distinction between *phenomena* and "the real truth" in *The Advancement of Learning*, they have adopted "another manner of severity and attention" and tried earnestly to see beyond appearances to realities (Bacon 2000a: 93).

In the case of *As You Like It*, the realities are partly historical and partly contemporary: patriarchy (Rosalind may work wonders in the woods, but in the end Duke Senior is restored as king on the mountain), land enclosures (thanks to daddy's money, Celia can buy Corin's master's sheepcote and turn it into a precursor of Marie Antoinette's Petit Hameau), and heteronormativity (at the very moment Hymen descends to bless Orlando's marriage to Rosalind, "Ganymede" conveniently disappears, ascending back to Olympus as it were, perhaps giving Hymen a high five as they pass in the air). What happens onstage in *As You Like It*—the witty speeches, the disguises, the gestures, the songs, the dancing, the playful epilogue—may not be repugnant to the phenomena, but they *are* repugnant to certain political preoccupations. I happen to share those political convictions—I'm against patriarchy, capitalist greed, and compulsory heterosexuality—but in the case of *As You Like It* I find "reality"—or what critics have regarded as reality—to be near-sighted, ear-plugged, and hand-cuffed.

Theatrical phenomena versus social facts, appearance versus reality, imaginative joy versus rational analysis: *must* we choose between these binaries? Why can't we embrace both? After all, aren't binaries supposed to be arbitrary? Why can't one hold fast to one's political commitments and revel in the play's phenomena at the same time? The problem is not really politics—after all, people who are passionate about their politics are usually passionate about art that affirms their politics—but the requirement to be cool, rational, and objective when faced with works of art. For that, we can carry blame back to the likes of Descartes, to the world as *he* liked it. About passion Descartes seems to have been of a mixed mind—he carried on a vigorous correspondence about the passions with James I's daughter Elizabeth, he dedicated to her his treatise on *The Passions of the Soul of Man* (1649), he recognized passions as "thoughts"—but on the whole Descartes preferred that objects of knowledge be "not merely clear but also distinct" (Descartes 1988: 174). Passions do not make the grade. Descartes' epistemological ideals were taken up by Enlightenment thinkers like Locke and Hume and were resisted by Romantic apologists like Shelley and Hegel, but the ologification and ographification of the humanities and social sciences in the nineteenth and early twentieth centuries (philology, psychology, aesthiology, historiography, semiology, narratology were all invented then) meant that Descartes' prescriptions about the proper objects of knowledge—that they be clear and distinct—ultimately carried the day.

Hence structuralism, with its search for the principles that underlie the superficial distractions of myths and stories. Hence Saussure's linguistics, with its attention to the formal system of language rather than the vagaries of individual utterances. Hence deconstruction, with its insistence on the arbitrariness of all forms of difference-marking. Hence Lacanian psychoanalytical theory, with its grounding of personal identity and its discontents in language. Hence political criticism, with its application of these axioms to gender, sexuality, race, ethnicity, and nationhood. Like Freud's unconscious, Jameson's "*political* unconscious" is, literally, undeniable. If you try to deny it, in that very act you are affirming its existence. All true enough—but not true through and through. What happens to sensations, feelings, emotions, aesthetic pleasure? To acknowledge these unclear and indistinct matters becomes an act of "false consciousness."

At least three reasons explain the distrust. For a start, aesthetics had been a primary concern of New Criticism, which held the field before post-structuralism. If critical practice proceeds as a dialectic, then post-structuralism figures as the antithesis to New Criticism's thesis. It is not surprising that both of New Criticism's main concerns, structural form and aesthetics, should be targets for attack under the regime of post-structuralism. A second reason is the personal nature of sensations and feelings. They are the possessions of individuals, bourgeois or otherwise, and hence cannot be generalized in the way Marx's base and superstructure can or Saussure's $s \neq S$ or Lacan's imaginary, symbolic, and real orders. Those apply to everyone; pity and fear are mine or yours. Perhaps the most telling reason for writing off sensations and feelings, however, is that they cannot be written. In Saussure's linguistics and in the critical models it has inspired, sensations and feelings are incidental to the main business at hand, on the order of pitch and rhythm in speech. What *really* matters is not individual variations in pitch and rhythm but the fundamental principles that govern all utterances. The critical dialectic that produced post-structuralism still lacks a coherent synthesis. An "affective turn"—a counterturn to the "linguistic turn" of the 1960s and 1970s—has been announced in the social sciences (Clough 2007: 1–33) and in performance studies (Massumi 2002: 23–45). *Phenomenal Shakespeare* takes its place in this counterturn. After the thesis of New Criticism and the antithesis of post-structuralism a synthesis can be found in phenomenology, specifically in the operations of "like."

⁝

The title *As You Like It* may have suggested itself to William Shakespeare as Author (WSA) through a line in Thomas Lodge's *Rosalynde* (1590),

7

WSA's primary source for the play's plot and many of its speeches. Striding into the reader's space in the brusque guise of "a soldier, and a sailor," Lodge in his epistle "To the Gentlemen Readers" takes the sixteenth-century author's usual stance toward critics: "If you like it, so." And if you don't, you're "a squint-eyed ass" (Bullough 1958: 160). "It" in WSA's title has received its fair share of critical commentary. (Does "it" = copulation?) "Like" we tend to take at face value, as a transitive verb, "to find agreeable or congenial" (*OED* 1989: "like," *v.*, 6.a). Certainly the play is full of that kind of liking. "I like this place," Celia says of the Forest of Arden (2.4.93). "And how like you this shepherd's life?" Corin asks Touchstone (3.2.11). It was by feigning a woman's changing passions, Ganymede tells Orlando, that he once cured a friend's love-sickness: he "would now like him, now loathe him; then entertain him, then forswear him; now weep for him, then spit at him" (3.2.400–2). In the epilogue the women are bidden "to like as much of this play as please you" (Ep. 12–13).

An exchange among Jaques, Duke Senior, and Touchstone reveals, though, how slippery "like" can be. Jaques is introducing the "motley-minded" Touchstone to the duke. The man swears that he has been a courtier, Jaques tells the duke, and to help prove that is so Touchstone volunteers, "I have had four quarrels, and like to have fought one" (5.4.46–7). Fortunately that one was prevented when the duelists met and discovered that the quarrel was based on "the seventh cause," i.e., a lie seven times removed from the original insult. Delighted with Touchstone's gift of separating words from their usual meanings, Jaques exclaims to the duke, "Good my lord, like this fellow." "I like him very well" is Duke Senior's reply (5.4.51–3). To "like" to have fought a duel is to like in a different way than Jaques and the duke "like" the motley-minded gentleman's wit. In a similar way Celia reminds Rosalind, "You know my father has no child but I, nor none is like to have" (1.2.16–17), and Touchstone says of the village priest, "he is not like to marry me well" (3.3.82–3).

In being "like" to have fought a duel, Touchstone "seems ready to," "pretends to," "looks as if he's near to" fighting a duel—a free-standing, intransitive state of affairs syntactically speaking (*OED* 1989: "like," *v.*, 2.2), but a dynamic, conjunctive state of affairs rhetorically speaking.

In the case of the village priest, "like" is an adjective, but it is used predicatively, to conjoin "now" and "the future" (*OED* 1989: "like," *a., adv.* [*conj.*] and *n.*², A.7). In its capacity to put two things together, "like" provides the basis not just for similes (where the "like" or "as" is explicit) but metaphors (where they are implied). To liken, to make alike, to make like one is something or is about to perform something: these actions are, after all, what similes and metaphors *do*. Duke Senior in his 2.1 pep speech to his co-mates and brothers in exile offers an example that is altogether characteristic of *As You Like It*. The duke reveals his route to the stage of the Globe via Lodge (the subtitle to *Rosalynde* is *Euphues' Golden Legacy*) and John Lyly (his *Euphues* and *Euphues His England* made verbal excess fashionable in the early 1590s) when he far-fetches a comparison from natural history to justify his current state of rustication: "Sweet are the uses of adversity/ Which, like the toad, ugly and venomous,/ Wears yet a precious jewel in his head" (2.1.12–14).

Earlier Charles the wrestler has performed a similar rhetorical feat of conjoining the human and the natural, the fictitious and the historical, when he reports that Duke Senior "and a many merry men with him" are in the Forest of Arden, where "they live like the old Robin Hood of England" (1.1.109–11). What is the syntactical function of "like" here? An adverb modifying "live"? A conjunction that coordinates "they live" with "[as] the old Robin Hood of England [lived]"? A preposition that relates "they" to "Robin Hood" via an implicit "like to"? The *Oxford English Dictionary* (*OED* 1989: "like," *a., adv.* [*conj.*], and *n.*²) recognizes all these syntactical slippages whereby what is technically an adjective or an adverb can function like a "quasi-*prep*[osition]" (B.1–5) and like a conjunction (B.6). The noun form of "like" (C.1–3) shapes up as the substantive result of these actions of conjoining A with B, of conjoining Duke Senior and his many merry men in fictitious present-tense France with "old" Robin Hood in historical past-tense England. The dynamic quality of "like," even as a noun, is suggested by several exchanges between Celia and Rosalind in 1.3. Adjectival, adverbial, prepositional, and conjunctive qualities converge in the peroration to the protest Celia lodges against her father's decision to exile Rosalind: "And wheresoe'er we went, like

9

Juno's swans/ Still we went coupled and inseparable" (1.3.74–5). To effect their escape together, Celia resolves to put on poor and mean attire and besmirch her face with umber. "The like do you," she urges Rosalind (1.3.113). Even better, Rosalind exclaims, she will "suit me all points like a man," complete with curtal axe and boar spear (1.3.115–17).

The refusal of "like" to stay fixed as a part of speech is probably to be explained by the word's origins as "body," "shape," "form" (*OED* 1989: "like," *a.*, *adv.* [*conj.*], and *n.*², etymology), an entity that is always in motion. The Old English word *lich* survived into the late fifteenth century to refer to a living body, especially the trunk as opposed to the limbs, as well as to a corpse. The word in the latter sense was resurrected by medievalizing English writers of the nineteenth century (*OED* 1989: "lich," 2) and survives still in the most common German word for corpse, *Leich*. Beneath all the modern uses of "like"—as verb, adjective, adverb, conjunction, quasi-preposition, and various combinations of the five—is the fundamental idea of *con*+formity, of fitting something *with* the body or fitting the body *with* that something. "I like this place": Celia perceives and expresses a certain relationship, a harmony, a conformity, between her body and the Forest of Arden. In all its forms, "like" is like that. With respect to sentences, "like" challenges the logic of syntax. With respect to fiction-making in general, "like" points up the fiction's status as a copy, a simulacrum, a mimesis of something that is not itself. With respect to drama in particular, "like" connects the pretending actor with the imagining spectator/listener. "I am like …" becomes "this looks like …," "this sounds like …," "this feels like …." *As You Like It*: the first word in the title sets up these dynamics.

With respect to epistemology, "like" insinuates a way of knowing that connects subject and object via the subject's body. That reciprocity is registered in the palindrome of "I like it" and "It likes me." The second form, now obsolete in standard English, is actually the older (*OED* 1989: "like," *v.*¹, etymology). "Like" functions in this case as an intransitive verb. "It" is doing the acting but has no direct object. "I" sneak into the proposition as it were by the side door, as "me," as the beneficiary or indirect object of the action being performed by "it."

Instead of observer → observed we get observed → observer. The first formulation, with "I" as the subject, "like" as a transitive verb, and "it" as the object, is now the more familiar, probably because it better fits our post-Cartesian epistemology in which the observer is very much in charge. "I like it" and "It likes me": the two phrases may seem to amount to the same thing, but the shift in emphasis from "I" to "it" should throw us off balance. The chiasmus challenges us to reconsider the linear subject → object relationship we take for granted and to rethink it in dynamic reciprocal terms. Instead of making a distinction between subject and object, "like" sets up an analogy. Perhaps, then, the best notation would be subject:object::object:subject. What Touchstone says about "if" (5.4.100–1) is no less true about "like": much virtue in "like."

:

Phenomenology as a school of philosophy favors *like*, not *is*. That difference becomes apparent when we compare three primal scenes of observation—one in Bacon, one in Descartes, and one in Husserl— and investigate which is closest to *As You Like It*.

In *The Advancement of Learning* Bacon may distinguish *phenomena* from geometrical demonstration, but he acknowledges "the ordinary face and view of experience" as the starting place and in so doing acknowledges the situatedness of the observer. Advancement in learning depends on the observer's moving forward in a deliberate, disciplined, and thorough way from direct observation to hypotheses to general principles. But firsthand experience is the starting point. The 182 aphorisms of *The New Organon* ("the new instrument" might be a more idiomatic translation of Bacon's Latin title *Novum Organum*) chart the way forward. "There are, and can be, only two ways to investigate and discover truth," Bacon declares in Book One, axiom 19. The first way—the erroneous way—"leaps from sense and particulars to the most general axioms" and then, from that seemingly secure position, backtracks to consider intermediate axioms, explanations that properly belong in between particulars and abstract principles. The method that Bacon advocates begins in the same place, with

11

sense and particulars, but rises "in a gradual and unbroken ascent to arrive at last at the most general axioms" (Bacon 2000b: 36). Abstract principles stay grounded in common experience.

For the fourth edition (1640) of *The Advancement of Learning*, expanded from two books to nine and translated into Latin, the engraver William Marshall, perhaps acting on instructions from Bacon's literary executor William Rowley, supplied both a frontispiece showing Bacon sitting in his study and an engraved title page laying out Bacon's program of observation. (See Figure 1.1.) The scene in the study is a posthumous confection based on a 1626 head-and-shoulders likeness engraved by Simon de Passe, but Bacon's posture and his accoutrements capture the essence of his method. Seated in a study bare of any objects but a drapery, a few books, and writing tools, Bacon stares out at the world (and the viewer) with frank intensity. The drapery, a standard prop in representations of scholars' studies, can be associated with revelations, as it is in Prospero's study in *The Tempest*, Act Five (Smith 2010). The books in this case are not tomes by recognized authorities but the very books that the sitter is in the process of writing as he looks out so intently. The book on the desk is *The Great Instauration*, the first part of which the reader of *The Advancement of Learning* actually holds in hand. On the title page itself light raking the objects from the left invites the viewer to apprehend a light side (left) and a dark side (right). Lined up top to bottom on the left are the "*Mundus Visibilis*" (the visible world) realized as a terrestrial globe, a sun face, and a monument featuring an obelisk inscribed "*Oxonium*" (Oxford) and "*Moniti Scientiae*" ("Admonitions to Science") resting on a base adorned with Oxford University's coat of arms, a stack of three of Bacon's scientific books, and a delta inscribed with History-Poetry-Philosophy along the outer edge and Memory-Imagination-Reason within. On the right, again reading from top to bottom, are the "*Mundus Intellectualis*" ("World of the Mind") realized as a globe of the three-quarters moon, the face of a quarter moon (with the light coming from the wrong side), and a monument featuring an obelisk inscribed "*Cantabrigia*" ("Cambridge") and "*Meliora Philosophiae*" ("Betterments to Philosophy") resting on a base adorned with Cambridge University's coat of arms, a stack of three of Bacon's legal books, and a delta inscribed with Natural-Human-Divine along the outer edge and Nature-Man-God within. (The association of Cambridge with divinity might be expected, given the university's reputation for religious controversy in the earlier seventeenth century.) That the world of the mind is cast in shadow should come as no surprise in a book that attacks "too great a reverence, and a kind of adoration of the mind and understanding of man: by means whereof, men have withdrawn themselves too much from the contemplation of Nature, and the observations of experience and have tumbled up and down in their own reason and conceits" (Bacon 2000a: 30). To ascertain truth, the shadowy intellect needs the bright world of appearances. At the top, in the title page's most striking detail, the World of the Mind shakes hands with the Visible World beneath a motto reading *"Ratione et experientia foederantur"* ("They are allied by reason and experience").

Included in the situatedness of the observer in Bacon's scheme are the *feelings* of the observer in the face of what he or she sees. Lorraine Daston and Peter Galison in their history of *Objectivity* point out how Bacon and other early scientists were attracted, not to the typical specimens and processes that claim the attention of modern science, but to the odd, the strange, and the monstrous (Daston and Galison 2007: 67). What interests Bacon in *Silva Silvarum, or A Natural History* (1627 and later editions) are phenomena that, if they were physical objects, might be collected in a Renaissance "Wonder Cabinet" and be responded to accordingly. *Silva Silvarum* contains 1,000 numbered "experiments," most of which are closer to what we would call "experiences," lively descriptions of this, that, and the other, along with reasoned explanations and, sometimes but not always, instructions for how to prove those explanations for yourself. There is a playful spirit about the whole enterprise, and affects are as present as effects. Take, for example, number 236, the first of several "Experiments in Consort touching the Imitation of Sounds." Speech sounds are so "curious and exquisite," Bacon observes, that it takes a long time and many trials for a child to learn to speak. "But all this dischargeth not the wonder": so hard is speech acquisition that you might think it happens—"exceeding strange" as the possibility may seem—through some kind of transfer

Figure 1.1 Francis Bacon, *The Advancement of Learning* (1640), frontispiece and title page engraved by William Marshall. Left: Bacon in his study. Right: the Visible World and the World of the Mind shake hands.

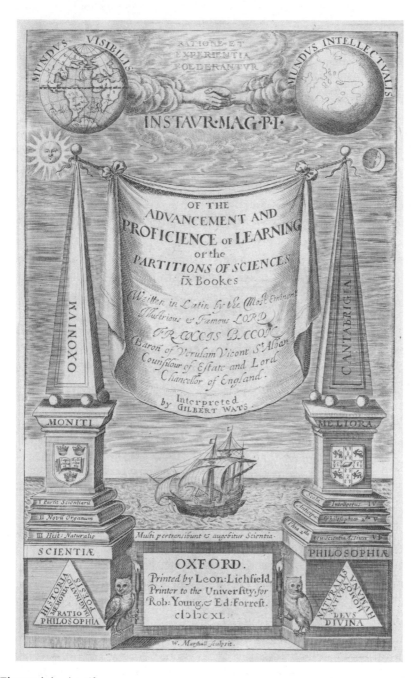

Figure 1.1 (*cont'd*)

15

of "spirits" from teacher to student (Bacon 1627: sig. I4v). A later series of experiments (numbers 904–11) argues that this is exactly what happens: "All operations by transmission of Spirits, and imagination have this; that they work at distance, and not at touch" (sig. II2). Wonder, Bacon says in still another experiment, touches off astonishment, which is occasioned by "the fixing of the mind upon one object of cogitation, whereby it doth not spatiate and transcur, as it useth" (sig. AA5v). That is to say, the mind, instead of moving from object to object as it usually does, becomes transfixed by a single object. The cause of that arrested movement is astonishment, and it has visceral effects: "an immoveable posture of the body; casting up of the eyes to heaven; and lifting up of the hands" (sig. AA5v). The scene of observation implied by *Silva Silvarum* is crowded with objects, playful, full of feeling, engagingly gregarious. Bacon welcomes wanderers among the thousand trees in his *Silva* (literally, "forest").

Descartes' scene of observation is lonelier, at least to start with. Descartes begins his *Meditations on First Philosophy* (published in Latin in 1641, a year after the expanded Latin edition of Bacon's *The Advancement of Learning*) just as Bacon does, with sense and particulars:

> although the senses occasionally deceive us with respect to objects which are very small or in the distance, there are many other beliefs about which doubt is quite impossible, even though they are derived from the senses—for example, that I am here, sitting by the fire, wearing a winter dressing-gown, holding this piece of paper in my hands, and so on. Again, how could it be denied that these hands or this whole body are mine? (*Meditations* VII.18 in Descartes 1988: 76–7)

There, however, Descartes parts company with Bacon. Where Bacon immediately turns outward toward the phenomena of the world, Descartes turns inward to consider the thinking observer—namely, himself. The six "meditations" are just that: six disciplined first-person exercises in which Descartes takes stock of his own mind. Famously, what Descartes discovers in the course of this inventory are two clear and distinct thoughts: (1) I exist because I think ("my essence consists solely in the fact that I am a thinking thing" [VII.78]);

and (2) I can think my body but my body can't think me ("I have a distinct idea of body, in so far as this is simply an extended, non-thinking thing" [VII.78]).

With respect to the world outside the mind (including the body itself) these two thoughts have had profound implications—and not only for Descartes personally. Instructed by Descartes, thinkers from Locke to Derrida have considered some thoughts more worth thinking than others. Descartes may recognize that "thought" (defined in the *Meditations* as "everything that is within us in such a way that we are immediately aware of it" [VII.160]) includes sensations, imaginings, emotions, and acts of will as well as intellection, but only one category of thought constitutes truth: perceptions that are "clear" and "distinct." Over and over in the *Meditations* Descartes uses these two criteria as he makes his way forward. In *Principles of Philosophy*, published three years later, he gives these terms precise definitions: "I call a perception 'clear' when it is present and accessible to the attentive mind .... I call a perception 'distinct' if, as well as being clear, it is so sharply separated from all other perceptions that it contains within itself only what is clear" (no. 45 in Descartes 1988: 174–5).

The trouble with sensations, imaginings, emotions, and acts of will is that, as thoughts, they are *not* clear and distinct. Quite the contrary. The same holds true for the perceived properties of all material things, including the human body. Only a few qualities—size, extension, shape, position, motion, substance, duration, and number—can Descartes perceive clearly and distinctly. And even these can change, as when the solid piece of wax he holds in his hands melts when he places it near the fire. As for color, sound, smell, taste, and tactility, "I think of these only in a very confused and obscure way, to the extent that I do not even know whether they are true or false, that is, whether the ideas I have of them are ideas of real things, or of non-things" (*Meditations* VII.43 in Descartes 1988: 92). The best way to know size, extension, shape, position, etc. is not through the senses but through geometrical diagrams of the sort Descartes includes in his *Optics*, published along with his *Discourse on Method* in 1637. Figure 1.2 shows how the relationship between viewer's eye and objects of vision can be plotted geometrically, via a series of triangles.

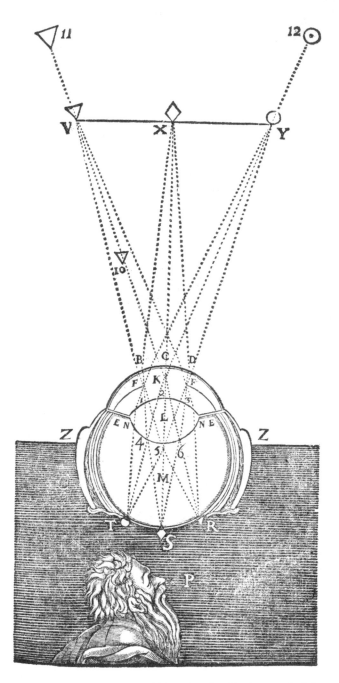

Figure 1.2 René Descartes, *Principia Philosophiae* (1644), Geometrical demonstration of visual perception as a function of focus, distance, and strength of light rays.

To gaze fixedly at object X in this figure is to relegate objects 10 and 12 to peripheral importance—literally, since the trajectory of the light rays in each case strikes the back of the retina in a peripheral position. On the other hand, object 10 might be judged to be closer than object X because the light rays coming from object 10 are stronger. By the same criterion, object 12 will be judged to be farther away.

The point of Descartes' analysis is the isolation of objects in the viewer's environment. What holds true for physical objects holds true for thoughts. Arithmetic and geometry, Descartes observes early in the first meditation, "contain something certain and indubitable" (VII.20)—*whether these things really exist in nature or not*. The illustration in Figure 1.2 is repeated several times in the course of the *Discourse on Method*. Left unexplained in each case is the gap between the meticulously dissected eye and the *owner* of that eye. What do those 80+ parallel lines at the bottom of the image indicate? Perhaps the night sky as the viewer at the bottom casts his gaze upward to stars or planets (points V, X, and Y at the top), his dissected eye functioning like a telescope. But the ambient darkness in which the viewer is situated also suggests the flesh in which the eye, protruding outward, is seated. Someone who knows how Saussure in his *Course in General Linguistics* represents waves of thought and sound (see Figure 2.5) may see a resemblance between Descartes' linear ambience and Saussure's wavy ambience. Descartes' viewer is a *situated* viewer, not the totally detached thinker familiar from Philosophy 101. But *where* is he located? In what context does he do his difference-marking? That is left ambiguous.

As a demonstration of his method, Descartes concludes *Meditations on First Philosophy* with a rehash of the arguments he arrived at intuitively, this time "arranged in geometrical fashion" (VII.160), with definitions, postulates, axioms, propositions, and demonstrations. Descartes does so at the request of one of the critics whose objections he takes up after the meditations proper are finished. In effect, Descartes goes over the same territory three times: once in the form of six private meditations, once in the form of a pronoun-trading dialogue (other thinkers—Johan de Kater, Marin Mersenne,

Thomas Hobbes, Antoine Arnauld, Pierre Gassendi, and Pierre Bourdin—write anonymously as "I" or "we" and object to Descartes as "you," to whom Descartes replies as "I"), and finally as a demonstration out of geometry.

In Part Two of *Ideas* (1913) Edmund Husserl sets in place yet a third scene of observation. He does so with a nod to Descartes' *Meditations.* Again we encounter the solitary thinker sitting in his study, on a particular day, in a particular season of the year (it was winter in Descartes' case, it seems to be summer in Husserl's). A photograph of Husserl in his study at Göttingen, where he was teaching when he wrote Part Two of *Ideas*, lets us look in on the scene of observation as Husserl describes it in words. (See Figure 1.3.) "I am conscious of a world endlessly spread out in space and having endlessly become in time," Husserl begins.

> I can let my attention wander away from the writing table which was just now seen and noticed, out through the unseen parts of the room which are behind my back, to the verandah, into the garden, to the children in the arbor, etc., to all the Objects I directly "know of" as being there and here in the surroundings of which there is also consciousness—a "knowing of them" which involves no conceptual thinking and which changes into a clear intuiting with the advertence of attention, and even then only partially and for the most part very imperfectly. (Part Two, §27, in Husserl 1982: 51–2)

What Husserl attempts here is a step-by-step framing of experience that begins with himself as a first-person observer and moves outward by degrees into the ambient world. Where Descartes looks inward, Husserl looks outward. And he does so by *degrees*: where Bacon surrounds himself with curiosities, where Descartes posits a geometrically plotted distance between himself and objects out in the world, Husserl recognizes a continuum in which the first-person observer is implicated in the many objects around him and—this is the key consideration—the objects are implicated in the observer. The objects exist in an infinite "horizon of indeterminate actuality" that surrounds the observer like a halo, like a mist (52). The ambient world, Husserl says, "is continually 'on hand' [*vorhanden*]

Figure 1.3 Edmund Husserl as the center of thought in his study at Göttingen (glass plate photograph, before 1916).

for me, and I myself am a member of it" (53, with original German from Husserl 1950: 58). As the observer casts attention on certain objects, in a particular moment, within a particular space, those objects move out of indeterminacy into presence, but they remain imbedded in the ambient world. They cannot be abstracted from that world and plotted on a graph any more than the observer himself can. The ambient world is, in Husserl's precise terms, "the world in which I find *myself*" (53).

By turning attention to this or that aspect, Husserl *frames* the ambient world. "Bracketing," "reduction," "putting in parentheses," and "*epochē*" (suspending judgment) are other terms Husserl uses for this act of attention-giving. In such acts of framing, all axioms, presuppositions, theories, and hypotheses are set aside. Instead, the observer attends to objects as they present themselves to him and, no less important, he attends to himself as he is present to objects. The stance is neither objective nor subjective but something in between. The result, in epistemological terms, is very close to "As it likes me." For phenomenologists, knowledge does not exist apart from the knower and the circumstances of coming-to-know.

As Husserl is careful to point out, the thing being attended to does not have to be a physical object. Take "the world of numbers." While he is occupied thinking about "pure numbers and their laws," Husserl observes, certain numbers and certain laws will come in and out of focus within a "partly determinate, partly indeterminate arithmetical horizon" (54). But the world of numbers can be dismissed; the "*natural world … the world in the usual sense of the word,*" cannot (54, emphasis original). The world "at hand," the world of things and people, is always present in its teeming plenitude. It is the always-present ground out of which figures emerge, the ground against which figures come to be known. In Husserl's mind (and in the minds of Martin Heidegger, Maurice Merleau-Ponty, and later phenomenologists) the natural world presents itself in the here-and-now. The observer can change his stance in time, just as he can in space, turning his attention backwards or forwards in time, but the time of knowing is always *now*. For all its insistent first-personhood, phenomenology as practiced in the twentieth century was essentializing in its claims about human perception and indifferent to cultural differences. (And indifferent to gender: the observer in these first-person writers is always a *he*.)

Husserl in *Ideas* assumes that the world at hand is present to other people in that world in the same way it is to him. He does, however, allow for individual differences in the way that the world at hand affects consciousness:

> Each has his place from which he sees the physical things present; and, accordingly, each has different physical-thing appearances. Also, for each the fields of actual perception, actual memory, etc., are different, leaving aside the fact that intersubjectively common objects of consciousness in those fields are attended to as having different modes, different manners of apprehension, different degrees of clarity, and so forth. (Husserl 1982: 55–6)

Husserl imagines an infinite world of possibilities, but he imagines that the phenomenological observer and his fellow observers occupy a "here" that is also a *now*.

What if we make allowances for people who share bodies and minds like ours but, who through an accident of time, do not happen to be physically present in the world about us? What about THWS and his original readers and audiences? Can we make any claim to share an "intersubjectivity" with them? The dominant way of going about academic business for the past 30 years provides a quick and definite answer: no. New historicism insists on the radical differentness of the early modern past, with its physical, public modes of punishment, its one-sex model of human reproductive organs, its fusion of heresy, treason, and sodomy, its belief in magic and witches. Lacanian psychoanalytical theory maintains that there is nothing natural about personal identity, that it is scripted by language, and that language in turn is scripted by culture. We speak a different cultural language; therefore we know a different cultural reality. Deconstruction would counter that all acts of meaning-making, including any attempt to reconstruct consciousness in the historical past, can happen only through difference-marking and that even the consciousness that seemed to be so present for Husserl is a function of language, an illusion made out of words. What common ground could there possibly be for "intersubjectivity"?

:

Now for the Retort Courteous. To new historicism, with its objectification and estrangement of the past, a counter argument is ready at hand in Jean François Lyotard's *Phenomenology* (1986, English translation 1991). Husserl in *Ideas* is keenly consciously of a past and a future that converge in the present: "This world, on hand for me now and manifestly in every waking Now, has its two-sidedly infinite temporal horizon, its known and unknown, immediately living and lifeless past and future" (52). Lyotard applies this observation to history. Objects of historical inquiry, Lyotard argues, are never really objects: a continuum of time connects the analyst with what she or he analyzes. As the analyst moves along the continuum, so too do the objects of analysis. Objects, no less than the analyst, are always in a process of becoming: "Just as we cannot assign some definitive meaning to a subjectivity, since this subjectivity is cast forward toward a future whose open possibilities will define it further, so the full meaning (the direction) of a historical situation is not assignable once and for all" (Lyotard 1991: 121). Past and future converge in the only practicable reference point along the continuum: now. We and THWS may not share a place, but we do share a time. If Lyotard is right (and I think he is), the main problem for "intersubjectivity" is not time but place.

One advantage of Lacan's psychoanalytical theory—an advantage for English professors if not for patients in psychotherapy—is the power Lacan accords to language. Personal identity, as Lacan understands it, is made out of language. During the first five or so years of life every speaking human being is inducted into what Lacan calls the Symbolic Order and, with that, into ways of being in the world that language dictates. My "I," seemingly so *there* when I speak, is actually the repository of everything that has been said to me and everything that I have heard others say. Lacan has in mind Language-with-a-capital-L, but culturally minded thinkers have seized on the corollary that different languages—or even the same language spoken at different times in history—dictate different ways of being in the world. Plausible enough. On the other hand, every speaking human starts with the same equipment for seeing and speaking: a body. And not just with a physical body but with an *image* of a body, and not just with the image of a body but with the image of *my* body, as I discover its separateness in the mirror of experience during the first 24 months of life. What the inert mass point is to physics, Lacan says, the *imago* is to psychology (Lacan 2006: 153). In Lacan's scheme of psychic development, perception through and *of* one's own body comes before speech.

The imposition of language creates—and this is Lacan's key observation—an existential dissatisfaction, a sense of alienation from the wholeness of being that each human speaker knew before Language. Works of art, Lacan claims, fascinate us precisely because they address and temporarily redress those dissatisfactions. Like Wordsworth's "intimations of immortality," certain moments in works of art give us access—tantalizing, all too brief access—to what Lacan calls, perversely perhaps, "the Real."[2] Rosalind and Celia's entry into the last scene of *As You Like It*, escorted by the god of marriage, shapes up as one such moment. "Then is there mirth in heaven," Hymen sings, "When earthly things made even/ Atone together" (5.1.106–8). "Atone," literally to-be-at-one, is the word that makes this momentary transcendence possible. And so does the fact of singing. Melody, rhythm, tone, the expression of air from the lungs into ambient space: these qualities are present in speech, but in music they overwhelm the more usual, more mundane *naming* functions of speech. The gap between *imago* and language in Lacan's scheme opens up, it seems to me, a space for phenomenology, for knowing-through-the-body that has a fraught, perhaps tragic relationship to knowing-through-language.

With respect to THWS and his original readers and audiences, the language in question may be early modern English, a language both

---

[2] Whether Lacan is reading Wordsworth or Wordsworth is reading Lacan is a nice question: "Shades of the prison-house begin to close/ Upon the growing boy,/ But he beholds the light, and whence it flows,/ He sees it in his joy" ("Intimations of Immortality from Recollections of Early Childhood," ll. 69–72, in Wordsworth 1982: 353).

like and unlike the contemporary English we speak in, think in, feel in, live in; but if Lacan is right, the existential situation we face *vis-à-vis* knowing-through-the-body versus knowing-through-language is the same as THWS and his contemporaries faced. "Intersubjectivity" does not require an impossible journey in some sort of time/space-ship, but that we master a language we partly know already, early modern English. Hence the frequent recourse in this book to the *Oxford English Dictionary*. As for the sixteenth- and seventeenth-century *imago*, we can come to know something about that through careful attention to visual images, to *ekphrasis* or picture-painting in poetry, to performance practices in the theater. We can insist on the body, even when the evidence at hand is not visual but linguistic. With its focus on the nexus between body and language, historical phenomenology may offer a glimpse into Lacan's "Real" in the same way that works of art do.

Deconstruction would seem to present a far more serious challenge to historical phenomenology and the possibility of "intersubjectivity" between sixteenth- and seventeenth-century readers and writers and their twenty-first-century counterparts. Derrida's entire critical project, after all, is an attack on *presence*, on Husserl's sense of the world as being present to him and himself as being present to the world in acts of framing. It was with Husserl, in fact, that Derrida began his life-long project, first with a translation of Husserl's *Origin of Geometry*, complete with a long critical introduction, and then with a critique of Husserl's "pure phenomenology" in *Speech and Phenomena*.[3] Geometry may seem an odd place to begin, but Husserl's interest in how geometry could be produced as an abstract closed system of thought, set apart from everyday experience, gave Derrida an opportunity to scrutinize Husserl's in-control self-present thinker. We have noticed already how Husserl claims to be able to move in and out of "the world of numbers" at will. *Ideas Pertaining to a Pure Phenomenology*: for Derrida it is the "pure" that presents the problem. A *sense* of presence there

---

[3] An accessible introduction to the development of Derrida's writing out his critique of Husserl is provided by Gayatri Chakravorty Spivak in her "Translator's Preface" to Derrida, *Of Grammatology* (Derrida 1997: ix–xc).

may be, Derrida concedes, but that sense can never be direct and unmediated. It is a function of the marking of difference that Derrida, following Saussure, finds in all acts of meaning-making. Far from being "pure," Derrida says in a rare moment of italicized directness, "*Phenomenological reduction is a scene, a theater stage*" (Derrida 1973: 86, emphasis original). With that *aperçu* I take Derrida to be referring to the secondhand status of the impressions that Husserl regards as just *being there*, "at hand." About those impressions, Derrida insists, there is nothing "natural" at all. What gets framed in Husserl's acts of *epochē*, according to Derrida, is an illusion, the elements of which—visual images as well as words—are not natural givens—things out there in the world—but man-made fabrications. To mark things off for attention you need a marker. And that marker, according to Derrida, is language.

In effect, Derrida doesn't destroy Husserl's phenomenology; he pushes it to its logical conclusions. In doing so, he opens up the possibility for a specifically *historical* phenomenology. Metaphysical presence, absolute knowledge: that may have been Husserl's goal, but it does not have to be ours. We can accept that knowing-in-place-in-time is like a theatrical scene. We can accept the speeches and the props in that scene as artifacts, not natural givens. We can accept the fact that presence is an illusion made with those speeches and props. But we can still be interested in the illusion of presence, and we can be interested in it in historical, culturally specific ways. We can take stock of the speeches and the props in just the way that Philip Henslowe inventoried the Lord Admiral's Men's props, costumes, and playbooks in 1598 or so (Foakes 2002: 316–25). Our relationship to the scene of knowing does not, in the first instance, put *us* at the center but THWS or the boy actor who played Rosalind in 1599 or the citizen's wife and her maid sitting in the third gallery at the Globe. We can insinuate ourselves into the scene-of-knowing, but we can never be at the center. The photograph of Husserl sitting at his desk in Figure 1.3, for example, may invite us as viewers to assume Husserl's subject position, especially when the photograph is placed alongside Husserl's first-person verbal description of his study in §27 of *Ideas*, Part Two. But we find ourselves, inescapably, behind Husserl's back.

We may be part of an intersubjective "field of perception" (Husserl 1982: 51), but we can never be at its center. Husserl, after all, is looking the other way. He doesn't even know we are there. And he is dead. Those considerations should not stop us, however, from projecting ourselves into the historically reconstructed field of perception as far as we are able. If Lyotard gives us permission to do so with respect to time (history is not *then* but *now*), Derrida does so with respect to place (the scene of knowing is *not-here*). Lacan, with his focus on the *imago*, encourages us to include the perception of one's own body as the precursor of speech.

::

Let us return to the epilogue of *As You Like It* and its playful ways with *I*, *he/she/he*, *you*, *they*, and *it*. Which of the three primal scenes of observation is most accommodating to the play of *like*? Certainly not Descartes', in which the thinking *I* is positioned in a precisely calibrated distance from the thought-about *it*, so that *it* is made to appear as clear and distinct as possible. Husserl's scene seems wide open when an actual performance is at hand. Bracketing the moment when the actor begins "It is not the fashion to see the lady the epilogue" turns attention toward bodies, space, time, and sound, toward the physical relationship between audience and actor, toward the costume, posture, gestures, and tricks of voice that create and uncreate the fiction, toward the *feeling* of what is happening. When the object at hand is not a performance but a printed text of *As You Like It*, the picture gets more complicated. Texts, after all, are not objects out there in the world like Husserl's desk or the objects behind his back in the room or the sounds of his children playing in the arbor. Texts are *representations* of such objects, and they come to us, albeit in the present, with a history. We need a strategy for moving from things-present to things-absent, from now to then, from particulars to a more general understanding. Bacon's scene of observation gives us what we need.

Historical phenomenology involves an understanding of "experience" that is closer to Bacon's than to Husserl's. For THWS and his contemporaries, "experience" was off-text, and it involved *doing* something rather than just *reading* about it. When Jaques in *As You Like It* tells "Ganymede" that he would like to become better acquainted, his interlocutor is dubious. They say you're melancholy, he/she/he retorts, and melancholics come in for more criticism than drunkards. Ah, but *my* melancholy is not like the scholar's, the musician's, the courtier's, the soldier's, the lawyer's, or the lady's.

> JAQUES … it is a melancholy of mine own, compounded of many simples, extracted from many objects, and indeed the sundry contemplation of my travels [trauells], in which my often rumination wraps me in a most humorous sadness.
> ROSALIND A traveller [Traueller]! By my faith, you have great reason to be sad. I fear you have sold your own lands to see other men's. Then to have seen much and to have nothing is to have rich eyes and poor hands.
> JAQUES Yes, I have gained my experience.
> ROSALIND And your experience makes you sad. I had rather have a fool to make me merry than experience to make me sad—and to travel [trauaile] for it too!
> (4.1.15–27, with original spelling from Shakespeare 1968: 218)

The oppositions Rosalind sets up here are six: traveling versus staying put, other lands versus my lands, eyes versus hands, experience versus foolery, sad versus merry, and travail versus repose. Bacon's essay "Of Studies" (1597), published two years before *As You Like It* was first acted, adds the more usual opposition of doing versus reading: books "perfect nature, and are perfected by experience" (Bacon 1987: 153).

Be that as it may, Rosalind's prejudice against experience was not uncommon. Her sentiments (and her word play on "travel" and "travail") are echoed by William Cornwallis in his essay "Of Censuring": "Experience doth much, but it is too full of scars and wounds, and is brought with gray hairs, and danger: when the other hath no less that hath travailed but in his study" (Cornwallis 1600: sig. H2v). Not a surprising sentiment from someone whose *Essays*, although inspired by Montaigne's (French editions 1580, 1588, and 1595, English translation 1603), read more like a commonplace book of *sententiae* worthy of Polonius. Montaigne's own essay "Of Experience" is much closer to the oldest (now obsolete) sense of the word "experience" as putting something (an object, a person, an idea) to the test (*OED* 1989: "experience," *n.*, †1). "There is no desire more natural, than that of knowledge," Montaigne begins the essay. "We attempt all means that may bring us unto it. When reason fails us, we employ experience" (3.13 in Montaigne 1613: sig. GGG6). Proceeding in his typical wide-ranging way, Montaigne puts this aphorism to the test, first by calling to mind a remembered testimonial from one of his favorite writers (in this case Martial in epigram 1.46: "By diverse proofs experience art hath bred,/ Whilst one by one the way examples led"), then by considering that experience, like reason, comes in many "shapes" ("Reason hath many shapes, that we know not which to take hold of. Experience hath as many"), then by using eggs' resemblance to one another to anticipate Derrida's difference-marking ("Dissimilitude doth of itself insinuate itself into our works, no art can come near unto similitude"), and so on for another 27,000 words in John Florio's English translation. Lots of words; lots of experience. It is from trials like Montaigne's that the more usual sense of "experience" today—knowing something in a subjective way (4.a)—derives. Montaigne proceeds by a kind of back-and-forth motion, touching now on what Socrates, Cicero, Aristotle, or another authority may have said, now on his own firsthand experiences.

With respect to subjectivity, Bacon's idea of experience, although governed by strict induction, is close to Montaigne's. The one thousand "experiments" in Bacon's how-to-do-it manual *Silva Silvarum* are presented as instructions—recipes, really—for how to put this or that observation to the test. The observation in each case isn't really a hypothesis, as it would be in a modern scientific experiment, but a "what if?" situation. The reason you should do the experiment is to try it out for yourself—in effect, to *experience* the experiment firsthand. Experiment number 363 is typical:

> Take a bladder, the greatest you can get; fill it full of wind, and tie it about the neck with a silk thread waxed; and upon that put likewise wax very close; so that when the neck of the bladder drieth, no air may possibly get in, nor out. Then bury it three or four foot under the earth,

in a vault, or in a conservatory of snow, the snow being made hollow about the bladder; and after some fortnight's distance, see whether the bladder be shrunk: for if it be, then it is plain, that the coldness of the earth, or snow, hath condensed the air, and brought it a degree nearer to water: which is an experiment of great consequence. (sig. N4)

Among Bacon's experiments having to do with perception, the one about the acquisition of speech, discussed above, presents the personal connection in even more intimate terms. For Bacon, experience doesn't come naturally, any more than it does for Husserl. Experience requires a plan. You don't just open yourself up to experience and then have it; you've got to *seek* experience, set up parameters, and try out possibilities within those parameters.

For experiments in historical phenomenology we can work within three basic paradigms. Each of the three involves a psychological subject set within what Husserl calls "the world at hand." The physical dimensions, temporal reach, and content of these worlds at hand will vary, of course, according to the main variable, the psychological subject, to wit:

- author ↔ world-at-hand (phenomenology of transcription)
- characters ↔ world-at-hand (phenomenology of representation)
- reader/sensor ↔ world-at-hand (phenomenology of reception).

Versions of all three of these paradigms have been tried out already. Caroline Spurgeon's once famous book *Shakespeare's Imagery, and What It Tells Us* (1935) may offer no direct acknowledgment of phenomenology as a philosophical movement, but it exemplifies the first paradigm by situating WSA within a phenomenal world of the sort that Husserl, Heidegger, and their disciples understood. Thus, a tabulation of all the images in CWWS indicates that THWS not only loved gardening but "was deft and nimble with his hands, and loved using them, particularly in the carpenter's craft, and, contrary to our ideas of most poets, he was probably a practical, neat and handy man about the house" (Spurgeon 1935: 205). (By contrast, Francis Bacon's images suggest a mind attuned to "everything touching the house and daily

31

life indoors, such as light and fire, furnishings, hangings, textiles, needlework, clothes, jewels, marriage, birth, death, parents, children and human relations generally" [16].) Old questions about whether THWS ever traveled to Italy or other places (see, for example, Lambin 1962 and Praz 1963)—questions that belong to the author ↔ world paradigm—have morphed in studies like Michele Marrapodi's *Italian Culture in the Drama of Shakespeare and His Contemporaries* (2007) into more sophisticated questions within the characters ↔ world paradigm as mediated by texts. Spurgeon may have been a proto-phenomenologist, but she was interested only in the author ↔ world paradigm.

To the third paradigm belong reader-response criticism as practiced by Wolfgang Iser, David Bleich, and others in the 1970s and more recent studies of early modern reading practices like Katharine A. Craik's *Reading Sensations in Early Modern England* (2007) and the essays collected in *The Practice and Representation of Reading in England* (Raven, Small, and Tadmor 1996). In Iser's and Bleich's analyses, the printed book with its words and conceptual gaps in effect becomes the world-at-hand in its totality. Present in a more tentative, less conclusive way is the world-at-hand that the reader creates out of those printed codes. Among these flirtations with phenomenology, only reader-response criticism has investigated the *process* of coming-to-know, and except for Craik only in cognitive terms. Touch, the feel of the book in the hand, is beyond notice in these studies, as are any other bodily sensations that might contribute to the reality-effect created through reading. In comparison with reading, the phenomenology of theatrical performance has been much better served in books like Bert O. States's *Great Reckonings in Little Rooms* (1987) and *Hamlet and the Concept of Character* (1992) and Alice Rayner's *Ghosts: Death's Double and the Phenomena of Theatre* (2006). Perhaps that is so because in theater the world-at-hand is palpably present: the reader becomes a sensor and the text becomes the bodies, actions, and speeches of other people, all of them sharers along with the sensor of the same intersubjective field.

The three core chapters in *Phenomenal Shakespeare* are offered as examples of how to *do* historical phenomenology, mostly within the second paradigm (characters ↔ world) and the third (sensor ↔ world) but with a glance or two into the first (author ↔ world). Within each paradigm the way of proceeding is the same. First you choose an *it*, an object of study, something as large as "the experience of reading in early modern England" or something mid-range like Francis Meres's reference to "Shakespeare's sugared sonnets among his private friends" (Ingleby, Toulmin Smith, and Furnivall 1909: 1:46) or something as specific as the couplet to sonnet 23: "O learn to read what silent love hath writ;/ To hear with eyes belongs to love's fine wit" (23.13–14). Then, like Husserl in his study, you should ground yourself with respect to the sensations represented in the object of study or implied by it. In the case of sonnet 23, that act of grounding would turn attention to the relationship among reading, seeing, and hearing—the relationship for *you*. Do you only see when you read? Do you hear? How do you coordinate seeing with hearing? How do you coordinate seeing and hearing with reading? Reading with remembering? And what about the "love" that is doing the writing—how might that influence the reading? Just what does it mean to *read* with love? Or write out sonnet 23 in your own hand, perhaps even hand what you have written to a friend. How does that act of manuscript transmission change your experience of the words? You might think of these meditations as warm-up exercises or, as one my students, Elizabeth Wilcox, likes to call it, "grooming," looking in the mirror before you open the door—or the book.

Next comes the framing, the bracketing, the putting-in-parentheses, and that requires first of all a clear sense of the paradigm within which you are working. Who is the psychological subject? With respect to sonnet 23, is it THWS? WSA? The "private friends" in Meres's remark? A contemporary purchaser of the 1609 quarto of *Shake-speares Sonnets. Never before Imprinted*? You as the reader of an edited text here and now? You as a replicator of the manuscript transmission implied by Meres? Whichever the paradigm, whoever the psychological subject may be, the next step is to take stock of the world at hand. In the cases of the first two paradigms, author ↔ world and characters ↔ world, that will involve a project of historical reconstruction. The evidence will be the same sorts of materials used in new historicism: polemical writings as well as literary texts, material things as well as verbal and visual representations of things, diaries and letters as well as published books, medical treatises as well as blazons of beauty, conduct books as well as play plots, court cases as well as fictions. No less important than books and things is an examination of the words that are used to designate the experience at hand. Again and again I find myself turning to the *Oxford English Dictionary* with its etymologies and obsolete meanings, not in an attempt to give meanings a historical fixity but to put back in motion all possible meanings of the word at hand. The very word "experience"—where it comes from, the various things it meant in 1600—should prompt us to stop short when we reach for that word so casually.

Peculiarly important to historical phenomenology are the stories that THWS and his contemporaries told themselves about perception, about what was happening in their bodies and brains when they looked, listened, read, and loved. From Aristotle's treatise "On the Soul" and its successors and from Galen's medical treatises the original consumers of CWWS inherited accounts of perception that involved the entire body, not just the brain. Central to such accounts was the very synesthesia described in the couplet to sonnet 23: "to hear with eyes." No less prominent was the word "wit," which served as a place-holder for what would later be called "mind," "psyche," and "consciousness." The qualifications in "love's fine wit"—both the "love" and the "fine"—become more than figures of speech in a physio-psychology that located the central processor in the heart, not the head.

"Psychology" as an early modern invention and the key ideas of that psychology have been usefully digested and summarized by Katherine Park (1988a, 1988b). Thomas Wright's summary in *The Passions of the Mind in General* (1604) is as handy as any. "Three sorts of actions proceed from men's souls," Wright explains, "some are internal and immaterial, as the acts of our wits and wills; others be mere external and material, as the acts of our senses, seeing, hearing, moving, etc.[;] others stand betwixt these two extremes, and border upon them both" (Wright 1971: sig. B4). External movements, starting with the eyes or the ears or the skin's surface, reach the brain via internal movements of an aerated fluid called *pneuma*, *spiritus*, or (Wright's preference) "purer spirits" that courses through the veins

34

(remember this was before William Harvey had demonstrated the pumping of blood through the veins by the heart) or, as the latest anatomical studies were suggesting, through nerve filaments or "sinews." The motions continue in the brain, where sensations of sight, hearing, touching, etc. are fused by "the common sense" into kinesthetic "images" in the imagination and are further shaped by memory into *phantasmata* or "fancies," which travel via *spiritus* to the heart, which determines the entire body's reaction—including the brain's. Once arrived at the heart, the fancies "pitch at the door" and signify the object that has been sensed externally. "The heart immediately bendeth, either to prosecute it, or to eschew it: and the better to effect that affection, draweth other humors to help him" (sig. D7). These "humors" are the body's four basic fluids: blood, yellow bile, black bile, and phlegm, each of which is seated in a different organ and causes the body to react in a certain way, desiringly in the case of blood, angrily in the case of yellow bile, sadly in the case of black bile, and sluggishly in the case of phlegm—or in some combination thereof. These *liquid* humors produce the *psychological* humors that we still recognize today, even though we would assign different names to the chemicals involved—serotonin, for example—if not to the felt result. A psychological subject experiences the rush of the liquid humors as a "passion" of one sort or another. It was only after the heart had added passion and the entire body had reacted accordingly that fancies were sent (via the spirits) back to the brain for judgment by the wit and actions by the will. Curiously, after all those sensations, waves, boilings, and coolings, Wright imagines operations of wit and will to be "internal and immaterial." Otherwise, the whole process is thoroughly corporeal: for THWS and his contemporaries, coming-to-know may have started as something external and material and ended as something internal and immaterial, but in between was something that partook of both. It was Descartes' maverick move, 40 years later, to try to eliminate that something in between. Investigations of pre-Cartesian psychology within the characters ↔ world paradigm have been provided by Michael Schoenfeldt (1999), Gail Kern Paster (2004), the essayists collected in Mary Floyd-Wilson and Garrett A. Sullivan (2007), and others.

It is within the third paradigm, reader/sensor ↔ world, that historical phenomenology comes into its own. For the phenomenology of reception, three temporal framings are possible: one limited to the historical moment in which the work in question was created and received, one trained on the analyst's own moment, and one opening the present into the past. If Lyotard is right, only the third is actually, practically possible. Past and present exist not as separate compartments but as relative points along a continuum that THWS and we (that's you and I) all occupy. Historical phenomenology embraces the openness of Lyotard's proposition. One happy result is the chance to combine early modern stories of perception (the synesthesia of looking, hearing, and reading in "wit") with the most recent cognitive research (the similar pattern of neural firings in discriminations among visual and aural stimuli, a state of flow that Michael Spivey [2007] calls "the continuity of mind"). As we have observed with respect to Husserl's scene of observation, it is perfectly possible for a twenty-first-century observer, equipped with cognitive theory, to insinuate herself into the intersubjective field of THWS's private friends, as long as the observer recognizes that she is an intruder. Potentially at least, the encounter can end in a critique of the observer's own period-bound assumptions.

You can't know anything apart from the way in which you come to know it: we can take the fundamental principle of phenomenology as practiced by Husserl, Heidegger, and Merleau-Ponty and apply it to the sixteenth- and seventeenth-century evidence available to us in the form of plays, poems, narratives, non-fictional writings, paintings, tapestries, embroideries, building designs, travelers' accounts, diaries, commonplace books, court records—indeed whatever evidence comes to hand. In the last analysis, however, the attention turns back on *us*. An historical phenomenology must inevitably be a *present* phenomenology, but not a *presentist* phenomenology if that means willfully turning one's back on the past. Among the traditional humanities subjects—classics, philosophy, history, literature—it would seem that history would have the best claim to objectivity. After all, the materials of history—state papers, wills, military records, census figures, maps—are *there*, ready to be seen and handled. Depending on where you live, you may be confronted on a daily basis with the material evidence of history in the form of buildings that still stand, sometimes after hundreds of years. In the case of documents as well as buildings, we *inhabit* the evidence. It is the shadow of the present cast back into the past as well as the analyst's orientation toward the future that makes it possible for historical phenomenology to stay rooted in the concerns, political commitments, and cognitive research of the present at the same time that it tries to make sense of the past, in the past's own terms.

2

How Should One Read a Shakespeare Sonnet?

Carefully, you might be thinking. Or skeptically, if your stance is deconstructive. Or reverentially if you're under the sway of Shakespeare as Cultural Icon (WSCI). Or referentially if you want to consider the social work the poem was doing in its own time. Or super-subtly if you want to know who "he" and "she" really were. I have in mind something more tech. Let us begin with a passage from one of the most famous poems printed in 1609 as *Shake-speares Sonnets*—i.e., "Sonnets by William Shakespeare as Author" (WSA). The passage in question can be communicated three different ways. The first way, be forewarned, doesn't work well in a book. You can find moving images of the entire sonnet at http://purl.org/emls/si-19/smitsonn.htm in an earlier, shorter version of this chapter (Smith 2009a). Otherwise, Figure 2.1 shows three stills that capture a big moment near the beginning. Any idea of just which sonnet is being communicated in these three images? How do you read those images? What do you look to for cues? Different forms of *techne* ask for different techniques of reading.

Version two of the same moment, shown in Figure 2.2, is perfectly suited to the codex you are holding in your hands. Once again, the mechanics of communication are cuing a certain kind of reading. Because you are an old hand at these mechanics, you can do the reading offhandedly, even with one hand tied behind your back. You don't need to think about what you're doing. For that reason, however, you may find it harder to isolate the cues you are being given and respond to them *as cues*. As you read the phrase, pay particular attention to how the first-person pronoun operates. Where do *you* stand in relationship

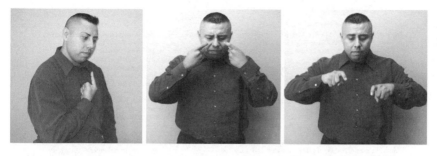

Figure 2.1   Crescenciano Garcia, Shakespeare sonnet number ???, version one.

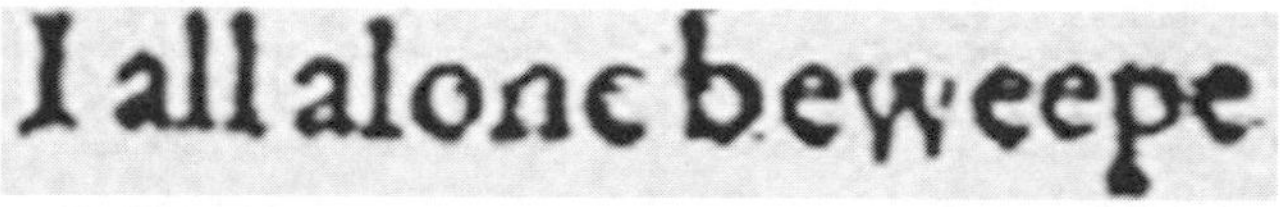

I all alone beweepe

Figure 2.2   William Shakespeare, sonnet number ???, version two.

to that "I"? Pronouns and the way they put people into place—"you" here versus "I" over there versus "he," "she," and "they" somewhere else again—will occupy us often in this chapter. To help you bracket the event of reading and see it strangely, the cues in Figure 2.2 have been enlarged by a factor of 2.

How did you do? Version number two is, of course, the first six pulses of the second line of sonnet 29 as it appears in the 1609 quarto of *Shake-speares Sonnets. Never Before Imprinted*—the one that begins "When in disgrace with fortune and men's eyes." You can view in Figure 2.3 the entire sonnet as imprinted, in context, in the quarto. What you witness in Figure 2.1 are the same sentiments, "I all alone beweep my outcast state," interpreted into American Sign Language (ASL) by Crescenciano Garcia of Los Angeles, California, as recorded in September 2006.

Version number three you will have to produce yourself. Take out a single sheet of paper, put a pen or pencil in your fingers, and copy out this text in your own hand:

> When, in disgrace with fortune and men's eyes,
> I all alone beweep my outcast state,

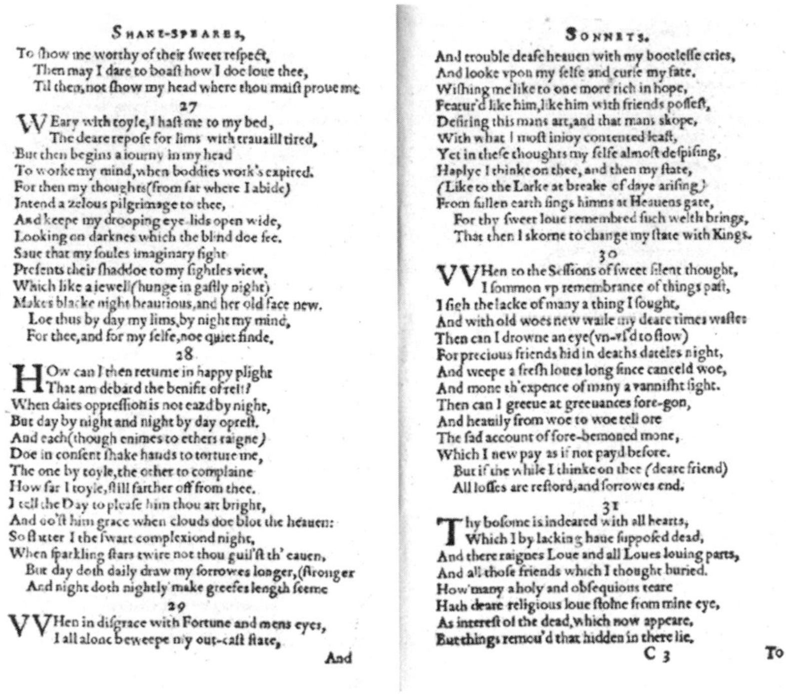

SHAKE-SPEARES,

To ſhow me worthy of their ſweet reſpect,
Then may I dare to boaſt how I doe loue thee,
Til then,not ſhow my head where thou maiſt proue me

27

WEary with toyle,I haſt me to my bed,
The deare repoſe for lims with trauaill tired,
But then begins a iourny in my head
To worke my mind,when boddies work's expired.
For then my thoughts(from far where I abide)
Intend a zelous pilgrimage to thee,
And keepe my drooping eye-lids open wide,
Looking on darknes which the blind doe ſee.
Saue that my ſoules imaginary ſight
Preſents their ſhaddoe to my ſightles view,
Which like a iewell(hunge in gaſtly night)
Makes blacke night beautious,and her old face new.
Loe thus by day my lims,by night my mind,
For thee,and for my ſelfe,noe quiet finde.

28

HOw can I then returne in happy plight
That am debard the benifit of reſt?
When daies oppreſſion is not eazd by night,
But day by night and night by day opreſt.
And each(though enimes to ethers raigne)
Doe in conſent ſhake hands to torture me,
The one by toyle,the other to complaine
How far I toyle,ſtill farther off from thee.
I tell the Day to pleaſe him thou art bright,
And do'ſt him grace when clouds doe blot the heauen:
So flatter I the ſwart complexiond night,
When ſparkling ſtars twire not thou guil'ſt th' eauen.
But day doth daily draw my ſorrowes longer,(ſtronger
And night doth nightly make greefes length ſeeme

29

VVHen in diſgrace with Fortune and mens eyes,
I all alone beweepe my out-caſt ſtate,

And

SONNETS.

And trouble deafe heauen with my bootleſſe cries,
And looke vpon my ſelfe and curſe my fate.
Wiſhing me like to one more rich in hope,
Featur'd like him,like him with friends poſſeſt,
Deſiring this mans art,and that mans skope,
With what I moſt inioy contented leaſt,
Yet in theſe thoughts my ſelfe almoſt deſpiſing,
Haplye I thinke on thee, and then my ſtate,
(Like to the Larke at breake of daye ariſing)
From ſullen earth ſings himns at Heauens gate,
For thy ſweet loue remembred ſuch welth brings,
That then I skorne to change my ſtate with Kings.

30

VVHen to the Seſſions of ſweet ſilent thought,
I ſommon vp remembrance of things paſt,
I ſigh the lacke of many a thing I ſought,
And with old woes new waile my deare times waſte:
Then can I drowne an eye(vn-vſ'd to flow)
For precious friends hid in deaths dateles night,
And weepe a freſh loues long ſince canceld woe,
And mone th'expence of many a vanniſht ſight.
Then can I greeue at greeuances fore-gon,
And heauily from woe to woe tell ore
The ſad account of fore-bemoned mone,
Which I new pay as if not payd before.
But if the while I thinke on thee (deare friend)
All loſſes are reſtord,and ſorrowes end.

31

THy boſome is indeared with all hearts,
Which I by lacking haue ſuppoſed dead,
And there raignes Loue and all Loues louing parts,
And all thoſe friends which I thought buried.
How many a holy and obſequious teare
Hath deare religious loue ſtolne from mine eye,
As intereſt of the dead,which now appeare,
But things remou'd that hidden in there lie.

C 3 To

Figure 2.3 William Shakespeare, sonnet 29, in *Shake-speares Sonnets* (1609).

And trouble deaf heaven with my bootless cries,
And look upon myself and curse my fate,
Wishing me like to one more rich in hope,
Featured like him, like him with friends possessed,
Desiring this man's art and that man's scope,
With what I most enjoy contented least:
Yet in these thoughts myself almost despising,
Haply I think on thee, and then my state,
Like to the lark at break of day arising
From sullen earth, sings hymns at heaven's gate;
For thy sweet love remembered such wealth brings
That then I scorn to change my state with kings.
(Shakespeare 2005: 782)

Come on, don't just think about it: *do* it. (And you can leave out the citation.) You may want to keep the sheet handy for reference as you read the rest of this chapter. Or perhaps pass it along to a friend.

In copying out sonnet 29 in your own hand (note the synecdoche) you've taken personal possession of the poem in just the way Francis Meres claims the contemporaries of The Historical William Shakespe are (THWS) did before the sonnets were printed in 1609. Meres, writing about WSA in 1598, refers to "his sugared Sonnets among his private friends" (Ingleby, Toulmin Smith, and Furnivall 1909: 1:46), suggesting that the sonnets circulated in manuscript copies at least a decade before they were printed. Surviving manuscript copies of individual sonnets attributed to WSA are mostly datable to later than 1609, not before, and many of them seem specifically indebted to *The Passionate Pilgrim*, which printed a small selection of the sonnets with an attribution to "W. Shakespeare" in 1599 (two editions), but Figure 2.4 shows how a handwritten copy of a sonnet, whenever someone (including you) wrote it down, presents an altogether different phenomenon from *The Passionate Pilgrim* or the 1609 quarto. The sonnet numbered 128 in the 1609 printing ("How oft, when thou, my music, music play'st") becomes, in this single sheet datable to 1625–40, something else again. (It comes from MS Rawlinson Poetic 152 in the Bodleian Library, Oxford, an eighteenth-century binding together of single sheets like this one and other small gatherings, most of them dating from the first half of the seventeenth century.) On the six-by-six-inch sheet five poems—all of them about the pains and the pleasures of love—have been written out in a neat italic hand. Vertical and horizontal creases suggest how the sheet might once have been folded for passing from hand to hand among the writer's friends.

In this sequence of five poems a pair of stanzas from John Dowland's song "Rest awhile, you cruel cares" precede the transcription of sonnet 128. "How oft, when thou, my music, music play'st" is in turn followed by two more love poems, "This is love and worth commanding,/ Still beginning, never ending" and "I bend my wits and beat my brain/ To keep my grief from outward show" (Shakespeare 1625–40: fols. 34–34v). The sonnet attributed in the 1609 quarto to WSA takes its place among works by other hands in a litany of ever mounting

Figure 2.4 William Shakespeare, "How oft, when thou, my music, music play'st," Bodleian Library, Oxford, MS Rawlinson Poetic 152, fols. 34–34v (1625–40).

desire. The first Dowland stanza asks for smiles; the second wants more: "Come grant me love in love's despair." "How oft, when thou, my music, music play'st" continues the progression toward physical closeness: the speaker uses a phallic pun ("saucy jacks") to fantasize about kissing first "the tender inward" of his lover's hands and then his lover's lips. The third poem carries the erotic fantasy even further: "twining arms, exchanging kisses,/ Each partaking other's blisses,/ Laughing, weeping, still together/ Bliss in one is mirth in either." If the third poem represents consummation, the final poem finds no release from the writer's desires: "I force my will, my senses I constrain/ To imprison in my heart my secret woe,/ But musing thoughts, deep sighs, or tears that flow/ Discover what my heart hides all in vain."

The sheet shown in Figure 2.4 is altogether typical of handwritten copies from the early seventeenth century. No two of these surviving manuscripts are the same. The handwriting in each case is different; so

Figure 2.4 *(cont'd)*

too is the "voice" that each manuscript implies. Erasmus claimed that in letters from friends in their own hand we "seem to be listening to their very voices and to be looking at them face to face" (quoted in Smith 1999: 117)—a sentiment repeated in one of the poems that John Deane of New College, Oxford, copied into a blank book in the 1630s. The poem, perhaps by Deane himself, celebrates the invention of writing, because "the deputed pen/ Did the tongue's office, and the eye turned ear/ To the dead voice" (quoted in Smith 1999: 117). According to testimonies like Erasmus's and Deane's, writing is an act of kinesthesia. On the part of the writer the hand does the work of the voice; on the part of the reader, the eye "hears" that absent voice.

Among the three versions of sonnet 29—Chris Garcia's, the 1609 quarto, and your handwritten copy—several large differences suggest themselves. In each case Chris Garcia's signing and the 1609 printed text can be read as oppositions, but in each case your written version

43

troubles those neat oppositions. The first difference is a matter of ontology: version one is an embodied act, whereas version two presents itself as a disembodied object. Sonnet 29 in ASL requires the physical presence of a signer: the signs do not exist apart from the signer's body. Signatures C2v and C3 in *Shake-speares Sonnets* may have required fingers, hands, arms, and a brain or two to make them, but the finished product exists quite apart from those bodies. The signs are impressed into the paper with lead and ink, and they remain right there, whether or not there is anyone around to see them, whether the book is open or closed. Version three, because you made it yourself, is somewhere in between. Should your text, 50 years from now, come into the hands of someone who never knew you, the inscription might have the same distance as the 1609 quarto does for us. But it is not the same to *you*. Those marks on the paper were made with your own hand; in the act of writing, those words became your words in a way not unlike Chris Garcia's writing the words in the air.

Media constitute a second difference. Sonnet 29 in ASL would seem to be communicated entirely through sight. When Peter Novak and his collaborators at Yale set out to translate *Twelfth Night* into ASL, the greatest challenge was finding visual equivalents for effects in the original text that depend on sound: rhyme, homonyms, songs (Novak 2008a: www.aslshakespeare.com, Novak 2008b: 74–90).[1] Since you can't communicate in ASL unless you can be seen, Malvolio's speaking while locked up "within" at 4.2.21ff. required some ingenuity. In the event Malvolio spoke by sticking his hands through a grate. By contrast, sounding goes on to some degree, if only subliminally, when speakers of aural English scan written texts like the 1609 printing of sonnet 29. Try to take stock of what was happening as you wrote out your own version of the text. Did you sound out the syllables in your head as you wrote them down? Did your lips move? Did you breathe differently from moment to moment? If so, you were sounding as you wrote and writing as you sounded. And yet, whatever happened at its making, your subliminally sounded text has left a visual record not unlike the 1609 quarto.

---

[1] I thank Joseph Roach for bringing the ASL Shakespeare Project to my attention.

Chronology shapes up as a third difference: Chris Garcia's signing brings Thorpe's 1609 text (very much there-and-then, especially as the text appears in Figure 2.3) into a here-and-now (or at least a here-and-now that once was, as captured on video and in still photographs). In the case of your own copy, there-and-then *becomes* here-and-now in slow motion as your hand writes the ciphers that contain the sounds.

A fourth difference is epistemological. How do the signs in each case get read? How is meaning constructed by the reader? The decoding process in each case is different. In version one what gets read is the signer's body, in particular his arms, hands, eyes, and mouth. In version two, what gets read is marks on a piece of paper. The marks in version three are somewhere in between: they are not objective marks on paper but indices of the body that made them. It was your index finger that guided the pen. The trace of your body lives on in the utterance as you decode the marks yourself or as another reader—your "private friend," perhaps—hears your voice in the marks as he or she reads the text. Your own coordination of unheard sounds with muscle movements in hands and arms recapitulates on paper what Chris Garcia accomplishes in the air. In linguistic terms, finally, versions one and two seem to confront us with two different organizations of signs: a language of words in version two versus a language of gestures in version one. As usual, version three is not so easy to categorize. With its evidence of a writing hand, version three presents a *combined* language of words and gestures—a creole, perhaps.

Due to the troubling presence of version three, it should be clear by now that the differences in how meaning is structured between versions one and two cry out for *de*-construction. In terms of ontology, reading a codex is no less an embodied act than watching Chris Garcia sign in ASL. The book is an object positioned in space 16 to 18 inches from my eye, something I hold in my hand, using my fingers and thumb as an easel. My body is positioned *vis-à-vis* the book in geometric space. The book remains an object "out there" even as I *in*-corporate "in here" the words printed on the page. Books, at least when they are being read, always exist within coordinates of space, time, and a human body. With respect to media, the distinction between vision+silence in Chris Garcia's signing versus vision+sound in my reading the 1609 quarto turns out to be a false dichotomy. Chris Garcia's interpretation of sonnet 29 is not just visual: it incorporates deliberate cheek and tongue "sounds" (scare quotes appropriate for users who lack hearing entirely) that are part of ASL. Look for them in the video at http://purl.org/emls/si-19/smitsonn.htm. To someone literate in ASL those clicks of the tongue and puffs of the cheek may not be heard with the ears, but they are felt in the muscles of the mouth and face—a circumstance that should make us consider that subliminal hearing of a printed text is not something that happens only in the ears, or even primarily in the ears: it involves muscle-memory in lungs, larynx, and mouth.

Those muscle-memories upset the chronological distinction between there-and-then and here-and-now. Far from standing apart as opposites, sounding and signing shape up as *analogies* that share certain commonalities. Both are somatic: the feel of sound-shaping in lungs, larynx, mouth, tongue, teeth, and lips becomes, in versions one and three, the feel of movement in hands and arms. In both of the bodily-signed versions meaning is made by precisely calibrated movements. As you wrote out sonnet 29 for yourself, you probably activated those muscle-memories in your chest and face, simultaneously with the muscle-memories in your arms and hands. You touched the poem—this 400-year-old poem—at the same time that the poem touched you.

If you were to act on Meres' hint and pass along your handwritten copy of the sonnet to a friend, that act of touching across the centuries would be extended to another person. "Sugared," "among," "private," "friends": with one exception, all of the key words in Meres' famous allusion have been subjected to critical scrutiny. "Sugared" awaits its expositor. What one was most likely to sugar in the days before coffee and tea was ordinary wine. In *Henry IV, Part One*, as in most of Shakespeare's works, sweet-talk is a property of wine—particularly of sack. "Sir John, sack-and sugar Jack" is how Poins greets the paragon of Knights Tipplers (1.2.112–13). "If sack and sugar be a fault," protests Falstaff later in the play, "God help the wicked" (3.1.475–6). "Sugared" seems an odd epithet for Shakespeare's often piquant and sometimes bitter poems. (Sonnet 29 is among the sweeter ones.) "Sugared" may have less to do with the sonnets' content than with the way they were passed from person to person.

Putting together Meres' "sugared sonnets" and Falstaff's "sack and sugar," we might conclude that reading a private friend's sugared sonnet would be like sharing a cup of sweetened wine. The scripted words are something to be brought to the lips, to be tasted, to be taken in through the mouth.

> Drink to me, only, with thine eyes,
> And I will pledge with mine;
> Or leave a kiss but in the cup,
> And I'll not look for wine.
> (Jonson 1947: 8:106)

The cup of wine, like the sheet of paper on which the poem is inscribed, is passed from hand to hand. Taken in hand and sounded, silently or aloud, with the lips, the poem itself becomes a kind of kiss. Ben Jonson's lyric invites the recipient to "read" the pledge in the face and to "read" the kiss in the cup, but the recipient can do so only by reading Jonson's lines on the paper. Face, cup, kiss, and handwritten paper fit within the same frame of experience. In its engagement of the senses, a manuscript leaf thus differs from a printed book. Meres' description suggests an experience that is as much tactile as visual, as much gustatory as aural. "When in disgrace with fortune and men's eyes,/ I all alone beweep my outcast state": if a sheet of paper bearing these lines is passed along to the "thee" of line 10, the poem itself becomes an act of reaching out, an act of touching, perhaps an act of kissing the eyes that see and the lips that sound the words that are not just words.

In different ways, then, touch is something that all three modes of communication share—even the printed book. We might distinguish the hand that holds the book from the hand that writes, or the lungs and mouth that subliminally sound a written text from the arms and hands that perform the text in ASL. Ultimately, though, touch is a function not of this body part or that body part but of the entire body.

As Helkiah Crooke, citing his favorite authority Aristotle, points out in his medical encyclopedia *Microcosmographia* (1615), touch "is not contained within any proper organ or instrument but equally diffused through the whole body" (531). One version of this whole-body sense of touch is known to modern psychology as "proprioception," defined by the *Oxford English Dictionary* as "the perception of the position and movements of the body" arising from muscle and nerve tissues (*OED* 1989: proprioception," *n.*). Proprioception is involved in all three modes of communication.

The most suggestive deconstruction of all concerns language, in particular the supposed distinction between a language of words in the 1609 quarto and a language of gesture in Chris Garcia's signing. As acts of decoding, reading marks on a page may not be so different from reading a signer's arms, hands, mouth, and eyes. To most linguists, both ASL and early modern English shape up as two distinct languages—no need for scare quotes with respect to the former. Each comes equipped with its own vocabulary and syntax. Considered as signs within a language system, arms, hands, mouth, and eyes do not operate differently than marks on a page: they *signify*. To understand the commonalities requires a readjustment of assumptions about the primacy of words. Classical rhetoric has taught us to think of gesture as something *added onto* words. Quintilian in his *Institutio Oratoria* distinguishes five "canons" or "departments" of rhetoric, in this precise order:

- *inventio* (invention of matter or arguments)
- *dispositio* (arrangement of those arguments)
- *elocutio* (the style with which the arguments are to be presented)
- *memoria* (memorization)
- *pronuntiatio* (delivery).

(3.3.1–3 in Quintilianus 1921: 1:382–4)

Invention of arguments is a thoroughly verbal enterprise. Feeling and affect come into consideration with arrangement and style. Memorization locates the resulting decisions in the speaker's body. Actions of the body—in particular, management of the speaker's arms and hands—come into play only as an *after*-thought. Thus Obadiah Walker's textbook *Some Instructions concerning the Art of Oratory. Collected for the use of a Friend a Young Student* (1659) advises, "Pronunciation ought to be accompanied with some decent action and comportment of your body. This action is especially of the eyes and the hands" (126). Chris Garcia's signing of sonnet 29 would seem to illustrate that chronology: first words, then gesture. (He is, after all, translating the sonnet from one language into another.) The case I wish to make here is, however, just the opposite. Gesture comes *first*.

:

To grasp that counter-intuitive proposition we need to distinguish two fundamentally different models of language. The first is the one that has held sway—in academic circles at least—since the linguistic turn of the late 1960s. In the transcribed lectures that comprise Ferdinand de Saussure's *Course in General Linguistics* the professor distinguishes two ways of framing the study of language. The more influential of these two frames in the late twentieth century was *langue*: a critical interest in the structures that make the marking of meaning possible, a synchronic framing of language in which particular utterances are less important than the deep structure that makes all utterances possible. In our fascination with these structural principles and the deconstruction they enable, we have forgotten the other framing of language described in Saussure's linguistics: *parole*, the diachronic consideration of language as it operates in time, language as particular utterances, language as process, language as dramatic event, language as speech-acts. Before *langue*, before *parole*, Saussure recognizes a primordial chaos of thoughts and sounds. The diagram shown in Figure 2.5—much less familiar than the tree and the horse that make every anthology of critical theory—comes from Part II, Chapter 4, of Saussure's *General Linguistics*. The letter A here designates what Saussure calls "the indefinite plane of jumbled ideas"; the letter B, "the equally vague plane of sounds" (122). Vertical lines indicate the cuts, the difference-markings that speakers make amid the chaos of thoughts and the plenitude of sounds. Saussure himself attended to the waves as well as to the lines, but most

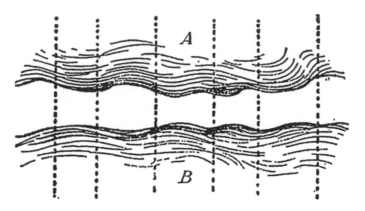

Figure 2.5 Cuts in *langue*, from Ferdinand de Saussure, *Course in General Linguistics* (1916).

of his disciples since the linguistic turn have not done so. Their attention has been trained exclusively on the vertical lines, on the markings of difference. What has been lost to view is what might come *before* and *between* those marks.

Saussure's figure was almost certainly inspired by a diagram in William James's *Principles of Psychology* (1890), which was translated into French in 1907, the very year Saussure began lecturing at the University of Geneva.[2] (See Figure 2.6.) James's figure plots the "stream of consciousness" that underlies a single utterance, "The pack of cards is on the table." The horizontal axis measures the time it takes a speaker to make this utterance, the vertical lines mark "the object in the mind" at a given instant, and the space between the horizontal line below and the curving line above envelops "the objects or contents of the thoughts" as they change through time (James 1890: 280). The curved line, with its peaks and valleys and its surge toward point 4′, plots the

---

[2] For this connection I am grateful to Edwin McCann, as well as for his counsel on the question of whether there can be thought without language. I am sorry to say I have refused his good counsel.

50

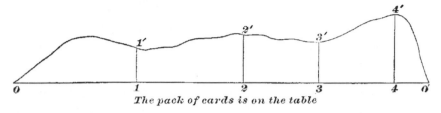

The pack of cards is on the table

Figure 2.6 "The stream of consciousness," from William James, *The Principles of Psychology* (1890).

successive aspects of the object as those aspects come to prominence (in the mind's eye, so to speak) at different moments. James's argument concerns the essential unit of the white space between the horizontal line and the curved line: "Whatever things are thought *in relation* are thought from the outset *in a unity*, in a single pulse of subjectivity, a single psychosis, feeling, or state of mind" (278, emphases added). Even though the speech may consist of individual words uttered in sequence, the whole idea is always present in the mind as a kind of "overtone," "halo," or "fringe" (281).

A second model of language, starkly in contrast to Saussure's *langue*, is provided by Lev S. Vygotsky (1896–1934), whose most famous book is *Thought and Language*, published in Russian in 1934, 18 years after Saussure's students first published in French his *General Linguistics* but just three years after the corrected third edition that provides the text for the English translations (1959, 1966, 1983) from which most participants in the linguistic turn have taken their direction. "Thought" and "speech": the two entities in Vygotsky's title are imagined, just as in Saussure, to exist on two "planes," one "external" (the spoken word) and one "semantic" (the internally experienced quality of thought). "These two planes do not correspond," Vygotsky insists.

> There is a second, inner, plane of speech standing beyond words. The independence of this grammar of thought, of this syntax of verbal meanings, forces us to see—even in the simplest of verbal expressions— a relationship between the meaningful and the external aspects of speech that is not given once and forever, a relationship that is not

constant or static. What we do see is *movement*. We see a continuous transition from the [internal] syntax of meanings to the [external] grammar of words, a transformation of sense structure as it is embodied in words. (Vygotsky 1987: 253)

Where Saussure, Derrida, and most of their followers see a "cut" or "bar," Vygotsky, like James, sees movement. Vygotsky regards speech, not as the *content* of "thought," but as the *completion* of "thought."

Furthermore, movement operates in two directions, not just from thought to words on the speaker's part but from words to thought on the listener's part. If external speech is produced by a movement from within to without, "inner speech" results from a movement in the opposite direction, from without to within: "It is a process that involves the evaporation of speech in thought" (257). Because of this two-way movement, Vygotsky can regard "inner speech," not as a natural phenomenon, as "that within which passeth show" in Hamlet's words (1.2.85), but as a cultural construction, a product of socialized speech (113). Hence his interest in how outer speech and inner speech overlap. Vertical planes is one model of thought and speech that Vygotsky proposes; two intersecting circles is another. The image in Figure 2.7, devised by David McNeill for his book *Gesture and Thought*, takes up the second model and realizes the relationship between thought and speech as a Venn diagram that mediates between "Speech-without-thought"

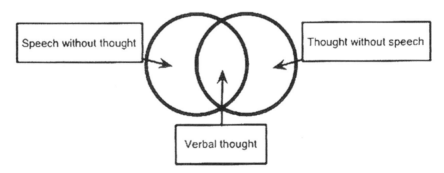

Figure 2.7   Speech without thought, Thought without speech, and Verbal thought, from David McNeill, *Gesture and Thought* (2005).

on the one hand and "Thought-without-speech" on the other. The overlap—relatively small in comparison with the other two areas—is what McNeill describes as "Verbal thought."

But wait. Can there *be* thought without speech? Not according to Derrida in *Of Grammatology* (1967, English translation 1974). Not according to Jerry Fodor in *The Language of Thought* (1975). Not, indeed, according to most other philosophers of language since the linguistic turn. Not according to those cognitive scientists who assume that the human brain is a particularly sophisticated computer, processing information via a sequence of 1 | 0 switches that work like Derrida's marks of *différance*. In both cases we are dealing with a "chain," not a flow. An alternative view, ultimately derived from William James, is emerging from the experiments of Michael Spivey, who argues in *The Continuity of Mind* (2007) that "the human mind/brain typically construes the world via partially overlapping fuzzy gray areas that are drawn out over time" (3). According to Spivey's findings, perception of language as well as perception of objects happens through constantly moving trajectories within a "state space" inside the brain—a space in which the two-dimensional planes and three-dimensional coordinates of Euclidean geometry are extended into the infinite-dimensional space needed to accommodate the possibilities of mobile thought. (James has anticipated this multi-dimensional model with his figure of a square wooden frame covered with a rubber membrane that can bulge in a third dimension as thought moves among the coordinates of time on one side and individual words on the other. See James 1890: 283.) When, to take a simple example, you hear the sound frequencies that your brain recognizes as /k/, /a/, /n/, and /d/, your neurons fire in a broad searching pattern until /l/ confirms the word as *candle* or /i/ confirms it as *candy* and the "wrong" circuits shut down. A similar process happens with objects. Is that two faces you are seeing, or a wine goblet? Instead of a 1 | 0 data-processor Spivey posits a constantly moving, *flowing* mind that works in sync with a constantly moving, flowing array of stimuli.

As it happens, the wave functions in Spivey's quantum-mechanics model of perception seem much closer to the circulations of *spiritus* in Thomas Wright's hydraulic model of perception (see Chapter 1) than they do to the 1 | 0 alternations in the computational model assumed by some cognitive scientists today. According to ideas derived from Aristotle's treatise "On the Soul" and Galen's physiological writings, external sensations were imagined by THWS and his contemporaries to be communicated to the brain by airy spirits, the body's vaporous internal communication system. In the brain these sensations were thought to undergo synesthetic fusion in "the common sense" and to be further shaped by fancy, memory, and imagination before being sent, again via airy spirits, to the heart. There desirable images cause the heart to dilate; repugnant images, to contract. In both cases the entire body responds to the resulting changes in body chemistry. Only in that altered state, when affect has been added to perception, does judgment come into play in the form of words, reason, and acts of will (Park 1988b: 464–84).

According to Spivey's experiments, the fuzziness that attends acts of perception carries over into acts of verbalization: "self-conscious thoughts are due to the language subsystem receiving its biased updates of the meandering, looping, and loop-de-looping mental trajectory and converting it (or collapsing its distributed wave function) into individual words and phrases" (2007: 328). Spivey, trying to describe his own internal monologues, notices "that the first few words of a sentence often ring clear in my head like a well-trained newscaster's voice, and the next several are somewhat vague or poorly enunciated, and the last few words of the sentence are left off entirely, because I've completed the thought for myself by then and finishing the linguistic version is unnecessary" (329–30). Not all thought-without-speech ends in speech-without-thought. It is in the in-between arena, what McNeill calls "verbal thought," that individual consciousness (thought-without-speech) intersects with regimes of verbal language (speech-without-thought).

∴

As they imply different ways of making sense of the world, Saussure's and Vygotsky's two models of language imply different ways of reading:

54

one strategy that is attentive to words, to Derrida's "arche-writing," to markings of difference, and one strategy that is attentive to gesture, to the origins of communication inside the human body, to the felt quality of thought *before* words. As a way of gauging the differences between these two strategies of reading, pronouns offer a particularly interesting test case. The insistent first-personhood of WSA's entire collection of sonnets is registered in sonnet 29. In this sonnet, as in all the others, it is precisely the repetitions of "I," "me," "my," and "mine" that produce the irresistible "subjectivity effect" that has been remarked by critics from Wordsworth to Joel Fineman.

Sonnet 29 is altogether typical of WSA's sonnets in the triangulated drama it plays out among "I," "he," and "thee." The twelve first-person pronouns in the poem's fourteen lines are contrasted in two ways, in two directions. In the octave "I" is played off against four—possibly five, possibly six—third-person Others:

> Wishing me like to **one more rich in hope**,
> Featured like **him**, like *him* with friends possessed,
> Desiring *this* **man**'s art and *that* **man**'s scope,
> With what I most enjoy contented least.

If "what I most enjoy" is the friend, then there are *six* third-person Others. In the sestet "I" turns from these assorted third-person Others to a single second person—"Haply I think on **thee**"—and with that shift in pronouns finds contentment that lasts even when the speaking "I" glances at third-person Others in the couplet: "For thy sweet love remembered such wealth brings/ That then I scorn to change my state with kings"—with, that is to say, "them."

My own head was turned by the linguistic turn, I have to admit, and this interdependency among pronouns inspired an essay, "I, You, He, She, and We: On the Sexual Politics of Shakespeare's Sonnets," which I published in 1998, with a reprint in 2000. The pronouns in WSA's sonnets may seem like fixed entities, I argued then, but "I" needs the "not-I" in order to *be* "I": "I" needs "thou," just as "I" needs "he" and "she," and "he" needs "she." And none of these supposedly fixed entities can stand alone: they are all implicated in each other. The distinctions among them keep breaking down, so that the "we" implicit in hetero-sexist (or, I would now add, homosexualist) readings of the sonnets doesn't hold up. All in all, I produced a standard exercise in decon-struction, informed of course by Saussure's model of language.

What happens to the pronouns if we read sonnet 29 using Vygotsky's model instead of Saussure's? They are still contingent, just as they are in Saussure's model, but they are contingent on bodies-in-space-in-time. I asked Chris Garcia to show me how he handled the pronouns in sonnet 29. In general, Chris explained, "I" is located by a tap of a finger on the breastbone. As Chris explained to me, the gesture toward the breastbone is much less important in the signing of the first quat-rain of sonnet 29 than the signs for "tears," shown as frames two and three in Figure 2.1. In this scheme, "I" does not exist apart from "tears." "I" and "tears" compose a single conceptual unit, in which the emphasis falls, not on "I," but "tears." What you see in the first frame of Figure 2.1 is the one moment in Chris's interpretation when "I" assumes unusual importance, as Chris signs "I alone": the tap to the breast is followed by a raised index finger for the number 1. Here is Chris's literal, if you will, translation of what he is signing in the poem's first two lines:

> when happen / mess–up / embarrass / eyes stare
> leave alone / tears / my life / look like / outcast

Where is "I" in this? Physically available for being gestured toward throughout the transaction, semiotically so in the sign for "alone," but generally speaking "I" is inseparable from "embarrass," "tears," and "outcast"—all three of which hover in a syntactically indefinite space somewhere in between adjective ("outcast"), noun ("tears"), and verb ("embarrass"). "I" as a pronoun is, literally, nowhere to be *seen*, except in "I alone." "Mess-up," "embarrass," and "eyes stare" *involve* "you" as well as "I." That is to say, they turn "I" into "you" and "you" into "I."

When it comes to pronouns, Chris's explanations of what he was doing made me see how linear and hence how redundant the English language is. The goal in signing, Chris told me, is to use as few signs as possible with movements between signs that are as fluid as possible.

As a signer Chris first creates a precisely delimited three-dimensional space with his hands and then proceeds to locate within that space himself, the people about whom he is speaking, and the people for whom he is signing. To indicate that a new idea applies to a given person requires only a small gesture toward the space that person occupies, actually in the case of listener/viewers and symbolically in the case of absent persons who are being spoken about.

It is the demonstrative pronouns in the second quatrain that best show the process of thought that begins with preparatory gestures and proceeds through various extensions of the speaker's body into space, before it ends with the definitive gesture that fixes the conception in the eyes of the listener/spectators. Let's follow Chris step by step:

> Wishing me like to one more rich in hope,
> Featured like him, like him with friends possessed,
> Desiring this man's art, and that man's scope,
> With what I most enjoy contented least.

The sequence begins with two fingers pointing to the chest, melded into the sign for "wish": a downward movement on the chest with five bent fingers. "One more rich in hope" starts out as four bent fingers in each hand at disparate heights. The lower hand attempts to rise to the same level as the higher hand. The index finger of the lower hand then points to the higher hand as if to say, "This—what?" Four bent fingers in each hand move down the chest in parallel to answer that question: "This *person*." A look at the video at http://purl.org/emls/si-19/smitsonn.htm will show you how important the ambient space is to the signer's rendering of this particular quatrain. The raised index finger of the formerly lower hand points to the higher hand to indicate the first "like him" and repeats that gesture to indicate the second "like him," as shown in Figure 2.8.

"This man" and "that man" are more complicated still—and they implicate the listeners/viewers in the poem's imaginative space. The first frame in Figure 2.9 shows the signer beginning his search for "this man." Here the gesture formally known as "two fingers outward" searches the listener/viewers. "This man" is found in the second frame

Figure 2.8   Crescenciano Garcia, Shakespeare sonnet 29, "Featured like him, like him with friends possessed."

Figure 2.9   Crescenciano Garcia, Shakespeare sonnet 29, "Desiring this man's art, and that man's scope."

of Figure 2.9, when the index finger points to him. In the third frame the search begins for "that man." While the two fingers are still "looking" in the direction of "this man," the speaker/signer has turned his attention in the opposite direction. Sweeping the listener/viewers with the two "looking" fingers, the speaker/signer finally turns his own gaze in the direction his hand has moved, as shown in the third frame of Figure 2.9. Finally "that man" is found. A pointing index finger in the fourth frame of Figure 2.9 says that the speaker/signer has found "that man"—the one he has been looking for among the listener/spectators. The sequence of gestures, like the English verbiage of the poem, reaches its climax when the speaker/signer communicates "Haply I think on thee," as shown in Figure 2.10. This Chris does by tapping an index finger on his temple, expanding outward in a circular

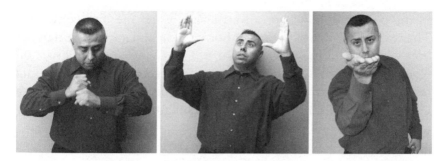

Figure 2.10   Crescenciano Garcia, Shakespeare sonnet 29, "Haply I think on thee."

motion with both hands, thus appealing directly to the listener/spectators, and at last gesturing toward them as "thee" in the sign you see in the third frame of Figure 2.10: a "supine open five hand" moving in their direction. The fact that in this particular shot the hand seems to be replacing Chris Garcia's mouth says it all.

Where can we locate Chris Garcia with respect to the two models of language? Chris was, of course, working out of a verbal text, WSA's sonnet 29 as it was printed in the 1609 quarto. Furthermore, he came to the task with trilingual expertise in spoken English and spoken Spanish as well as ASL. Chris began, then, in the left-hand circle of David McNeill's Venn diagram, in the arena of speech-without-thought. (See Figure 2.7.) But by returning speech to the body, Chris's interpretation reclaims the right-hand circle, thought-without-speech. If, in Vygotsky's scheme, words are an analogue of thought, Chris provides gestures that are analogues of speech. In effect, Chris ends up occupying a position in the overlap between the two arenas in McNeill's diagram. From that position Chris makes forays into the other arenas. Most of those forays are into the arena of thought-without-speech. Only in rare moments, as when he sets up the simile in line 11, does Chris's reading veer into the arena of speech-without-thought.

Metaphors, which link things present with things *not* present, would seem to present a challenge for remaining within the overlap between thought and speech. As logical (or perhaps quasi-logical) operations, metaphors require words. Take for example "Like to the lark at break of day arising / From sullen earth / sings hymns at heaven's gate."

In the poem the indication of a metaphor and the bird come first. The word "like" signals the metaphor up front and locates the transaction within the arena of speech. In ASL, by contrast, the transaction would begin holistically, in the arena of thought. First the earth would be contextualized, then the bird would be put in it. It would be more idiomatic in ASL, Chris explained, to render the lines this way:

> Compare / round earth / quiet / sun rise / shine
> Bird awake / inspire / chirp / sing / offer up / towards heaven

In his interpretation Chris chose the harder course of emphasizing the contrivance of the concept and starting with the bird, which at first lacks the usual spatial context:

> compare / same bird / sit quiet / earth / sun rise / light beam

Chris's solution puts the spatiality of earth in ASL in exactly the same syntactical position it occupies in WSA's early modern English: fourth.

"Haply I think on thee, and then my state": the occasion for this metaphor begins with Vygotsky's "inner speech" ("I think on thee") and ends with external speech ("sings hymns at heaven's gate"). Chris's realization of the sequence is plotted in the three frames of Figure 2.10. Chris's literal translation of the line may seem radically disjointed—"paratactic" is the technical word—when judged by usual English syntax:

> happen / imagine you / then self state

But ASL renders that thought with unusual fluidity, amplitude, and compression. Frames one and two locate "imagine" as a turning-inward followed by an opening-out. The third frame extends this opening-out into the viewer/listener's space. A striking illustration of James's claim that the entirety of a thought is present throughout an utterance of that thought is to be found in the second frame, when Chris interprets the second phase of "imagine" with two raised hands.

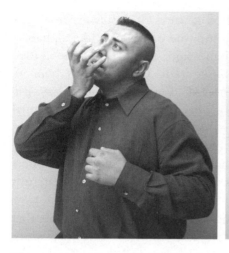

Figure 2.11   Crescenciano Garcia, Shakespeare sonnet 29, "Sings hymns at heaven's gate."

"Think on thee" and "sings hymns," in Chris's interpretation, are similar events. The two frames for "sings hymns" in Figure 2.11 show a
visual homology that repeats the earlier literal homology of "imagine
you" (for "think on thee") and "offer up" (for "sings hymns"). These
repeated gestures of *in/out/up* endow both events with a feeling of
exaltation that pulses throughout the thought. There is good evidence
that Chris's gestures for both "think on thee" and "sings hymns" would
have been read by seventeenth-century watchers/listeners, centuries
before the invention of ASL, as signs of triumph.

⋮

Thanks to the paucity of information about early modern acting
techniques, John Bulwer's twin treatises *Chirologia: or the Natural
Language of the Hand* and *Chironomia: or the Art of Manual Rhetoric*,
although published 28 years after THWS's death, figure on the horizon of most students of early modern drama. A sample plate (usually
the first of the publication's six plates) appears in many books about
early modern theater, usually with a casual comment about how
modern viewers would find early modern acting technique stilted

and artificial, as witness the codified gestures that Bulwer shows for expressing various passions. The composite plates look like alphabets of a sort, alphabets made up of hand-signs rather than letters. (See Figure 2.12.) The Latin captions—see items C (*Ploro*), D (*Admiror*), and P (*Triumpho*)—suggest a visual dictionary or vocabulary list. *Chirologia* and *Chironomia* have both been regarded as a professional manual—*literally* a "handbook"—that seventeenth-century orators (and presumably stage actors) could use. That may be true of the second treatise, *Chironomia*, but what the first treatise, *Chirologia*, offers is a complete, reasoned philosophy of language—and one that runs counter to Saussure and Derrida.

In *Chirologia* Bulwer regards hand gestures, not as ornaments that occur *after* verbal signifiers, as most modern histories of theater assume, but as meaning-formations that occur *before* verbal signifiers—and that often outpace them. Bulwer's deployment of the word "difference" gives an uncanny sense that he has read Derrida's *Of Grammatology*: "whatsoever is perceptible unto sense, and capable of a due and fitting difference; hath a natural competency to express the motives and affections of the mind, in whose labors the hand which is a ready midwife takes oftentimes the thoughts from the forestalled tongue, making a more quick dispatch by gesture" (Bulwer 1974: 17). Bulwer instances the firing of a piece of ordnance, in which the eye perceives the blast before the ear hears the report. The reason for the primacy of gesture is not just a function of light rays' traveling faster through the air than sound waves do: it has to with the embodiedness of thought. What the hand is expressing is not just a certain "signified," to use modern terminology, but "signifying," *the trajectory of thought* that ends in that "signified."

Bulwer emphasizes the power and temporal immediacy of fancy in the sequence that leads from sensation to common sense to fancy to memory to imagination to judgment. Fancy (or fantasy as we might term it today) operates as a species of Vygotsky's thought-without-speech: "For when fancy hath once wrought upon the hand, our conceptions are displayed and uttered *in the very moment of a thought*" (Bulwer 1974: 17, emphasis added). What is more, hand gestures are closer than words to "the true nature of things":

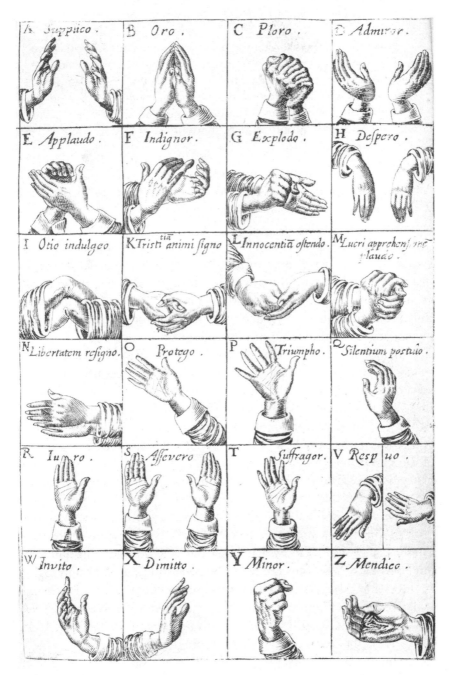

Figure 2.12 John Bulwer, *Chirologia* (1644), Chirogrammatic Plate A.

63

all these motions and habits of the hand are purely natural, not positive [i.e., "posited," "put out there"]; nor in their senses remote from the true nature of the things that are implied. The natural resemblance and congruity of which expressions result from the habits of the mind by the effort of an impetuous affection wrought in the invaded hand which is made very pliant for such impressions. (16)

That is to say, hand gestures, more than words, are imbued with what Antonio Damasio has called "the *feeling* of what happens." In keeping with Bacon's goals in *The Advancement of Learning*, Bulwer has no anxieties about presenting his "natural" language of the hand as a universal language. I do not share Bulwer's aspirations in that regard, nor do I wish to romanticize users of ASL (or any other sign-language for that matter) as being in touch with a primitive essence that the rest of us have lost. I do think, however, that ASL in conjunction with Bulwer's twin treatises can make us aware that language begins, not in mental acts of marking, but in movements of the body.

I am not alone, I suspect, in having assumed that what Bulwer's charts illustrate are passions, as if such-and-such a gesture somehow equaled such-and-such a passion. Wrong. What the images demonstrate are, in Hamlet's words, "actions that a man might play" (1.2.84). At the end of his introduction to *Chirologia,* Bulwer sets up a phrase "For with our hands we …" and follows it with *more than 200 verbs.* All of the gestures described and illustrated in *Chirologia* are expressed as first-person verbs ("I …") and represent only a small selection of the more than 200 that Bulwer has catalogued. The relevant first-person verbs for WSA's sonnet 29 are *ploro* ("I beweep"), *admiror* ("I admire," "I think on thee"), and *triumpho* ("I exult," "I sing hymns at heaven's gate"). Let us consider these one by one. Figure 2.13 illustrates the three pivotal verbs, abstracted from the plate in Figure 2.12 and placed in chronological sequence with respect to sonnet 29. *Ploro* (frame one) is derived from Francis Bacon's *Silva Silvarum, or A Natural History* (published posthumously in 1627, with reprints in 1628, 1631, 1635, and 1639), the text that in fact inspired Bulwer's entire project. According to Bacon, wringing of the hands as a sign of weeping has a physiological cause. "To wring the hands," Bulwer explains,

Figure 2.13 Chirograms for William Shakespeare, sonnet 29, from John Bulwer, *Chirologia* (1644).

is a natural expression of *excessive grief* used by those who *condole, bewail*, and *lament*. Of which gesture that elegant expositor of nature [Francis Bacon in *Silva Silvarum*] hath assigned this reason: sorrow which diminisheth the body it affects provokes by wringing of the mind, tears, the sad expressions of the eyes, which [tears] are produced and caused by the contradiction of the spirits of the brain, which contradiction doth strain together the moisture of the brain, constraining thereby tears into the eyes; from which compression of the brain proceeds the HARD WRINGING OF THE HANDS which is a gesture of expression of moisture. (1974: 32, emphases original)

Throwing up the hands to heaven in the gesture *Admiror* (see frame two) "is an expression of *admiration, amazement*, and *astonishment*, used also by those who *flatter* and *wonderfully praise*, and *have others in high regard*, or *extol* another's speech or action" (33, emphases original). *Admiror*, it is worth noting, is a so-called "deponent verb" in Latin: it exists only in passive-voice forms, even though what it signifies is generally understood to be in active voice. Literally translated, *admiror* ought to mean "I am admired." Deponent verbs in Latin, Emile Benveniste has argued, are vestiges of middle-voice verbs in Greek and other Indo-European languages. Middle voice covers situations in which, as Benveniste puts it, "the subject is the *center* as well as the *agent* of the process; he *achieves* something which *is being achieved* in him .…. He is indeed *inside* the process of which he is the agent" (Benveniste 1971: 149). Other examples that seem to occur in all Indo-European

65

Figure 2.14 Chirograms for William Shakespeare, sonnet 29, from John Bulwer, *Chironomia* (1644).

languages are the verbs for "to be born," "to marry," and "to converse." *Admiror* in sonnet 29 involves not just the speaking "I" but the "thee" who inspires the speaking "I," like a lark, to sing hymns at heaven's gate. In deponent verbs the inscribed personal pronoun is implicated in third person or second person. *Triumpho*, finally, is, as Bulwer puts it, "to put out the raised hand, and to shake it, as it were into a shout."

The gestures described in *Chirologia* are, Bulwer claims, "purely natural, not positive." Hence the appropriateness of first person to designate the subject. One is "invaded" by the passion, one "suffers" the passion. (*Patior*, from which the English word "passion" derives, is another deponent verb.) The gestures catalogued in *Chironomia* are, by contrast, contrivances: they are "posited," put forward as artistic devices. Rather than accepting these gestures as the irreducible elements of body-language, Bulwer takes a step backward in *Chironomia* and attempts to isolate the "canons" of hand gestures by isolating several dozen different combinations of finger and hand positions and assigning them Roman numerals. The result is not "sufferings" expressed in first-person verbs but performances expressed in *third*-person verbs. *Chirologia* catalogues gestures that occur *before* words; *Chironomia*, gestures that occur *after* words. And those post-verbal gestures happen, not in first person ("I do this or that"), but in third ("*he* does this or that"). Thus the same gesture that "naturally" signifies *Ploro*, "I weep," in *Chirologia* becomes *Dolebit*, "*he* sorrows"—or rather "he *will* sorrow"—in *Chironomia*. (See the first frame in Figure 2.14.) Why Bulwer or his engraver chose future tense for this particular gesture is not clear. Because an assumed passion has to be premeditated? *Admiror*, "I admire," becomes *Admiratur*, "he admires" (frame two). The closest equivalent in *Chironomia* to *Triumpho* is *Exclamationem aptat*, "he makes an exclamation" (frame three).

Why "he makes an exclamation" rather than "I exult"? The shift in personal pronouns suggests two shifts in perspective. One shift is on the speaker's part, as he consciously manipulates the canon of signs made by fingers and hands to act out a certain passion and thus becomes someone else: "I" becomes a dramatic character, a "he." And the speaker doesn't just exclaim; he *makes* an exclamation. The other shift occurs on the spectator/listener's part, as he or she admires—that deponent verb again—the speaker's artifice: for the listener, the impassioned speaker is someone else, a "he." *Chirologia*, then, belongs to Vygotsky's pre-verbal arena of thought-without-speech. *Chironomia*, with its calculated moves of turning words into gestures, belongs to the post-verbal arena of speech-without-thought, in the sense that "thought" has been reduced to words, and words have been reduced to gestures. The shift in pronouns is eloquent: "I"+verb is *pre*-verbal, "he"+verb is *post*-verbal. Why should that be so? The answer points to Lacan's notion of words as an estrangement, as an imposition on bodily wholeness. It is verbal language that turns the first-person actor into a third-person subject.

Along with the change in person in Bulwer's second treatise comes a change in gender that Lacan would also understand. The figures on the engraved title page to *Chirologia* are female, while those on the title page to *Chironomia* are male. The conceits must be Bulwer's, since the engraver, William Marshall, produced detailed work like this only when someone else was supplying the visual and intellectual ideas (Griffiths 1998: 164). The detail in Figure 2.15 shows Natura Loquens ("Speaking Nature") on the left and Polyhymnia (the muse of singing and rhetoric) on the right. "*Hinc latices!*" ("Hence the stream!") Natura's hand is saying; "*Digitisque loquor Gestumque decoro*" ("I speak with fingers and adorn gesture") say Polyhymnia's fingers and arm. Between them a female hand/face is spewing Natura's stream into the *Cisterna Chirosophiae* ("Handwisdom's Reservoir").

The male quartet on the title page to *Chironomia* (see detail in Figure 2.16) are much more self-conscious about how they use gesture. The Greek orator Demosthenes regards himself and his hands in a

Figure 2.15   William Marshall (engraver), title page (detail) to John Bulwer, *Chirologia* (1644).

full-body mirror (labeled "*Actio*," action) which is being held up by Andronicus (presumably Livius Andronicus, credited with being the first Roman to turn satiric diatribes into dialogue and drama), while Roscius the famous Roman actor and Cicero the famous Roman orator take note and practice their own gestures. No doubt about it: "natural" language is being gendered female, "posited" language male.

:

"Nouns and pronouns," exclaims Will Summer in Thomas Nashe's play *Summer's Last Will and Testament*, "I pronounce you traitors to boys' buttocks!" (Nashe 1965: 74). For THWS and his male contemporaries the *Verfremdungseffekt* of language was something they experienced through—and on—their bodies. To get pronouns into schoolboys'

Figure 2.16   William Marshall (engraver), title page (detail) to John Bulwer, *Chironomia* (1644).

heads a schoolmaster needed to use other parts of schoolboys' bodies, the lower parts. It is the same parts of the anatomy—the lower parts— that Hugh Evans has in mind in *The Merry Wives of Windsor* when he tries to show off his pedagogical handiwork to Mistress Page by quizzing her son William:

EVANS   Show me now, William, some declensions of your pronouns.

WILLIAM   Forsooth, I have forgot.

EVANS   It is *"qui, que, quod."* If you forget your *"qui"*s, your *"que"*s, and your *"quod"*s, you must be preeches. Go your ways, and play; go.

MISTRESS PAGE   He is a better scholar than I thought he was.

EVANS   He is a good sprag memory.

(4.1.68–76 in Shakespeare 2005)

69

What made pronouns so difficult for William Page and his fellow schoolboys was the fact that the pronouns he was learning and the rules that applied to them referred not to the English that they spoke without thinking about it but to the Latin that was beaten into them. If Latin was in the head (or supposed to be), English was in the buttocks. English grammarians before, during, and immediately after THWS's time had problems with pronouns, because in Vygotsky's terms they thought in spoken English but spoke (for scholarly purposes at least) in Latin thought.

William Lily's formulation of the rules of grammar and syntax, first published in collaboration with Erasmus in 1513, became the model for all English schools, thanks to royal proclamations by Henry VIII (in 1543), Edward VI (in 1547), and Elizabeth (in 1559) that in effect made Lily's explanation of the Latin language *the* explanation of language—English as well as Latin—for the entire kingdom. In *An Introduction of the Eight Parts of Speech* (1543 edition) Lily defines "a pronoun" in terms that were repeated verbatim by John Brinsley, Clifford Leech, and other pedagogues of the sixteenth and seventeenth centuries—including, presumably, Hugh Evans at Windsor in 1597 and Simon Hunt at the King's New School in Stratford-upon-Avon in the 1570s, when THWS was likely a student there. "A pronoun," says Lily, "is a part of speech much like a noun, which is used in showing or rehearsing" (sig. B4v). The catalogue of 15 pronouns that Lily proceeds to give, along with the categorizations and rules of use that go with them, are all in Latin. Of the 15 pronouns, eight are "primitives, for because they be not derived of any other." These include *ego* (I), *tu* (familiar you), *sui* (its own), *ille* (that one there), *ipse* (the very one), *iste* (that one beside you), *hic* (this), and *is* (he). Lily also calls them "demonstratives, because they show a thing not spoken of before." The other six pronouns—*hic* (this), *ille* (that), *iste* (the one beside you), *is* (he), *idem* (the same), and *qui* (who)—are "relatives, because they rehearse a thing that was spoken of before" (sig. B4v). Hence Lily's basic definition of a pronoun as a part of speech which is used in one of two situations: "showing" or "rehearsing."

Lily's distinction here between *pointing at* something and *saying* something does not bear close scrutiny. John Brinsley catches the ambiguity in the question-and-answer dialogue he stages in *The Posing of the Parts* (1615):

Q.   Can *hic, ille, iste,* and *is* be both demonstratives and relatives?
A.   Yes, in respect of the diverse uses to which they serve: that is, both to show and to rehearse.

(Brinsley 1615: sig. D4)

After all, *hic, ille, iste,* and *is* are the same words, conjugated in different grammatical situations in exactly the same way. It is the grammarian who decides whether they are showing or telling. If they are "relatives" *now,* they were "demonstratives" *then.* Pronouns may occupy the place of a noun, but they are at bottom spatial indicators of just the sort Chris Garcia makes with his hands. The difference between a demonstrative and a relative is only a matter of time. Despite Lily's neat tables of declensions—structuralism *avant la lettre*—it is not hard to deconstruct pronouns. Really, I hesitate to contradict Erasmus and Lily, but it seems to me that what *all* pronouns do is "show." It is well and good to distinguish persons and things that are being referred to *now* and things that were referred to *then,* but wasn't that *then* once a *now?* You can't have *rehearsing* without having once *shown.* We confront here the kind of infinite regress familiar to us from deconstruction. What all pronouns do at bottom, I would argue, is show. As Thomas Blundeville puts it in *The Art of Logic* (1617), "This, or That, and such like Pronouns, do point out a thing, as it were with the finger, when proper names oftentimes do fail" (5). Hence the startling immediacy of "*this* man's art" and "*that* man's scope," of the demonstration implicit in "featured like *him,* like *him* with friends possessed."

In Saussure's terms, Lily and his successors, with their tables and rules, were trying their damnedest to analyze *langue.* As long as they stuck to Latin, they could pretty much do that. But the distractions of *parole* could easily put them off track, especially when they were trying to rationalize pronouns. Erasmus and Lily may have assumed that they were talking about *ego,* but really they were talking about *ick* and *I.* It was, after all, Erasmus's Flemish and Lily's English, not Cicero's Latin, that needed free-standing pronouns like "I," "thee," "he," "she," and "it."

Fortunae fugiens iras oculosque virorum
Sicubi desertum me miserumque fleo.
(Shakespeare 1913: 29)

Like Chris Garcia's signing of sonnet 29, Alfred Thomas Barton's 1913 translation of the same poem into Latin deflects attention from the speaking "I" to what the speaking "I" is *doing*. Word by word, Barton's translation reads

Of Fortune / fleeing / outrages / and eyes of men /
If anywhere deserted / myself / and wretched / I weep for ….

Who is doing the fleeing? Who is deserted? Who is wretched? The reader does not find that out until the very end of the main clause, in the definitive verb *fleo*, "I weep for." It is the *-o* suffix to the root verb *flere* that fixes the first-personhood of the statement. The only pronoun present in the transaction is the reflexive *me* that stands as the direct object of the verb *fleo*: "I weep for myself." English syntax demands a much more forcefully present "I"—and much sooner in the transaction. Who is in disgrace with fortune and men's eyes? The reader finds out at the beginning of line 2, in what feels like a spondee rather than an iamb: "I all alone."

A tension between *langue* and *parole* is played out on every page of Ben Jonson's *An English Grammar*. For the "grammar" part of his project Jonson is indebted to the Latin education he received at Westminster School. In this endeavor he proceeds deductively from the rules. Thus nouns in English are reckoned to have number, gender, case, and declension just as they would in Latin. But the "English" part of his project inspires Jonson to pay careful attention to actual speech. For that, Jonson proceeds inductively from numerous quotations. It is the *parole* of English speech, not the *langue* of Latin grammar, that leads Jonson to the curious conclusion that the articles in English—*a*, *an*, and *the*—function as pronouns. Thus in Chapter III Jonson explains the "syntax" of how *a*, *an*, and *the* are joined to substantives. "In these two pronouns," he argues, "the whole Construction almost of the Latins is contained" (Jonson 1947: 8:535). Which is saying a lot, since

Latin does not use articles. Perhaps it is the prefix *pro-* in the term *pronoun*—literally, "before" or "in front of"—that leads Jonson to treat articles as the paradigmatic case of pronouns.

In THWS's time people in England, France, Germany, and the Low Countries could sometimes kill one another over pronouns, especially pronouns that *show*. "Much divinity in pronouns," Martin Luther was often quoted as saying (Boys 1610: sig. H2; Adams 1619: sig. §§§4). The passage being cited—although one wonders how many of the people doing the citing knew it directly—occurs in Luther's commentary on Galatians—in particular his commentary on verse 4, where Paul refers to Christ, "who gave himself for *our* sins"—not that man's sins or this man's sins but *our* sins and hence *my* sins. "We find very often in the scriptures," Luther observes, "that their significance consists in the proper applications of pronouns, which also convey vigor and force" (Luther 1963: 26:33–4).

The instance that could provoke murderous thoughts was the phrase "*Hoc est corpus meum*": the Latin Vulgate translation of the words Christ is reported, in the gospels of Matthew, Mark, and Luke, to have uttered at the Last Supper—"This is my body"—had found its way into the liturgy of the mass by the twelfth century and provided the occasion for sustained debate among Catholic and Protestant apologists in the sixteenth and seventeenth centuries. The demonstrative *hoc*, as Catholic writers liked to point out, is neuter in gender and hence refers to *corpus*, the neuter word for "body," and not *panis*, the masculine word for "bread," which would take the masculine demonstrative pronoun *hic*. (All a matter of *hocus pocus*, Protestant detractors said.) Nicholas Sander in *The Supper of Our Lord Set Forth According to the Truth of the Gospel and Catholic Faith* (1566) gives this interpretation a classic statement. Christ's "deed of taking bread, and of blessing," Sander argues,

> showed his words to be directed unto that which was in his hand, or lay before him (which was bread before). It must needs be, that the pronoun *this* so showed to his Apostles the thing already subject unto their eyes, that much more it served to teach their understanding verily, this which appeared to them bread to be in substance, at the ending of the words, his own body. (sig. YY1v)

Protestant polemicists like Daniel Featley in *Transubstantiation Exploded* (1638) will have none of this:"it seems to be very absurd to say that the pronoun *this* doth not demonstrate something present. But our Lord took bread, and reaching it, said, 'Take eat, this is my body.' He seems therefore to have demonstrated bread" (sig. I5).

I wish to embrace the Catholic argument. *Hoc* can refer, not just to the thing in front of the speaker, but to the process through which that thing acquires a name and comes to figure in speech. As Sander puts it,"we teach the pronoun *this* to serve both to the eyes and to the understanding of the Apostles: to their eyes, in pointing to the form of bread which they saw; to their understanding, in teaching that substance which was present under that they saw, to be his own body straight when it was so named" (sig. YY1v). *Hoc*, that is to say, gestures toward a process—a process by which thought becomes word.

The *OED* states in more eloquent and precise terms what we heirs of Erasmus, Lily, and Jonson learned in grammar school: a pronoun is "a word used instead of a noun substantive, to designate an object without naming it, when that which is referred to is known from context or usage, has been already mentioned or indicated, or, being unknown, is the subject or object of inquiry" (*OED* 1989: "pronoun," *a.*). Note the positions of "object" and "subject" in this definition: a pronoun is regarded as something *there*, a bounded entity, an object that stands in for another object. But the prefix *pro-* is not so solid. What is that *pro-* and what does it do to the *-noun* to which it is attached? As Bulwer, Barton, and Chris Garcia all remind us, pronouns are implicated in actions. The Latin word *pronomen* belongs to a class of constructions that all involve a verb. Thus, a *pro-consul* was, originally, a person *acting in the place of* a consul. Similarly with *pro-dictator, pro-gubernator, pro-praetor*—and *pro-nomen* (*OED* 1989: "pro-", *prefix*[1], II.4). The fundamental work of pronouns, to point, is registered in these constructions. A consul consults, while a pro-consul consults in the place of *that* person. A noun names, while a pro-noun names in the place of *that* thing or *that* person. Pronouns, as words that point, are implicated in space and time.

:

Among the standard eight parts of speech, the one with which pronouns have the most affinity is not, finally, nouns or verbs, but prepositions. The Latin *pro-* is cognate with the Greek πρό, meaning forward, before, in front of, earlier than (*OED* 1989: "pro.," *n.*[1], *prep.*, and *a.*, etymology). Pronouns don't just name substantives; they *locate* them. In that respect they function as prepositions. According to Michel Serres in *Angels* (1995) and *The Troubadour of Knowledge* (1997), prepositions point up the conditionality of knowledge. Objects of knowledge don't just exist *over there*; they exist in certain temporal and spatial relationships to the knower. Prepositions, literally, *pre-pose* the knower's body. They *position* it *before*, both temporally and spatially, and implicate the body in ways of knowing the world that are far more complicated than the subject/object binary implicit in nouns, in the act of naming. In Serres' formulation, "weaving space, constructing time, they are the precursors of every presence" (Serres 1997: 146).

To understand how this works, consider the prepositions in sonnet 29: "in" (line 1), "out" (2), "with" (3), "upon" (4), "like to" and "in" (5), "like" (6), "with" (8), "in" (9), "on" (10), "like to," "at," and "of" (11), "from" and "at" (12), "with" (14). Each of these prepositions, in Serres' terms, pre-*poses* "I" *vis-à-vis* various other persons and things. "I" may weep, admire, and triumph, but "I" does so in certain spatial and temporal relationships. The most remarkable of these situations occurs in line 4: "I all alone beweep my outcast state." Figure 2.1 shows how Chris Garcia manages that reflexive action. We see him here in mid-sequence, between projecting two looking fingers outwards toward the listener/viewers and turning those looking fingers upon himself. In that gesture he establishes the contingent nature of the speaker, located within his own body but reaching out in a gesture of inclusiveness toward the bodies of others.

To understand these relational ways of knowing, we need, not a dictionary or a grammar book, but something like the "Spatial Relations Alphabet" that Dana Chodzko has designed. Working in

Figure 2.17 Dana Chodzko, "Spatial Relations Alphabet," installation, San Francisco, California (2001).

Abiquiu, New Mexico, and teaching sculpture at the Institute of American Indian Arts in Santa Fe, Dana identifies herself primarily as a sculptor, despite the varied media in which she works. It is spatial relationships rather than particular materials that distinguish her work. The installation shown in Figure 2.17, displayed in the Andrea Schwartz Gallery in San Francisco in 2001 and in the Rotunda Gallery of the New Mexico State Capitol Building in 2006, invited visitors to make their way among objects straight, curved, and round ranged within an open white space. Making their way among the curved lines positioned against the wall and on the floor, passing the red ball resting atop a waving plane, viewers were drawn, at some point or another, to a wall displaying 35 square panels, each of them a different combination of red circles and black lines. In effect, the panels provided visitors with a two-dimensional key, a short-hand guide, to the four-dimensional experience of walking around the installation. The grid shown in Figure 2.18 was Dana's first sketch of the whole idea.

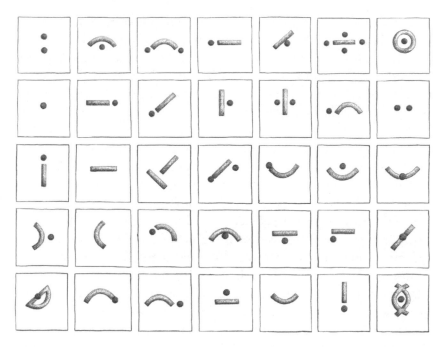

Figure 2.18 Dana Chodzko, "Spatial Relations Alphabet," preliminary sketch, graphite on paper (2000). In other versions Dana Chodzko has keyed the diagram as follows: top row (left to right) *about, above, across, after, against, among, around*; second row (left to right) *at, before, behind, beside, between, beyond, by*; third row (left to right) *down, during, except, for, from, in, into*; fourth row (left to right) *near, of, off, on, over, past, through*; bottom row (left to right) *throughout, to, toward, under, until, up, with.*

Each of the 35 units in Dana's Spatial Relations Alphabet realizes one of the common English prepositions as a combination of a red circle (or circles) and a black line (or lines). According to Dana's own explanation, circles indicate objects, and lines indicate movements, but the essential experience is in the white spaces. "In school I memorized the prepositions to the tune of Yankee Doodle and never forgot them," Dana explains. "They became a metaphor for a big question about the spaces between the points. Is the rhythm of a song created by the notes or by the space in time between the notes? Is the news determined by events or by reactions to events? Something happens between two points that often becomes more important than the points themselves" (Chodzko 2001). Each preposition involves an object that is extended in space and time in a distinctive way. Thus "across" (top row, third panel from the left) shows a red circle that is moving/has moved in an arc from left to right, and "with" (bottom row, last panel) shows a red circle that is moving/has moved through two arcs that define an interior.

Where is the viewer/reader in each case? That depends, just as it did in the installation, on how you move and where you stand. In most cases the circle or circles seem not only to indicate objects but to offer subject positions. As such, the circles occupy the place of pronouns: "I" or "it" or even "you," depending on where you position yourself. You can project yourself into the action or regard it from a distance. Consider "from" in row three, panel five. The combination of red circle and outwardly, upwardly curved black line suggests the action in "*from* sullen earth." Who or what the red circle *is* seems less important than the white space, the relationship between circle and line. Like the letters in a normal alphabet, the units in Dana's Spatial Relations Alphabet are combinable. Putting together the sign for "up" (last row, next-to-last panel) and the sign for "on" (fourth row, middle panel) captures the outward-then-inward action of "look *upon* myself." The fundamental nature of all the signs—and the actions they represent—is perhaps best represented in the sign that Dana has labeled "around" (first row, last position) but which Chris Garcia and I agree would more aptly signify "about" (first row, first position). *Ab* + *out* means, at bottom, a movement *around the outside*: Anglo-Saxon *be* (by) + *utan* (outside) (*OED* 1989: "about," etymology).

To read sonnet 29 with an eye toward the pronouns and prepositions is not unlike walking among the straight, curved, and round objects in Dana Chodzko's installation. The reading and walking "I" is not a free agent, however independent-minded he or she may wish to be. "I" may begin in isolation, "all alone," but my seeming isolation is in fact self-reflexive: I "look upon myself." Then "I" must negotiate my way among those third-person Others—"him," "*him*," "*this* man," "*that* man," perhaps even "what I most enjoy"—before confronting the energizing presence of "thee." So unsettling is that confrontation to my proprioception that I lose myself in the syntactical ambiguities of the final quatrain.

::

What is sonnet 29 *about*? What is going on as I move around the out-side? It is not about "myself," "this man," "that man," "thee," and "they," but about them all *vis-à-vis* the red circle, the speaking "I." Think about the situation of the speaker with respect to the *pro-* in the pronouns he invokes. Forward, before, in front of, earlier than: it's the pronoun that comes *first*. It's the pronoun that is *closer*. The person or object being named is further away in space and/or time. The pronoun occupies the middle distance. "He" and "she" in WSA's sonnets hover somewhere in between the speaker and the people to whom the speaker is referring. Think then about the situation of the reader. In the cases of the "he" and the "she" of WSA's sonnets, the reader never goes the whole dis-tance. The reader is left in the last of the situations described in the *OED*'s definition of "pronoun," a situation in which the noun, "being unknown, is the subject or object of inquiry."

Where, then, should we locate the subject position in WSA's son-nets? What name can we put to the space that the reading subject occupies? WSA gives us the phrase in line 10: "Haply I think on thee, and then my state." The lines that follow introduce a syntactical ambi-guity that demonstrates how speech-without-thought in sonnet 29 has not actually transcended thought-without-speech. In the 1609 quarto printing the phrase "Like to the lark at break of day arising" is put within parentheses—marked off as a simile—so that there can be no doubt about who or what is doing the singing at heaven's gate. Not the speaking "I," not the lark, but "my state." Chris Garcia prob-ably speaks for most readers of the poem in assuming that it is the lark who is doing the singing, or perhaps the speaking "I" in the guise of a lark. Thus Chris interprets the line as

bird / wake / inspire / chirp / sing / offer up / towards heaven.

Stephen Booth in his commentary on the sonnets wants to keep in play all three possible actors: "I," "lark," and "my state." The general context and the common knowledge that birds fly, Booth observes, "make any punctuation powerless to deny that *state* and *lark* are both singers and risers. However, both the Q punctuation and the line-end pause between *arising* and *From* carry a syntactically blurred image of the speaker's state sending hymns aloft from the earth, sending up hymns to heaven" (Shakespeare 2000: 181). Katherine Duncan-Jones in the Arden Three edition uses italics to register mild surprise at the syntax: "Instead of importuning heaven, as in I. 3, the speaker, or his *state*, now praises God" (Shakespeare 1997: 29). The three iterations of the word "state" are central to Helen Vendler's reading of the poem in *The Art of Shakespeare's Sonnets*. "State" is one of two key words, she observes, that resonate between the couplet and the rest of the poem (the other key word is "sings"), and it is the very word that encapsulates the speaker's self-analysis, as he moves from the social world of "my outcast state" to the natural world of "my state,/ Like to the lark" and ends with "my state," not to be compared with kings', in the final line. This third iteration, Vendler proposes, incorporates the earlier two states, the social and the natural, and offers "an integrated model of the 'whole' world" (1997: 161).

"State," I would agree, best describes the speaker's situation—but in a thoroughly physical, thoroughly grounded way. "State" has its origins in the Latin verb *stare*, to stand. So "my state" means, physically as well as psychologically and ethically, "how I stand." Sonnet 29 is one of the citations in the *OED* for "state" in the more abstract sense of "A combination of circumstances or attributes belonging for the time being to a person or thing" (*OED* 1989: "state," *n.*, I.1.a). But "state" is also "A condition (of mind or feeling); the mental or emotional condition in which a person finds himself at a particular time" (I.2.a). "My state" is what I find when I "look upon myself." As such, "state" gets us closer to the dynamics of the speaker's situation in sonnet 29 (and in the sonnets in general) than does the rigid (if unstable) geometry of "I," "you," "he," "she," and "we." Above all, "state" reminds us that thought is not just words but bodily gesture, an extension of the speaker's body into ambient space. The relationship of "I" to "thee," "he," and "she" is a matter of "in," "out," "with," "at," "from," and "like to."

With respect to the body, "I," "he," and "thou" merge into that useful but now rarely heard pronoun "one." "One" *purports to be* third person, but it *functions as* an amalgam of "I" and "you." It exists some-where in between "I" and "you." It implies mutual understanding. It pointedly excludes "them." How should one read a Shakespeare sonnet? By realizing that difference-marking might not be the begin-ning of meaning-making. By embracing middle voice. By attending to pronouns. By assuming the subject position of "one."

3

Carnal Knowledge

Just the facts, ma'am: law is concerned with observable events. What is needed, ideally, to make a charge stick is an eye-witness. Next best is a demonstration that the event in question probably, likely, surely, almost certainly happened, beyond a reasonable doubt. Either way, the viewpoint is supposed to be objective or as close to objective as possible. The magistrate or the jury may get to hear what the charged person has to say for himself or herself, but that testimony figures as just one aspect of a case that is being considered from the outside, from the standpoint of an observer. Thus Sir Edward Coke in the third part of his *Institutes of the Laws of England* (1644), summarizing centuries of legal practice for law students in London's inns of court, can be quite precise about what constitutes rape, sodomy, and bestiality. In the case of "buggery" (a category that for Coke embraces bestiality as well as sodomy), you've got to be careful how you frame the indictment: "there must be *penetratio* [penetration], that is, *res in re* [the thing in the thing], either with mankind or with beast, but the least penetration maketh it carnal knowledge" (Coke 1644: sig. I5). Ejaculation, Coke goes on to say, is not enough to secure a charge of buggery, any more than it is with rape. To demonstrate carnal knowledge, you've got to have penetration. And for that, in a court room at least, you've got to have an observer—even if that observer is the supposed victim of the crime.

Indictments in the assize courts in the counties around London during the reigns of Elizabeth I and James I provide plenty of evidence of this circumstantiality, this framing of sexual acts from the outside. The indictment of Nicholas Nicholas [*sic*], shoemaker, of Reigate, Surrey, for the rape of Elizabeth a Lyffe, also of Reigate, on October 20, 1559 is a case in point. The assize-court records for March 1560 show that Nicholas was indicted by a grand jury a few weeks later for having used a pruning tool and a dagger to force Elizabeth (who was the wife of Thomas a Lyffe, a weaver) to a field called "le yowes" ["The Yews"?], where he allegedly raped her. Despite a bond from her husband and a local farmer to produce Elizabeth as a witness, Nicholas was acquitted, as were most men indicted for rape in the sixteenth century (Cockburn 1975–85: 5:49). Apparently Coke's rule of penetration was, in this case as in others, hard to prove. Elizabeth a Lyffe is typical of the victims in the Elizabethan records in being described as someone's wife or daughter or servant, suggesting that rape was often construed as a property crime. Ages of the victims, specified in about half the cases, range from 4 to 40, with an average of just over 10—precisely the age of consent specified in the statute against rape (Coke 1644: sig. I5v).

Sodomy, sexual acts between two males, was no different with respect to the young ages of the alleged victims and the low rate of convictions. The entry concerning Remily Clerke of St. Thomas's parish, Southwark, in July 1584 is typical. For naming the victim Coke's *A Book of Entries: Containing Perfect and Approved Precedents* (1614) uses the phrase *puerum masculum* ("male boy") in its sample indictment for sodomy and as a precedent cites a case where the "boy" in question was 16 (Coke 1614: fol. 352). Accordingly Clerke's alleged victim, Richard Wooly, is designated in the court records as "a boy" (Cockburn 1975–85: 3:261). For the four indictments for sodomy in the assize-court records, the ages of the victim are specified in all cases but one: they are 5, 8, and 10. One has to think twice about all those representations of Cupid as a plump young boy or about characters like Viola/"Cesario" in *Twelfth Night*, described by Malvolio as being "in standing water between boy and man" (1.5.154).

Sexual acts with animals merited the same attention to external details but surprisingly (considering the animal's inability to testify) yielded a higher conviction rate. At the Chelmsford Assizes on June 29, 1573 Robert Cock (*sic*), laborer, was indicted for buggery. According to the record, on May 29, 1573 he drove a brown mare into a corner of a deep pit in the marsh at Rivenhall and committed buggery with it (Cockburn 1975–85: 3:636). The gender of the horse (female), its color (brown), the physical location of the sexual assault (a corner in a deep pit in a marsh): these circumstantial details were important enough to be recorded in the summary of this case. Cock was convicted and hanged. The court record doesn't say so, but presumably in this case, as in others, there was a third-person witness, someone who saw the act between Cock and horse and could testify to penetration. The tally of animals who figure in the assize-court records for Elizabeth's reign in the home counties is cows 11, horses 9, pigs 3, sheep 1, dogs 1, and goats nil.

Many of Coke's young readers in law would have known a differ-ent take on such matters as readers of Ovid-inspired narrative poems like the 1,194-line *Venus and Adonis* first published in 1593 with no one's name on the title page but with a dedication signed "William Shakespeare"—i.e., William Shakespeare as Author (WSA). Like other poems in the same vein, WSA's seems to have been written and printed with just such young male readers in view. Francis Beaumont was only 17, and had only recently been admitted to study law in the Inner Temple, when he published (anonymously) in 1602 his version of Ovid's tale of the erotic fusion of the water nymph Salmacis and the preternaturally good-looking Hermaphroditus into a single female/male body. "I hope my poem is so lively writ," he tells his readers in the preface, "That thou wilt turn half-maid with reading it" (Beaumont 1602: sig. A4). Another poem in the same vein, George Chapman's *Ovid's Banquet of Sense* (1595), is dedicated to the gregari-ous friend of poets Matthew Royden and carries commendatory poems by John Davies of the Middle Temple and Thomas Williams of the Inner Temple. A young male coterie—perhaps specifically a young male coterie of law students—is likewise implied in *Venus and Adonis*, with its dedication to Henry Wriothesley, Earl of Southampton (20 years old and unmarried at the time), and its presentation of the poem as a child ("the first heir of my invention") for which Southampton is cast as godfather. If Southampton likes what he reads, WSA will honor him "with some graver labour"; if not, WSA will "never after ear so barren a land" (Shakespeare 2005: 224). "Heir" is a legal term, but in combination with "labor" and "ear" the underlying conceit is sexual: writing and publishing a poem is like conceiving and giving birth. In Plato's *Symposium* one encounters the underlying idea here, that a man who is "pregnant in soul" will give birth to works of wisdom "when he makes contact with someone beautiful and keeps company with him" (209.b–c in Plato 1997: 489–90). A male readership associated with the law—a male readership who live together, study together, recreate together—is assumed or implied in all these Ovidian excursions.

The long-term popularity of *Venus and Adonis*, however, implies a readership, female as well as male, far beyond the circle of Francis Beaumont and his law-school buddies. By the time Beaumont's *Salmacis and Hermaphroditus* appeared in 1602, WSA's *Venus and Adonis* had already gone through five editions—well on its way to a record 18 printings down to 1675, the most among any of WSA's printed works. *Venus and Adonis* not only marked WSA's debut in the book stalls; it proved to be his best known piece of writing in his own lifetime. Francis Meres in his 1598 catalogue of WSA's works gives *Venus and Adonis* pride of place and associates WSA with the poem's inspirer: "*Ovid* lives in mellifluous & honey-tongued *Shakespeare*, witness his *Venus* and *Adonis*, his *Lucrece*, his sugared Sonnets among his private friends, etc." (Ingleby, Toulmin Smith, and Furnivall 1909: 1:46, italics original). Only then does Meres turn to WSA's plays. By 1675, when the last free-standing edition of *Venus and Adonis* was issued, the third part of Coke's *Institutes*—admittedly a much more expensive book—had gone through just six printings. The reason is not hard to seek. What *Venus and Adonis* offers that Coke's *Institutes* does not is an *inside* account of rape (an attempted one anyway), sodomy (perhaps), and bestiality (achieved)—an account that goes beyond what those sexual acts *look* like to describe what they *feel* like.

From WSA's preface to the opening lines to the closing lines *Venus and Adonis* insinuates itself into the third paradigm of phenomenal knowing that we set in place in Chapter 1: reader/sensor ↔ world-at-hand. As an explicitly erotic text, the poem offers us telling evidence of how The Historical William Shakespeare (THWS) and his readers experienced their bodies. "To thought," Merleau-Ponty observes, "the body as an object is not ambiguous; it becomes so only in the experience which we have of it, and pre-eminently in sexual experience, and through the fact of sexuality" (1962: 167). The ambiguity concerns the boundaries of body and self. I am an object to others but a subject to myself, and I try to present myself to others as a subject. Sexual desire, according to Merleau-Ponty, heightens this basic existential situation. A third-person observer upsets the mutual "fascination" in this economy of two (167). The kind of evidence brought forward in court records, medical books, conduct books, and Saussure-inspired readings of literary texts brings in this unwelcome third-person observer. From that third-person standpoint sexual acts are all about bounded bodies that can be read from the outside. By contrast, *Venus and Adonis* makes its readers complicit within an economy of two. It refuses the third-personhood in which Coke and company take refuge. As *Venus and Adonis* heightens ambiguity about the boundaries of the self, so it blurs the boundary between the body and the world-at-hand.

Coke and WSA offer two different kinds of texts that require two different kinds of reading: a juridical reading in the case of *Institutes of the Laws of England*, an ecological reading in the case of *Venus and Adonis*. Ecological? Where are the plants? Where are the animals? Where, for that matter, is nature? "Ecology" may be a term used most often in connection with botany and zoology, but it is derived from the Greek word *oikos* ("house") and can be applied more generally to the conditions of inhabiting. Niklas Luhmann has applied ecology to social systems in *Ecological Communication* (1989); Timothy Morton, to acts of interpreting the ambient world without recourse to an entity called "nature." The word "ambience," in Morton's reading, "suggests something material and physical, though somewhat intangible, as if space itself had a material aspect" (Morton 2007: 33). Morton's coinage "ambient poetics" provides a useful handle for interpretation within the paradigm of reader ↔ world-at-hand. An ecological reading of *Venus and Adonis* will attend not just to the paradigm of characters ↔ world-at-hand (as fascinating as that may be in this case) but also to the paradigm of reader ↔ world-at-hand. It will start with the printed book itself and move out by degrees into the ambient world, a world that includes bedchambers as well as studies; ears, eyes, and mouths as well as genitals; psyche as well as soma. The result will be a version of carnal knowledge quite beyond Coke's ken. Nonetheless, it is Coke who provides the key term for the enterprise: penetration.

:

Let us begin with the book itself. The various printings of *Venus and Adonis* insinuate the book as a physical object into the reader's phenomenal space in ways that vary from edition to edition. The unique surviving copy of the original 1593 printing in the Bodleian Library, Oxford, presents to the reader's eye a planar surface of $7\frac{3}{8}''$ × $5\frac{1}{4}''$ (a little over 38 square inches) per two-page opening. The book is thin and light: only $\frac{1}{8}''$ thick, it weighs about 2 ounces. Compared with a folio of Virgil or Ovid, or with the 1623 folio of WSA's collected plays, *Venus and Adonis* is, in more ways than one, *light* reading. The 1593 *Venus and Adonis* is a "handy" book, and it got even handier in the course of its publishing history. The first four editions were printed as quartos (i.e., the printer's standard sheet of paper was folded twice to make up a signature), the next six editions shrank to octavos (the same sheet folded three times), the next edition, dated 1636, was smaller still, a sexto-decimo (folded four times). Surviving copies of octavos average about $5''$ × $3''$ (for a surface area of about 15 square inches, more than 50 per cent smaller than a quarto). The Folger Library copy of the sexto-decimo of 1636 measures only $4\frac{3}{8}''$ × $3\frac{1}{12},''$ giving a surface area of $12\frac{3}{4}$ square inches, about 85 per cent of the surface area of the octavo editions, but only a third of the surface area of the quarto editions. (See Figures 3.1 and 3.2.) Because more pages are needed for the smaller-format editions (despite a decrease in the size of the type), the weight remains about the same: 2 ounces, small enough and light enough to be slipped into a pocket and carried next to the reader's body.

Now as in 1593, the reader's experience of these books in all their various sizes is both out there in the world and in here, inside the body. The printed codex itself is an object positioned in physical space,

Figure 3.1   William Shakespeare, *Venus and Adonis*, 15th edition (1636), cover.

something one holds in one's hands, something one keeps at a certain distance from one's eyes. (For most people that distance is between 12 and 18 inches.) The reader's relationship to the codex can thus be plotted like a figure in a geometry book. The text is "justified" in physical space, in the same way a digital text is justified in electronic space, with precisely calibrated left and right, top and bottom margins. A book remains an object even as the reader, literally, *in*corporates the words printed on the page by taking them in through the eyes. How the reader uses his or her hands in this operation is more variable, depending on the edition. A quarto is just large enough that two hands are required to hold the book, unless the reader lays the book

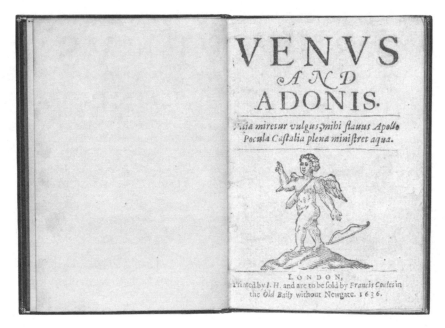

Figure 3.2   William Shakespeare, *Venus and Adonis*, 15th edition (1636), flyleaf and title page.

on a table. Even so, the book might require two hands to hold the book open, especially if it were hardbound and tightly sewn. The pages of an octavo, by contrast, and a sexto-decimo can be kept open with the thumb of one hand, the other four fingers acting as an easel.

Printing technology in THWS's time (an iron chase was required for holding the type in place) meant that text and illustrations were always framed by white space. The Bodleian copy of the 1593 edition, even though it has been radically cut down in the course of rebindings, still provides half-inch margins all the way around. Prints like those shown in Figures 3.5, 3.6, and 3.7 likewise came with wide margins, but purchasers often trimmed them down, right to the plate mark, so that the image merged into its new surroundings, whether that was a blank page in a printed book or the plastered wall above a fireplace. In modern print technology the elimination of margins around a printed image is known as a "bleed." Even without the

Figure 3.3 William Shakespeare, *Venus and Adonis*, 1st edition (1593), within the visual field of the Bradford table carpet (probably London, early seventeenth century), Victoria and Albert Museum.

technology needed to eliminate margins, books like the 1593 quarto "bled" into the environments within which they were read. Take, for example, Figure 3.3, a composite image that shows the 1593 quarto of *Venus and Adonis* laid open for reading on top of a corner of the early seventeenth-century Bradford table carpet in the Victoria and Albert Museum (inventory T.134-1928). The book is open to sigs. G2v–G3, where Venus opens her eyes to behold the dead body of Adonis and "the wide wound that the boar had trenched/ In his soft flank" (1052–3).

As it happens, the border of the Bradford table carpet shows to the left a hunting scene in which a rider holds his lance at the ready to pierce a charging boar. If you were reading the 1593 quarto of *Venus and Adonis* while it rested on the table, 18 inches from your eyes, you could not, of course, take in the entire visual field in a single glance as a camera can. You would stay focused on the book. Indeed, many people would say that the book's power to absorb the reader is the very thing that recommends books as companions in waiting rooms, airplane cabins, and other tedious environments. Occasionally, however, you will look up and look

Figure 3.4 William Shakespeare, *Venus and Adonis*, 15th edition (1636), within the visual field of the Bradford table carpet.

away, and if what you see is appealing, you may find it hard to turn back to the book. (I, for one, find it impossible to read in the midst of beautiful scenery.) If you happened to be reading the 1593 *Venus and Adonis* while seated at a table on which the Bradford carpet was spread, your peripheral vision, even while you stayed focused on the book, could take in the 46″ × 30″ swath of carpet shown in Figure 3.3—perhaps even more. I have based these dimensions on my own peripheral vision at age 62, which has deteriorated by 10 degrees from the 100°-lateral and 60°-medial field it once commanded (Harrington 1971).[1] And of course if you looked up from the book you could see even more. Figure 3.4 shows how much larger the visual field looms when the book in question is the smaller sexto-decimo of 1636, opened to the same passage on sig. D1. The Bradford table carpet is an apt and historically plausible prop, but the field-effect is present—potentially at least—wherever and whenever someone reads a book. A phenomenological investigation will attempt to reconstruct the likely visual fields and gauge their influence

[1]   I am grateful to Michael Quick for the reference to Harrington and for information on lateral and medial fields of vision. For measuring my own fields of vision I thank Joshua Sapkin, MD.

on the experience of reading. Those visual fields include objects that might be physically present while the book was being read—objects like the lid in Figure 3.9 or the playing card in Figure 3.10 or the wall painting in Figure 3.11 or the music book in Figure 3.12 or the bed furnishings in Figures 3.13, 3.14, 3.15, and 3.16. The perceptual fields might also include visual images of the story—the prints in Figures 3.5, 3.6, and 3.7, or the painting in Figure 3.8.

Attentiveness to acts of seeing is cued by the printed text itself. *Venus and Adonis* unapologetically casts the reader as a voyeur. Take, for example, this exclamation from the narrator amid the throes of Venus's frustrated wooing:

> O, what a sight it was wistly to view
> How she came stealing to the wayward boy,
> To note the fighting conflict of her hue,
> How white and red each other did destroy!
> But now her cheek was pale, and by and by
> It flashed forth fire, as lightning from the sky.
>
>   (343–8)

Subsequent stanzas complete the cinematic sweep of body parts: one of her hands heaving up Adonis's hat, the other hand leaving its print on his cheek, the war of looks as her eyes press upon him and his eyes refuse to see, the combat as his white hand is held back by hers like "A lily prisoned in a jail of snow,/ Or ivory in an alabaster band" (362–3). The white-on-white effect points up how either or both of the figures here—he and/or she—can become objects of the reader's lascivious gaze, regardless of the reader's own gender. And it all happens on the sly. "Wistly to view": the word "wistly" usually means "intently" (*OED* 1989: "†wistly," *adv.*), but it also suggests silently ("whistly," *adv. arch.*) as well as "wishly" or longingly. This is a scene of voyeurism: I as reader am both *over there* with the characters I read about and *right here* with the book in my hand. In effect, WSA invites the reader to take the position of Beaumont's Salmacis, hiding in the woods to watch Hermaphroditus undress, or Chapman's protagonist Ovid, sequestered in a bower to spy on Julia as she bathes. In those poems the voyeur is located within the fiction; in WSA's poem the voyeur spies into the fiction from without. If *Venus and Adonis* and WSA's second narrative poem, *The Rape of Lucrece*, published the next year, don't look like pornography by today's standards, it is because they are so wordy. Pornography, we assume, is visual: it circulates over the internet as .jpg or .mpg files. Yet both of WSA's texts (they pulse through the ether as .pdf or .doc files) present scenes of sexual predation—an experienced woman's attempt to seduce an adolescent boy in *Venus and Adonis*, a soldier's rape of his friend's wife in *Lucrece*—and both of them grant the reader a morally safe distance from the scandalous events they get to enjoy. *Morally* safe, perhaps, but not *ethically* safe, if we remember that *ethos* means the character or spirit of people in a certain place, the "genius" of a system or institution (*OED* 1989: "ethos," 1). The inns of court constituted just such an ethos. The ethical knowledge on offer in *Venus and* Adonis is situated knowledge, knowledge-in-a-surround. Readers of the poem were—and are— inescapably *implicated* in what they read. The voyeur may begin in comfortable isolation, but the erotic text, through its very nature as an erotic text, stares back. *Venus and Adonis* gives you the eye.

:

From the very first stanza, in which "Sick-thoughted Venus makes amain unto him,/And like a bold-faced suitor 'gins to woo him" (5–6), the poem presents itself as a scene of seduction. Adonis's resistance, like Lucrece's in the later poem, is part of the thrill. For that, we have WSA to thank. In Ovid, Adonis is altogether happy to take the love-goddess as his mistress; WSA's Adonis, quite a different character, prefers his mates' company to Venus's—"Hunting he loved, but love he laughed to scorn," as the poem's fourth line succinctly puts it—and in that refusal WSA's Adonis generates sexual energy that drives the narrative and impels the reader through another 1,190 lines. Refusal is, of course, the energy-source in Petrarchan love poems. For a poet at least, "no" is a much more powerful word than "yes." The "prithee"/"no" alternations in the story are allied with a distinctive rhythm of speech/action. Venus's oratorical dilations—running to 17 stanzas and then some when she warns Adonis not to hunt the boar

(611–715)—alternate with stretches of ekphrasis, picture-painting with words, that are anything but still-lifes. It is a paradox that Ovid should be the inspiration for so many images in Renaissance paintings and engravings. Ovid may be a master of ekphrasis, but he is obsessed with life-in-motion, with chases, changes, metamorphoses. With each shift in the characters' situation, with each turn of the page, the reader shifts location and is drawn deeper into the scene at hand.

The multiple possibilities for voyeuristic pleasure in WSA's *verbal* pictures can be experienced in *actual* pictures of Venus and Adonis that are contemporary with the poem and its 18 editions. Titian's composition (1554), showing a nude Venus from behind, and Adonis, outfitted for the hunt, breaking off from her embrace and pulling away to the right, may be the most famous image today. (More than 30 painted and engraved versions survive, including paintings in the Prado, the National Gallery in London, the Metropolitan Museum, the National Gallery in Washington, and the Getty.) The images that THWS and his readers were likeliest to see, however, came in prints circulated out of Antwerp and in tapestries, embroideries, and designs on utilitarian objects that were often based on prints from the continent, especially the Low Countries (Wells-Cole 1997: 3–124, Griffiths 1998: 21–2). The varying postures that Venus and Adonis assume in these images are not without affinities to "the sixteen pleasures" depicted in Marcantonio Raimondi's engravings after designs by that rare Italian master Giulio Romano, published in Italy as a set in 1524 and given a dramatic turn ("Where are you going to put it? Please tell me./ Behind or in front?") in sonnets by Pietro Aretino the next year (Lawner 1988: 72). Both the original set of prints and the set with Aretino's verses were apparently destroyed on orders of Pope Clement VII, but the reputation of *I Modi* reached faraway England and made "Aretino" a by-word for salaciousness. Prints illustrating the story of Venus and Adonis show forms of foreplay that *I Modi* carry to various conclusions. Those modes of foreplay can be classified into three types, each coordinated with a particular erotic object in WSA's poem. In all three modes the viewer/reader is implicated as a participant.

The first mode, in the poem as in the prints, makes Venus the erotic object. Venus's blazon of her own body ("Within the circuit of this

ivory pale,/ I'll be a park, and thou shalt be my deer" [230–1]) presents
in inked words what Jacob Matham's print, published at Haarlem in
1600, presents in inked lines and hatchings. (See Figure 3.5.) Nude
except for boots, necklace, bracelet, earrings, a halter just below her
breasts, and a discreet but curiously stiff fold that covers her vagina,
Venus figures as the center of the viewer's gaze. Adonis's doting
embrace and Cupid with his now–slack bow, conform perfectly with
Ovid's version of the story, in which Adonis is an altogether willing
lover. So does the proleptic vignette on the left, which shows Adonis,
legs spread, being gored by the boar. Tree trunks (Ovid's poplars),
shadows, and draped fabric make the scene of Venus and Adonis's
embrace seem part bower and part curtained bed. In addition to a
disused spear and hunting horn, the foreground presents a small single
flower. A proleptic anemone? At the visual center of the composition
is Adonis's right hand, which forms the lower point of an inverted
triangle created by Venus's right hand as she plays with Adonis's hair

Figure 3.5 Jacob Matham, *Venus and Adonis* (1600).

95

and by Adonis's left hand as he enfolds Venus in the fabric spread out beneath them and touches her neck.[2]

In the second mode Adonis becomes the erotic object—but always *post coitu*. One look at Philips Galle's version in Figure 3.6 explains why. To a Renaissance artist's eye the dead Adonis invited the same treatment as the dead Christ, with Venus cast as a grieving Mary.

Figure 3.6 Philips Galle, after Anthonis Blocklandt, Venus and Adonis suite, image 4 (1579).

[2] Among other versions of this template, many of them Italian, the best known in THWS's time were probably two prints by Giorgio Ghisi, who worked in France in the 1550s and 1560s (Boorsch 1985: 19). Ghisi's print of Luca Penni's "Venus and the Rose" (1556, Bartsch 15.400.40) shows a frontally nude Venus standing in a pool of water and being pricked by a rose bush's thorns while she looks over her shoulder at a jealous Mars, club in hand, chasing a distraught Adonis. The original copper plate survived until the nineteenth century, when it was destroyed under papal order. A later print by Ghisi (c. 1570, Bartsch 15.402.42), after a design by his brother Teodoro, shows Venus and Adonis in poses very much like the ones they assume in Titian's painting.

In effect, Ovid's scene of mourning becomes a pagan *pietá*. The suite of four prints from which this image comes was designed by Anthonis van Blocklandt and was engraved and published by Galle in 1579, after he had taken over Hieronymus Cock's prolific publishing house. It was from Cock's "Aux quatre vents" that many prints blew the relatively short distance across the channel to England in the sixteenth and seventeenth centuries. The cast-off hunting implements in the foreground of Galle's print, including a curiously phallic scabbard, now appear as religious relics of Adonis's sacrifice. An attendant angel is suggested by the extra-large wings of Cupid, who strokes Adonis's hair while Venus kisses his forehead. A heavenly ascent—for Venus at least—is anticipated by the swan-powered chariot to be seen in a break in the clouds to the left. In Blocklandt and Galle's print Venus not only participates in the scene but observes it from afar.[3] These visual arrangements are replicated in the last third of WSA's poem, when Venus seizes on Adonis's dead body as the occasion for a 19-stanza oration (1051–164), followed by an abrupt leave-taking that lands Venus in the same detached position she occupies in the upper left of Galle's print.

A third mode, perhaps the most enticing of all, makes Venus and Adonis *both* available for erotic contemplation. Crispijn de Passe's print in Figure 3.7, from a suite of 134 illustrations to Ovid's *Metamorphoses* published singly (1602–4) but designed to be collected in book form, drapes the lovers' flesh with folds of cloth in the image above but in the verses below plays up the erotic frisson of the disparities in age and power: "Fired with love, the goddess Venus follows the fair Adonis,/ Now harrying harmless game/ Then resting in the boy's lap, happy,/ Pressing long kisses on his rosy cheeks" (Veldman 2001:

[3] To judge by productions from the School of Fontainebleau, the French seem to have been particularly fond of the dead Adonis. There are versions of this template by Léon Davent (1540s, Bartsch 16.324.47), Jean Mignon (1540s, Bartsch 16.398.58), and Étienne Delaune (1569), all after designs by Luca Penni, and by Antonio Fantuzzi (1540s, after a design by Rosso Fiorentino, Bartsch 16.402.69) and an unknown engraver (1540s, after a design by Giulio Romano, Bartsch 16.406.77). Penni's three designs put Venus in a separate heavenly sphere as she looks down on Adonis's appealing disposed flesh.

Formofam fequitur flagrant Dea Cypria Adonim, Inq; finu inuetnes requiem modo ducere gaudet,
E i nuncumbelles follicitare feras. ~~~ | Ofculaque inrofeis figere longa genis ~~~

Figure 3.7   Crispijn de Passe, *Venus and Adonis*, from a series of 134 prints after Ovid (1602–4).

no. 94).[4] According to Anthony Griffiths, de Passe carried on a lively trade with England from various locations on the continent (Griffiths 1998: 17–18). Adonis's reluctance in WSA's poem would seem to militate against such scenes of mutual delight as de Passe presents, but in practice that delight is transferred to the voyeur, who is invited to hold in view two erotic objects at the same time. The economy of two is maintained, but the viewer is invited to shift between the available subject positions, now occupying *hers*, now occupying *his*. The final subject position is *ours*—theirs and mine.

Multiple erotic possibilities of just this sort—possibilities in which the viewer is triangulated—are offered by Van Dyck's double portrait of Sir George Villiers, Duke of Buckingham, and his wife Lady

[4]   The third image in Philips Galle's suite shows Venus, Adonis, and Cupid in a mutual embrace, a veritable family of love. The two lovers gaze at Cupid rather than at each other. For his part, Cupid's gaze is trained on Adonis. In the meantime, the viewer gets to gaze at Venus's lithe limbs and ripe buttocks and Adonis's small Grecian penis and large testicles.

Katherine Manners as Venus and Adonis, dating from 1620–1, when Van Dyck was making his first trip to England and WSA's poem was in its fourteenth edition. (See Figure 3.8.) No premonitions of disaster attend Buckingham's visual and brachial embrace of Lady Katherine, whose bright red wrap also helps to draw attention—erotic and otherwise—to her. The same pose that Lady Katherine assumes in the picture Buckingham himself had assumed for the past five years as he enjoyed the political favor and reputedly the sexual attentions of King James I. James's autograph letter to Buckingham addressing him as "my sweet child and wife" (December 1623?) has by now become an anthology piece in histories of sexuality (Bergeron 1999: 173–5). Other letters indicate that hunting and deer parks, along with bedrooms, figured prominently in the imaginative world James shared with Buckingham.

In a letter written to Buckingham, probably in 1622, just after Van Dyck's double portrait was painted, James describes how he "rode this afternoon a great way in the park without speaking to anybody and the tears trickling down my cheeks, as now they do that I can scarcely see to write" (Bergeron 1999: 150). James urges "my only sweet and dear child" to invite Lady Katherine to come to Buckingham's country house, Newhall, in eight to ten days' time—but not before James and Buckingham have enjoyed their own rendezvous the very next day. "Remember thy picture," James urges, "and suffer none of the Council to come here. For God's sake write not a word again and let no creature see this letter" (150). James's letters to Buckingham gesture toward an off-the-page life in which hunting, deer parks, male bonding, erotic pleasure, and a female third party all have a place— a scenario not unlike that in *Venus and Adonis*. James, like Adonis, loved going out hunting with the boys above all else, statecraft included. In this case, however, the female figure seems not to have occasioned the resentment that Adonis feels toward Venus. Indeed, James refers to "Kate" as his daughter and is solicitous about her pregnancy, hoping that she will bring forth "sweet bedchamber boys to play me with" (149)—an exquisite example of middle voice. Villiers's first appointment, it should be noted, was as the king's cupbearer, a role that Ganymede performed for Jupiter.

Figure 3.8 Anthony van Dyck, Sir George Villiers and Lady Katherine Manners as Venus and Adonis (1620–1).

In historical fact, then, as in Van Dyck's visual fiction, Buckingham could function as both erotic object (*vis-à-vis* James) and erotic agent (*vis-à-vis* Lady Katherine). Add to the scenario the wistly voyeur in WSA's *Venus and Adonis*, and the possibilities become giddy-making. In her speeches of seduction Venus speaks to the reader as well as to Adonis, just as Van Dyck's Lady Katherine beckons the viewer. Or does Lady Katherine transfer to the *viewer* the gaze that Buckingham bestows on *her*? If so, and if the viewer is male, Van Dyck's portrait, like WSA's poem, uses a female intermediary to effect a homoerotic trans-action between two men in just the way Eve Sedgwick finds in WSA's sonnets (Sedgwick 1985: 28–48). Or perhaps the wistly viewer's gaze stops at Lady Katherine. If so, and if the viewer is female, the economy of two doesn't require a male at all.

None of the 18 editions of *Venus and Adonis* down to 1675 con-tains cuts of the sort devised by Matham, Galle, and de Passe, but beginning with the fifteenth edition in 1636, readers were con-fronted on the title page with a Cupid figure who invited them into the story in just the way Van Dyck's Lady Katherine invites the viewer into the picture space. (See Figure 3.2.) Cupid may have got onto the title page quite by accident—a printer's whim—but there he remained, in recut images down to 1675. Cupid's slack bow is being dropped from his left hand, while his right hand, index finger raised, points upward, seemingly toward the epigraph from Ovid's *Amores* 1.15 that introduces all editions of the poem from 1593 to 1675: "*Vilia miretur vulgus; mihi flavas Apollo/ Pocula Castalia plena ministret aqua*" ("Let base conceited wits admire vile things,/ Fair Phoebus lead me to the Muses' springs," as Marlowe translates the lines in *All Ovid's Elegies*) (Marlowe 1981: 2:339). The reader who takes the book in hand is cast as a connoisseur, a knowledgeable person. Knowledgeable about what? About Latin and Ovid and high culture, perhaps. But more certainly about the amorous affairs that the poem treats: in fine, carnal knowledge. If Ovid's metaphor about the Muses' Castalian spring can be taken at face value, the knowl-edge offered by *Venus and Adonis* is knowledge that can be *tasted*. Positioned on the title page as an intermediary, a host of sorts, Cupid gestures toward the reader and invites the reader into the book. Reading the book, the figure implies, will be like falling in love.

:

"The least penetration maketh it carnal knowledge": Coke has in mind a very small physical space—as small perhaps as half an inch— but the word "penetration" suggests a range of spatial relationships that could in fact extend hundreds of feet. Coke's knowledge is determined by an outside view—and a fixed view, at that. He speaks, before the technology was available, as if a photograph could be taken, capturing the precise moment of the very least penetration. What Coke wants is documentation of penetration, a visual fact frozen in time. But penetration is not like that. The root sense of "penetrate"—from *penus* (the inmost part of a house) + *intrare* (to get into)—is an action, a movement, a process (*OED* 1989: "penes," *prep.*, etymology; "†peni- tissim," *adj.*, etymology; "penetrate," *v.*, etymology). It was in the *penus* that the *penates*, the household gods, were kept. Penetration is less about *there* than about *getting there*.

Almost as early as the use of "penetrate" in the physical, transitive sense of getting into or through a space (*OED* 1989: "penetrate," *v.*, 1.a) is the psychological, intransitive sense of gaining specifically "intellectual or spiritual access, insight or knowledge" (1.b). Affect is added to that knowledge when WSA's Proteus in *The Two Gentlemen of Verona* describes how Sylvia took the news of Valentine's banishment. Before her father, Sylvia wept, knelt, wrung her hands, sighed, and groaned, Proteus tells Valentine, but nothing "could penetrate her uncompassionate sire" (3.1.230). The *Oxford English Dictionary* cites this passage as the earliest instance of "penetrate" as "to touch the heart or feelings" (*OED* 1989: "penetrate," *v.*, 3). That affect-laden sense of penetration is on Cloten's mind (along with anticipated carnal knowledge of a more physical sort) when he hires a string-player and a singer to make music outside Imogen's window and tells them to "penetrate her with your fingering" and "with tongue too" (*Cymbeline* 2.3.13–14). Cross-species penetration figures in Prospero's reminder to Ariel that, trapped by Sycorax in a cloven pine, "Thy groans/ Did

make wolves howl, and penetrate the breasts/ Of ever-angry bears"
(*Tempest* 1.2.288–90). The metamorphosis and the aural reverbera-
tions described by Prospero are worthy of Ovid. Carnal knowledge in
WSA's scenes of penetration is not just fleshly knowledge but *passionate* knowledge. Flesh and spirit refuse to remain in separate locations.
In all these senses—physical, psychological, emotional—carnal knowledge is about space and movement. In each case an inward space
(vagina, anus, ears, heart) is penetrated by something or someone
moving in from an outward space.

Within the second paradigm of characters ↔ world–at–hand *Venus
and Adonis* charts Venus's invasion of the geographical domain belonging to Adonis, the wooded chase, and an unsuccessful attempt on her
part—an anatomically doomed attempt—to invade Adonis's body.
The original story in Ovid's *Metamorphoses*, Book Ten, makes the setting explicit. Here is the scene in Arthur Golding's translation of 1567,
the one used by WSA: "Through tushy grounds and groves,/And over
hills and dales, and lawns and stony rocks she roves,/Bare-kneed with
garment tucked up according to the wont/ Of Phoebe, and she
cheered the hounds with hallowing like a hunt" (Ovid 1567: sig. P3v).
("Tushy" means "tusky," as in the tusks of a boar [*OED* 1989: "tusky,"
adj.].) Venus shadowed Adonis as he hunted. The setting in WSA's
poem is the same: it begins as "Rose-cheeked Adonis hied him to the
chase" (3). The scene of Venus's wooing in Ovid, the shade of a poplar
tree, becomes in *Venus and Adonis* a version of the *locus amoenus* familiar from pastoral poetry. "Witness this primrose bank whereon I lie,"
Venus tells Adonis: "These forceless flowers like sturdy trees support
me" (151–2). Here is not only an anticipation of Perdita's "bank, for
love to lie and play on" in *The Winter's Tale* (should "Love" be capital-
ized? is it Venus herself who is lying there?) but just such a cozy bower
as bed hangings provided in England's cool, damp climate.

The phenomenal space of reader/sensor ↔ world–at–hand within
the third paradigm was, in the sixteenth and seventeenth centuries,
likewise a retreat to a bower. In houses of the period, the rooms most
removed from public spaces outside the house and communal spaces
within the house were likely to be bedchambers, which increasingly
were to be found upstairs or at the back. In general, privacy was a

scarcer commodity in THWS's England than today, and bedchambers and the closets attached to them provided one of the few living spaces where—under certain circumstances at least—privacy could be found (Richardson 2006: 82–103, Orlin 2007: 105–11, 306–26). Fynes Morrison, comparing house-building practices all over Europe, comments on the way the houses of London's aldermen and chief citizens are "built all inward," with shops toward the street and living quarters to the rear (quoted in Smith 1999: 59). Robert Greene's narrative *Thieves Falling Out, True Men Come by Their Goods* (1615) tells the story of a citizen's wife who attempts to seduce a clothier by inviting him in for a drink. First she takes him upstairs to a sitting room and then, after drinking and kissing have commenced, through a series of chambers ever more remote from outside light and prying eyes. The first chamber beyond the sitting room is not dark enough. (The clothier, it seems, can only perform in the dark.) Next comes a bedchamber with its curtained bed: "then I carried him into a further chamber, where drawing a curtain before the window, and closing the curtains of the bed, I asked him smiling if that were close enough" (Greene 1615: sig. F1v). No. Finally she takes him to a "back loft, where stood a little bed, only appointed to lodge suspicious persons" (sigs. F1v–F2). This, too, is not dark enough or private enough to avoid God's eyes, the clothier says, and he berates his would-be seducer as an adulterer.

In grander houses the sequence of rooms was even more precisely laid out. Public reception rooms gave way to privy chambers, which in turn gave way to withdrawing rooms, which in turn gave way to bedchambers, which in turn gave way to closets (Girouard 1978: 110–16, Orlin 2007: 306–26). In the case of royal palaces this sequence measured political status: the farther a courtier could move toward the monarch's bedchamber and closet, the greater his or her power. James's immediate impulse when he met George Villiers was to make him a "gentleman of the king's bedchamber," as the title went. The move was at first blocked by James's earlier favorite, Robert James Carr, sometime page, later Earl of Somerset, who had started out in James's retinue as a "groom of the king's bedchamber."

Short of the bedchamber, the story of Venus and Adonis could be enjoyed in a variety of chambers, amid a variety of activities, through a variety of sensations. One might think of them as chambers for foreplay. Philippe Millot's oval engraving (see Figure 3.9) was probably devised for use as a pattern by goldsmiths or silversmiths. The image of Adonis kissing Venus while Cupid chains his leg would have made an apt design for a watch case, a hand mirror, or a large locket for wearing the miniature portrait of one's beloved around one's neck. The fruit, flowers, female nudes, and nut-eating squirrels that surround the central scene compose the sort of design that THWS's readers knew as "antic work," designs that take the "antique" figurations of Roman wall paintings as inspiration for flights of fantastic imaginings (Smith 2009b: 148–53). It is just such a combination of classical motifs and *jeux d'esprit* that Theseus has in mind in *A Midsummer Night's Dream* when he dismisses the strange metamorphoses in the woods outside Athens as "antique fables" ("antic" in many modern editions) and "fairy toys" (5.1.2). More ominous elements of the story in Millot's engraving—Adonis's sprawled body being discovered by Venus in her chariot—are kept in the background. That very moment, however, is the one chosen by Stephano della Bella for the four of spades in his set of 52 playing cards inspired by stories from Ovid.[5] (See Figure 3.10.) On her own, Venus figures as the queen of diamonds, Narcissus as the one of hearts, Pyramus and Thisbe as the two of diamonds, Jupiter and Ganymede as the six of hearts, Salmacis and Hermaphroditus as the eight of diamonds. As for the game at hand, who plays, who cheats, what is trumps, whether the cards are kept close or laid down, what the forfeit might be: these decisions are left to the user of della Bella's deck.

Card-playing and sexual flirtation might have gone on in the "Venus and Adonis room" in the White Hart Inn at St. Albans, Hertfordshire, but the main pursuits there, according to the Swiss traveler Thomas Platter, would have been eating, drinking, fiddling, and smoking tobacco—in that order (Platter 1937: 170). St. Albans, an easy day's ride north of London, lay astride the Great North Road and boasted many inns, of which the White Hart is one of several survivors.

---

[5]   For information on the design of seventeenth-century playing cards I am grateful to Gina Bloom.

Figure 3.9   Philippe Millot, design for a pendant cover, watch case, or box lid (1610–12), magnified.

Figure 3.10 Stephano della Bella, Venus and Adonis as the four of spades, playing card from a suite of 52 (1644).

(Whether Francis Bacon ever partook of the inn's oral and aural pleasures is doubtful, but he bore the title Viscount St. Albans and lived a little over a mile away at Gorhambury.) Wall paintings in the White Hart, uncovered in 1985, mainly depict birds, beasts, and foliage but include the detail shown in Figure 3.11, which has been plausibly read as the death of Adonis and—more of a stretch perhaps—as a contemporary illustration of WSA's poem. The poor condition of other parts of the wall painting make interpretation difficult, and Venus is nowhere to be seen today, but the image in Figure 3.11 does seem to correspond to the moment in Ovid before the boar does his goring. Adonis has speared the boar with his hunting staff, the boar has removed the staff and has turned on Adonis.

None of this is directly represented in WSA's poem, of course. Still, the story of Venus and Adonis provides perfect surroundings for

Figure 3.11 Detail of mural painting in the White Hart Inn, St. Albans, Hertfordshire (late sixteenth century).

indulging in oral, aural, and tactile pleasures. In one stanza at least Venus imagines the scene of her tryst with Adonis as just such a chamber, a secluded room in which all five senses might be banqueted. "But, O, what banquet wert thou to the taste,/ Being nurse and feeder of the other four!" she exclaims to Adonis.

> "Would they not wish the feast might ever last,
> And bid Suspicion double-lock the door,
> Lest Jealousy, that sour unwelcome guest,
> Should, by his stealing in, disturb the feast?"
> (445–50)

Later references to drink—"that sweet coral mouth,/ Whose precious taste her thirsty lips well knew" (542–3)—continue the conceit. Platter comments on the English preference for privacy from other patrons while eating and drinking. It is customary in London's ale houses, he notes, "to erect partitions between the tables so that one table cannot overlook the next" (1937: 189). Until the advent of big-screen televisions, small rooms remained the norm in most older pubs. Mistress Quickly's establishment in Eastcheap had its Pomegranate Chamber (*1 Henry IV* 2.5.36–7); the White Hart at St. Albans, its Venus and Adonis Chamber.

Kinesthetic pleasures with Venus and Adonis are also made available in John Bartlet's four-voice song "The Queen of Paphos Ericine in heart did rose-cheeked Adone love," as printed in *A Book of Airs with a Triplicity of Music* in 1606. (See Figure 3.12.) The book's size is handy for using in a sitting room or music room, and the format encourages bodily contact. Unlike the Venus and Adonis Chamber at the White Hart, a connection with WSA's poem in this case is all but certain, since Bartlet's song turns on unrequited love:

> The Queen of Paphos Ericine
> in heart did rose-cheeked Adone love,
> He mortal was but she divine,
> and oft with kisses did him move,
> with great gifts still she did him woo,
> but he would never yield thereto.
> (Bartlet 1606: sig. F2v)

("Rose-cheeked Adonis" makes his appearance in the third line of WSA's poem, and Paphos rather than Ovid's Citheria is Venus's destination in WSA's next-to-last line.) The melody, assigned to the Canto voice in the left-hand score in Figure 3.12, shapes a passion that declines on the phrase "he mortal was" but immediately rises to a climax on the phrase "but she divine." Another, less dramatic climax concludes the first stanza, as the rising phrase "with great gifts still she did him woo" finds its falling contrast in "but he would never yield thereto." Succeeding stanzas repeat this falling/rising/rising/falling contour to express alternations between hope and disappointment. The most affecting alternation comes in the last stanza, in which the

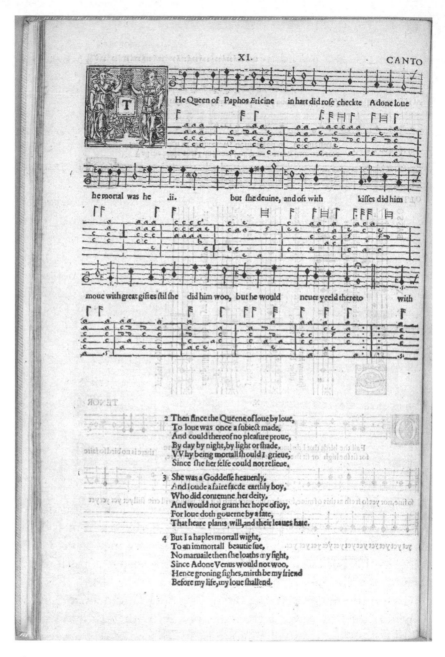

Figure 3.12 John Bartlet, "The Queen of Paphos Ericine in heart did rose-cheeked Adone love," from *A Book of Airs with a Triplicity of Music* (1606).

110

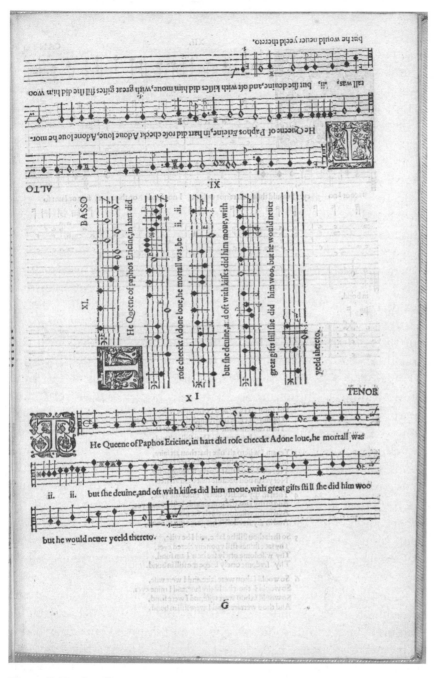

Figure 3.12 *(cont'd)*

111

singer identifies with Adonis's mortality in the face of his own mistress's "immortal beauty," but ultimately takes on Venus's role as frustrated lover. The climatic rise in pitch comes on the phrase "No marvel then she loathes my sight" (sig. F4v).

Bartlet has scored the song for four voices (in addition to the high Canto, there is a lower-pitched Alto, a lower-still Tenor, and a lowest-of-all Basso), plus a lutenist and viol-player if they are available. In effect, the disappointed lover's passion becomes the four singers' collective passion as they sing together—or the six musicians' collective passion if instrumentalists accompany the singers. For the singers, the very act of making music would be an oral pleasure as they roll the words in their mouths. For the instrumentalists it would be a tactile pleasure. For all of them, the pleasure would also be aural, as it would for anyone who happened to be present to listen (assuming, that is, that the musicians were good). Considering the way that Bartlet's score is printed, with the Canto and Tenor parts facing in one direction, the Alto part in another direction, and the Basso part in a third, the pleasures at hand might be tactile as well. Printing arrangements like this, common in music publishing at the time, allowed multiple musicians to share one book—but at very close quarters. If the book lay open on a table and four singers were ranged around it, there would be plenty of opportunity not only for looking closely at each other's faces but for grazing arms and touching hands and knees under the table. In this respect, the Canto and the Tenor would have enjoyed particular license, since they are seated on the same side of the table, their hands and knees out of the others' sight. The Tenor part in Bartlet's score would likely have been sung by a male; the Canto part, though scored in the treble clef, could as readily have been sung by a male countertenor as by a soprano.

Kinesthetic pleasures of hearing, seeing, and feeling also attend the sounds in WSA's poem. Aural pleasure joins visual and tactile pleasure when Adonis suddenly speaks and inspires Venus to exclaim, "Thy mermaid's voice hath done me double wrong./ I had my load before, now pressed with bearing:/ Melodious discord, heavenly tune harsh sounding,/ Ears' deep-swect music, and heart's deep-sore

Figure 3.13 Triumphant Venus, detail of bed valence, English (late sixteenth century).

wounding" (429–32). WSA's Venus does not need Lacan to tell her about interchangeability among orifices and between orifices and wounds.

If under-the-table play with Bartlet's score were successful, penetration to the bedchamber might come next. Of all the spaces within which *Venus and Adonis* can be imagined, a bedchamber is the ultimate destination, the *penus* in psychological as well as physical terms. I have noted already the way the draperies in Matham's print (Figure 3.5) have been arranged to look like bed curtains. Surviving fragments of bed hangings like the valences shown in Figures 3.13, 3.14, 3.15, and 3.16 suggest the continuities between WSA's fictional setting and the curtains that enclosed the beds in which THWS and his contemporaries slept, dreamed, and made love. The triumphant Venus in Figure 3.13, from English-made hangings contemporary with WSA's poem, joins five other goddesses—Ceres, Flora, Juno,

Figure 3.14   Adonis hunting the boar, from an embroidered valence (English or French, 1570–1629).

Pallas, and Diana—in a continuous procession against a dark-green background, amid flowers, shrubs, and sprays of leaves that are as large as the goddesses are. Mercury accompanies Pallas, just as Cupid, his bow drawn back for a shot, accompanies Venus.

The protagonists in Figures 3.14 and 3.15, depicting highlights from the story of Venus and Adonis (in Figure 3.14 Adonis spears the boar; in Figure 3.15 Venus and her attendants mourn the dead Adonis while just out of the frame to the upper right Venus looks on from her chariot in the heavens), may be decorously clothed in late sixteenth-century costumes, but the plants and animals on the valence are even more voluptuous than in Figure 3.13. Note the monkey plucking oranges in Figure 3.14. A companion panel tells the back-story, in which Myrrha seduces her father, conceives Adonis (a rabbit inhabits the foreground), and is turned into the tree out of which Adonis is

Figure 3.15   Venus and attendants lamenting the dead Adonis, from an embroidered valence (English or French, 1570–1629).

later born. A visual passage on that valence (see Figure 3.16) shows the bed where the seduction took place, complete with woven hangings and breast-baring caryatids. The setting for Myrrha's incest matches, item for item, the scene for lasciviousness inventoried in John Marston's and John Webster's 1604 play *The Malcontent*: "sweet sheets, wax lights, antic bed posts, cambric smocks, villainous curtains, arras pictures, oiled hinges, and all the tongue-tied lascivious witnesses of great creatures' wantonness" (Marston and Webster 1604: sig. C3v). One thinks of Venus's asking Suspicion to double-lock the door.

Embroidered in England in the late sixteenth century, both the Venus and Adonis panel and the Myrrha panel were acquired by the Victoria and Albert Museum in 1904 from the rector and wardens of the church of St. Mary the Virgin at Purley-on-Thames, Berkshire, near Reading. According to a letter from the rector on file in the V&A Department

Figure 3.16 Cinyras king of Cyprus in his incestuous bed, from an embroidered valence showing the story of Myrrha (English or French, 1570–1629).

of Furniture, Textiles, and Fashion, the Venus and Adonis panel "has for some years been hung in the vestry and is <u>said</u> to have been used as an altar cloth" (Victoria and Albert Museum 1904: T.10475/04, emphasis original). Philips Galle may not be the only person to have seen the *pietá* of St. Mary the Virgin in Venus's lament over Adonis's corpse.

Continuities with wool-and-silk hangings like these are woven into the verbal texture of *Venus and Adonis*. "Here come and sit," Venus invites Adonis in the third stanza, "where never serpent hisses;/ And, being sat, I'll smother thee with kisses" (17–18). The garden that she implies here, unwittingly casting herself as Eve, first becomes a metaphor (she feeds on the steam of Adonis's breath, "Wishing her cheeks were gardens full of flowers,/ So they were dewed with such distilling showers" [65–6]) and then a physically realized place of pleasure, a "primrose bank" (151). The garden motif can extend to clothing, as witness the green sleeves that Marlowe bestows on Hero: "wide sleeves green, and bordered with a grove,/ Where Venus in her naked glory strove,/ To please the careless and disdainful eyes,/ Of proud Adonis that before her lies" (Marlowe 1981: 2:431). In such a context, Venus's comparison of her body to a deer park (229–40) is not so far-fetched. "Park work" was a term used in inventories to designate tapestries depicting hunting tracts like the one James I describes in his letter to Buckingham. Other terms for tapestry designs—"*mille fleurs*" (a thousand flowers), "verdure" (green-work), "boscage" (forest-work)—suggest that the flora and fauna in Figures 3.13 and 3.14 could command as much attention as the "histories" depicted in front of them—or rather, *amid* them (Smith 2009b: 45–6, 147–8). In such situations it is not always easy to tell the figure from the ground. Venus and Adonis in Figures 3.14 and 3.15 are implanted in a teeming, fecund landscape just as they are in WSA's poem.

In the wedding poem that Edmund Spenser wrote for his marriage to Elizabeth Boyle in 1594 (one year after the first publication of *Venus and Adonis*) the scene of sexual consummation is a "bridal bower and genial bed" (line 399 in Spenser 1989: 678) presided over by Genius, the congenial god of genitals and generation. The word "bower" figures frequently in Spenser's "Epithalamion," covering the full range of the word's meanings from dwelling or abode (*OED* 1989: "bower," *n.*[1], (1)—specifically an inner apartment (2), more specifically a bedchamber (2.a), more specifically still a *lady's* bedchamber (2.b)—to an arbor or leafy covert (3). As for the "bridal bower" in which the marriage is consummated, the furnishings of the bed itself have been specified a few stanzas earlier: "Lay her in lilies and violets,/ And silken curtains over her display,/ And odoured sheets, and arras coverlets" (ll. 302–4). Within that surround Elizabeth Boyle appears to the bridegroom's eye in an Ovidian guise, "Like unto Maia, when as Jove her took,/ In Tempe, lying on the flowery grass,/ Twixt sleep and wake" (ll. 307–9).

:

Having penetrated to the bedchamber, one could be said, in a material history, to have gone all the way. But in a phenomenological framing the body still awaits its penetration, and beyond the body the psyche of the lover. In Donne's "Epithalamion Made at Lincoln's Inn" the bride stripped of her clothing and laid on the bed is presented as a sacrificial lamb: she "at the bridegroom's wished approach doth lie,/ Like an appointed lamb, when tenderly/ The priest comes on his knees t'embowel her" (ll. 88–9 in Donne 1978: 6). The penetration is presented in even more graphic terms in Donne's epithalamion for the marriage of Princess Elizabeth to the Count Palatine on St. Valentine's Day 1613. In terms reminiscent of "The Ecstasy" the bride's taking off her clothes is imagined as a soul stealing unseen from the body and the bridegroom's coming as a cosmological phenomenon that nonetheless involves the fabrics of the bed: "he comes, and passes through sphere after sphere,/ First her sheets, then her arms, then an anywhere" (ll. 81–2). Donne's pastoral epithalamion for the marriage of Robert Carr (late groom of the king's bedchamber) to Frances Howard in 1613 likewise represents the unclothing of the bride and bridegroom as a disclosing of souls.

Venus and Adonis moves toward sexual consummation in just the way these wedding poems do. In the numbered stanzas of an epithalamion—stanzas that follow the wedding day events one by one—the climax is easy enough to locate. But where does the climax come in *Venus and Adonis*? Not in Venus's attempted rape. The boar succeeds where Venus does not. It is Venus herself who reads Adonis's dead body as a sexually violated body, the boar's thrusting Adonis through the groin. She takes her cue from Ovid, who describes Adonis's death in blatantly sexual terms:

> By chance his hounds in following of the track, a boar did see,
> And roused him. And as the swine was coming from the wood,
> Adonis hit him with a dart askew, and drew the blood.
> The boar straight with his hooked groin the hunting staff out drew
> Bestained with his blood, and on Adonis did pursue
> Who trembling and retiring back, to place of refuge drew.
> And hiding in his cods his tusks as far as he could thrust
> He laid him all along for dead upon the yellow dust.
>
> (Ovid 1567: sig. P6v)

"Cod" is still a current word (although "not in polite use") for the scrotum or, in the plural "cods," for testicles (*OED* 1989: "cod," *n.*[1], 4). (Hence codpiece.) Ovid's own phrase for where the boar thrusts his tusks is *sub inguine*, "under the front part of the body between the hips" (Lewis 1879: *inguen*, general meaning). Virgil and Livy use *inguen* to refer to the groin (Lewis 1879: *inguen*, I.A), giving most English translators the demure cue they need, but Ovid in his *Fasti* (or "Festivals") and Horace and Juvenal in their satires apply the word more specifically to "the privy members" (I.B), giving the translator, Arthur Golding, *his* cue. In *Fasti*, Book Two, when the horned (and horny) forest-god Faunus feels his way around the darkened bedroom of Hercules and Omphale and, fooled by the touch of the gauzy gown Omphale has put on Hercules, climbs into the wrong bed, it is Faunus' *inguen* that stands erect (Ovid 1959: II.346).

The "wide wound" that Venus sees first when she opens her eyes to the sight of Adonis's dead body (1051–3) is given a rhetorical turn 60 lines later. The point of view remains hers:

> "'Tis true, 'tis true; thus was Adonis slain;
> He ran upon the boar with his sharp spear,
> Who did not whet his teeth at him again,
> But by a kiss thought to persuade him there,
>> And, nuzzling in his flank, the loving swine
>> Sheathed unaware the tusk in his soft groin."
>> (1111–16)

Or so it seems to Venus. And so perforce it seems to the reader. What evidence is there otherwise? The encounter of Adonis with the boar happens, as it were, offstage. The reader, along with Venus, hears evidence *before* the fact—the hounds and the horns—and sees evidence *after* the fact—the boar with his "frothy mouth, bepainted all with red,/ Like milk and blood being mingled both together" (901–2), the bloody dogs with their hanging tails (913–24)—but the fact itself remains elusive and all the more fascinating for that.

The word "flank" both in the third-person description of Venus's original view and in her first-person lament would seem to deflect attention from Adonis's *inguen* to more decorous territory several inches above, but "wound" is a sexually loaded word (Partridge 2001: 289), and Venus, the second time around, puts the site of the wound just where Ovid locates it. The flank attracts the boar's nuzzling; the groin gets the tusks. Whether or not the Venus of sonnets 4, 6, and 9 in *The Passionate Pilgrim* (published in 1599 with an attribution to WSA, the same year as the fifth edition of *Venus and Adonis*) can be identified with Venus in the more familiar poem from the Collected Works of William Shakespeare (CWWS), she nonetheless confronts the same reluctant lover, betrays the same casualness about flank, thigh, and groin, and displays, in sonnet 9, the same propensity to equate wound with vagina:

> Fair was the morn, when the fair queen of love,
> [   ]
> Paler for sorrow than her milk-white dove,
> For Adon's sake, a youngster proud and wild,
> Her stand she takes upon a steep-up hill.
> Anon Adonis comes with horn and hounds.
> She, silly queen, with more than love's good will
> Forbade the boy he should not pass those grounds.
> "Once," quoth she, "did I see a fair sweet youth
> Here in these brakes deep-wounded with a boar,
> Deep in the thigh, a spectacle of ruth.
> See in my thigh," quoth she, "here was the sore."
>   She showèd hers; he saw more wounds than one,
>   And blushing fled, and left her all alone.
>   (Shakespeare 2005: 808)

In his encounter with the boar Adonis not only receives a wound; he gains a new body part. His emasculation—in Venus's eyes at least— goes beyond castration. Adonis's body has been penetrated, and the reader is invited to gaze on his wound/ vagina with the same fascination as on Nature's "addition" of a penis to the hermaphroditic "master-mistress" of the poet's passion in sonnet 20. Eighteen editions suggest that few readers, confronted with that spectacle, took Adonis's cue and blushing fled.

Gender seems less important than species when it comes to the poem's climax. Venus's description of Adonis's being gored by the boar is a moment of cross-species love-making that fits with the frequency of such moments not only in Ovid's *Metamorphoses* but in court records concerning buggery. In summaries of the assize court proceedings in the counties around London during the reign of Elizabeth, indictments for sex with animals outnumber indictments for sex between males on the order of seven to one. During the 45 years of Elizabeth's reign there were only four sodomy indictments out of the 12,725 indictments on record but 30 indictments for buggery with animals (Cockburn 1975–85: *passim*). Dympna Callaghan has argued that representations of cross-species desire, far from being limited to *Venus and Adonis*, strike at a fundamental anxiety about the boundary between "human" on the one hand and "nature" on the other (Callaghan 2003: 58–78). What does seem striking about *Venus and Adonis*, however, is who is doing the acting. In the court records it is the human who penetrates the animal; in WSA's poem it is the animal that penetrates the human. The result in both cases is an extreme instance of the confusion of bodily boundaries that fascinates Merleau-Ponty.

:

The move toward the bedchamber shapes up as an act of penetration giving ever more intimate access to the *person* at the end of the sequence. In early modern English, as now, "person" could refer to three distinct, possibly contradictory things: the living physical body as opposed to its clothing and other accouterments (*OED* 1989: "person," *n.*, II.4.a), a role in a play or in some other social entity (I.1), and the individual self (II.3.a). Carnal knowledge in *Venus and Adonis* certainly involves persons as bodies and persons as speakers, but it is the poem's implied sense of person as self that is the most telling. Carnal knowledge: a psychological dimension to that word was no less present to THWS and his contemporaries than the strictly material sense of *res in re*, thanks to Paul's obsession with carnality in his New Testament epistles to early Christian churches.

All of these congregations were struggling to find and hold an identity *vis-à-vis* the adherents to traditional Greek and Roman religion (and to Judaism) among whom they lived in Rome, Corinth, and elsewhere. Paul's repeated gambit is to contrast the bodiliness of the other religions with the spirituality of Christianity. Thus Paul urges Christ's sacrifice as a cancellation of Mosaic law, "Which stood only in meats and drinks, and divers washings, and carnal ordinances" (Bible 1967: Hebrews 9:10). Writing to the church at Rome, the imperial capital of worshipers of Venus and her ilk, Paul distinguishes the fleshliness of the body from an indwelling spirituality: "For I delight in the law of God after the inward man: But I see another law in my members, warring against the law of my mind, and bringing me into captivity to the law of sin which is in my members" (Romans 7:22–3). The result is a strongly felt struggle between, on the one hand, the body with its unruly members (including for males *the* member among members) and, on the other, "the inward man."

In that contrariety, explored in such thorough and affecting detail by Augustine, is to be found the beginnings of modern European consciousness (Taylor 1992: 127–43). For Marlowe, WSA, Beaumont, Chapman, and their readers, the more immediate result was an ambivalence about carnal knowledge. Knowing-through-the-body presented itself as a way of apprehending the world—and *enjoying* it—but Paul's words made that knowledge seem as uncomfortable as it was intense. Othello speaks to that ambivalence when he protests to the duke that he wants Desdemona to accompany him to Cyprus— Venus's isle—"not/ To please the palate of my appetite,/ ... / But to be free and bounteous to her mind" (1.3.261–5). As events prove, he is wrong about his person.

To walk today through the file of rooms in a sixteenth- or early seventeenth-century house like Knoll in Kent or Montacute in Somerset or Hardwick Hall in Derbyshire or Ham House in Surrey or even THWS's birthplace in Henley Street, Stratford-upon-Avon, and arrive at a bedchamber is to find oneself in a space that seems at once familiar and strange. And so with the mental space that the physical space implies. The familiar part of the sixteenth- and seventeenth-century scene of sexual play is archetypal. Sexual acts then and now, one might say, are fundamentally about *res in re*: penetrating another person with one's own person or having one's own person penetrated by another person. But really, that would not be saying very much. Such a statement gets no farther than Coke. It leaves out the inward man. It leaves out the culture within which the inward man and inward woman find their conscious being. It leaves out the feelings that the culture fosters and the feelings that the culture suppresses. It leaves out the internal imaginings. It leaves out the words. Most important, it leaves out the possibility that penetration can happen through orifices other than vagina and anus—like the eyes one uses to read a book, the ears one uses to hear music, the mouth one uses to speak.

More interesting than the continuities with twenty-first-century sexual imaginings are the differences. The aspects of sexual experience that seem peculiar to THWS's time and place can all be investigated with respect to Adonis's wound. Let us take another, valedictory look at that. First we encounter the third-person fact—or at least the third-person fact as it presents itself to Venus's eyes. "Murdered with the view" (1031), her eyes turn back "Into the deep dark cabins of her head" (1038) and deliver her to darkness and a series of violent metaphors. She has refused to let the horrible vision penetrate her brain and "wound the heart with looks" (1042). When she finally opens her eyes again, they have ceased to be passive *receptors* of light (which Aristotle believed to be the case) and have become active *projectors* of light (which Plato believed) (Smith 2009b: 17). "From their dark beds," the narrator says, "once more *leap* her eyes" (1050, emphasis added). The searching beams that she casts forth find their object in Adonis's wound. Her eyes,

> … being opened, threw unwilling light
> Upon the wide wound that the boar had trenched
> In his soft flank, whose wonted lily-white
> With purple tears that his wound wept was drenched.
> > No flower was nigh, no grass, herb, leaf, or weed,
> > But stole his blood, and seemed with him to bleed.
> > > (1051–6)

In Venus's tearful view Adonis's body has already begun to bleed into the verdure—or rather to *weep* into the verdure, since Adonis's wound figures, in Venus's eyes, as just such an eye as her own *three* eyes—not only the two upper ones but the lower one as well. Hair-bedecked, oval, and moist, the lower eye, according to Biron in *Love's Labour's Lost*, is "one that will do the deed/ Though Argus were her eunuch, and her guard" (3.1.193–4, cited in Partridge 2001: 130–1).

The second sight of Adonis's wound comes 50 lines or so later, as the climax to a nine-stanza speech in which Venus searches for words to articulate her grief. Here is how she begins, with a double vision created by her tears: "'My tongue cannot express my grief for one,/ And yet,' quoth she, 'behold *two* Adons dead'" (1069–70, emphasis added). Here is how she ends, still speaking in soliloquy, finding both the acceptance ("'Tis true, 'tis true") and the verbal formula ("*thus* was Adonis slain") she has been searching for:

> He ran upon the boar with his sharp spear,
> Who did not whet his teeth at him again,
> But by a kiss thought to persuade him there,
> > And, nuzzling in his flank, the loving swine
> > Sheathed unaware the tusk in his soft groin.
>
> "Had I been toothed like him, I must confess
> With *kissing* him I should have killed him first;
> But he is dead, and never did he bless
> My youth with his, the more am I accursed."
> > (1111–20, emphases added)

Again the mouth occupies an equivocal position in erotic affairs. In giving words to the spectacle Venus consoles herself by closing the gap between the viewer and the viewed—between her eye and Adonis's "eye"—and by taking the position of the boar. Implicitly she invites the reader who, fictionally at least, "hears" her soliloquy to do the same. The double wound that presents itself to Venus's double vision—first a weeping eye, then a male vagina—suggests five distinctive aspects of Renaissance sexual imagination: (1) gender fluidity, (2) violence,

(3) cross-flow of sexual passion with religious passion, (4) flirtation with bestiality, and (5) a state of mind that I would call "ambient swoon."

:

Gender fluidity in *Venus and Adonis* should by now come as no surprise. Feminist theory in the mode of Judith Butler (1990) and Queer theory as deployed by Jonathan Goldberg (1992) and others begin with the axiom that words are unstable as markers of gender and sexual identity. Even biological sex, Thomas Laqueur (1990) has demonstrated, was not a natural given in Galenic physiology, which imagined "female" to be the default state out of which "male" emerges when the adolescent body heats up and rod and cods descend. A Galenic body is assumed in *Venus and Adonis* when Venus hails Adonis in the poem's second stanza as "Stain to all nymphs, more lovely than a man" (9). All in all, the stanza resonates with sonnet 20, addressed to "the master-mistress of my passion" (20.2). That epithet seems just right for a person endowed by Nature with a woman's face, heart, and eyes but possessed with male traits, too: a sanguine skin tone ("a man in hue" [20.7]) and a penis ("Till nature as she wrought thee fell a-doting,/ And by addition me of thee defeated/ By adding one thing to my purpose nothing" [20.10–12]). Nature is likewise confused with respect to Adonis: "Nature that made thee with herself at strife/ Saith that the world hath ending with thy life" (11–12). The only way of remedying the death of beauty, in *Venus and Adonis* as in the sonnets, is for the beautiful androgyne to procreate. This Adonis refuses to do. Instead, his gender is finally decided in the boar's attack, his species is established in his transformation from human into a flower, and Adonis's beauty lives on as an anemone. The flowery beds of the *locus amoenus*—first a bank of "these blue-veined violets" (125), later "this primrose bank" (151)—compose a surround teeming with plant life. The same surround was replicated in bed curtains, as witness Figures 3.13, 3.14, and 3.15. Amid such fecundity, gender fluidity comes naturally. The homoeroticism that haunts Virgil's second eclogue, Spenser's "Januarye" in *The Shepheardes Calender*, and Rosalind's sheep cote in

As You Like It suggests that today's "metrosexual" has a counterpart in the Renaissance "pastorsexual."

More startling than fluidity with respect to gender and species is the violence that THWS and his contemporaries admit within the folds of pastoral and the folds of bed curtains. Violence, specifically sexual violence, courses throughout Ovid's *Metamorphoses*: Eurydice is bitten by a snake and dies before the consummation of her marriage, Orpheus is torn to pieces by the women of Thrace after he introduces homosexual love among their men, Apollo's beloved Cyparissus literally pines away after accidentally killing the god's favorite stag, Jupiter falls in love with Ganymede and wafts him to heaven clutched in an eagle's talons, Hyacinthus is pierced through when he runs to catch his lover Apollo's javelin, Venus turns the human-sacrificing people of Amathus into bulls and the unsacrificing people of Propoetides into stone but rewards her devotee Pygmalion by bringing to life the statue he loves, Myrrha seduces her father Cinyras and is turned into the weeping myrrh tree out of which Adonis is born, Hippomenes and Atalanta are transformed into lions when they neglect Venus's altars, Adonis fails to heed Venus's warning and is gored by the boar—and all this just in Book Ten. No wonder Golding says that Book Ten "doth contain one kind of argument/ Reproving most prodigious lusts of such as have been bent/ To incest most unnatural" and "doth show/ That beauty (will they nill they) aye doth men in danger throw" (Ovid 1567: sig. A4). Those warnings, posted at the very beginning of Golding's translation, were designed, not to stop people from going any farther, but to help them justify what they were about to read.

Ovid's violence insinuates itself into narrative poems like *Hero and Leander* (he drowns in the sea, she joins him there by throwing herself off her tower), *Ovid's Banquet of Sense* (as punishment for falling in love with Julia he is exiled to become Touchstone's "most capricious poet honest Ovid ... among the Goths" [*As You Like It* 3.3.6]), and *Salmacis and Hermaphroditus* (he is fused forever with a woman he disdains)—and into the bed furnishings that were inspired by those episodes. Adonis's death in Figure 3.14, as in WSA's poem, is true to form. Among the Victoria and Albert Museum's other holdings are a coverlet showing Lucrece's banquet (T.125-1913) and embroidered

126

panels (once part of a set of bed curtains) depicting Venus and Adonis, Pyramus and Thisbe, and Narcissus (T.219A-1981, T.219B-1981, T.219C-1981). A valence at Blickling Hall, Norfolk, shows Europa's rape by Jupiter in the guise of a bull—"rape" in the fundamental sense of *raptus*, getting carried away (Clabburn 1988: 29). What are we to make of these choices in decor? They suggest a decorum in sexual play that was anything but decorous by the standards of later centuries. To judge from artifacts like those shown in Figures 3.13, 3.14, and 3.15, the space within the bed curtains—the phenomenal space of sexual play—was not only fluid with respect to gender and species but charged with pleasurable violence. Or at least the purchasers of those fabrics hoped it would be. Who knows how often reality lived up to Ovid's ideal?

The implied terrain of *Venus and Adonis* is not just a *locus amoenus* (those primrose and violet banks for love to lie and play on); it is also a hunting park. Ovid's terrain is much more the latter, rich with details of bowers and grasses, stones and brambles as Venus stalks Adonis in his hunting. In effect, the events in Ovid's story take place in a fictional space that belongs to Adonis; the events in WSA's story, in an ambiguous space that is now hers (the flowery bank), now his (the chase), now hers again (the scene of Adonis's metamorphosis into an anemone). Venus's space supplies the flowers that so handily lend themselves to becoming familiar metaphors and similes; Adonis's space, the animals that insinuate themselves into the landscape of desire in stranger, more disturbing ways.

Only slightly more outrageous than Adonis's cheeks as red and white roses is Venus's conceit of her body as a deer park where Adonis can graze and feed (229–40). Hunting is explicitly excluded from that space: "Then be my deer, since I am such a park;/ No dog shall rouse thee, though a thousand bark" (239–40). Adonis, then, will no longer be the hunter but the hunted. And so he proves to be later in the poem. The temperature rises considerably when Adonis's tethered horse catches sight of a lusty mare, breaks his restraints, and gallops off in hot pursuit (259–324). We should follow their example, Venus urges (385–408). The narrator's description of the lusty stallion wavers between the patently animal ("Thin mane, thick tail, broad buttock, tender hide" [298]) and the metaphorically human ("Then, like a melancholy malcontent,/ He vails his tail that, like a falling plume,/ Cool shadow to his melting buttock lent" [313–15]). Those "likes" implicate the human in the animal and the animal in the human, even as the "melting buttock" keeps the animal's body fully in view. (One thinks about those nine horses in the bestiality indictments.) Adonis's reply to Venus's object lesson would seem, at first blush, to separate humankind and love on the one hand from animals and hunting on the other: "'I know not love,' quoth he, 'nor will not know it,/ Unless it be a boar, and then I chase it'" (409–10). An attentive reader remembers that detail. As matters fall out, human and boar, love and hunting prove to be anything but opposites. In all sorts of ways, then, Adonis's pursuit of the boar is set up beforehand to be the sexual encounter that Venus makes it out to be after the fact. Cross-species encounters were woven into the imaginative refuge supplied by bed curtains, a refuge that entwines human subjects with plants and animals. As such those encounters figure prominently in the phenomenal space of Renaissance sexual play.

The culmination of the first four aspects of Renaissance sexual imagination—gender fluidity, violence, religious passion, and cross-species desire—elucidates the fifth: a state of mind and body that might be called "ambient swoon." "State," as we observed in Chapter 2, is a whole-body experience, a stance, a way of standing *vis-à-vis* one's surroundings. Every stance implies a *circum*-stance, a surround within which mind and body are situated. For the readers of the first 18 editions of *Venus and Adonis* the circumstances of making love were interweavings of fancy, memory, and imagination like those in Figures 3.13, 3.14, and 3.15.

The mythical identity that Spenser bestows on his bride, "Like unto Maia, when as Jove her took,/ In Tempe, lying on the flowery grass,/ 'Twixt sleep and wake" (ll. 307–8), suggests not only the Ovidian inspiration of an arras like the Sheldon "Judgment of Paris" hanging today in the British Galleries in the Victoria and Albert Museum (T310-1920) but the liminal state of mind induced by the surroundings of flowers and verdure. In such circumstances it is natural that the moment of consummation should be realized, not through direct description of body against body (that would be Coke's viewpoint) but through images like those in Donne's epithalamions: a priest emboweling a lamb in "Epithalamion Made at Lincoln's Inn," the Count Palatine passing through sheets, arms, "then anywhere" (l. 82), the Count and Princess Elizabeth after the sexual consummation as having exchanged genders ("Here lies a she sun, and a he moon here" [l. 85]) and having risen as two phoenixes (l. 99) from the heat of their encounter. In *Paradise Lost* the reunion of Adam and Eve (after all, they began as one flesh) is a similar state of kinesthetic swoon within "their blissful bower," woven with verdure and flowers: "These lulled by nightingales embracing slept,/And on their naked limbs the flow'ry roof/ Show'red roses, which the morn repaired" (4.690, 772–4 in Milton 1998: 463, 466). The metamorphosis in *Venus and Adonis* asks to be read in this light. In all these cases one loses oneself not just in one's sexual partner but in an ambient surround of gods, mortals, plants, animals, and things in between.

::

Tears, blood, sap, semen: these are the liquids that dissolve the boundaries in *Venus and Adonis*. The double vision that Venus experiences as she opens her tearful eyes to the sight of Adonis's gored body has been anticipated not only in the tears of frustrated desire that Venus has shed in her wooing (false tears, Adonis has claimed) but in the cooling touch of tears ("He burns with bashful shame; she with her tears/ Doth quench the maiden burning of his cheeks" [49–50]) and their taste ("Dost thou drink tears, that thou provok'st such weeping?" [949]). The wide wound disfigures Adonis's flank, "whose wonted lily white/With purple tears that his wound wept were drenched" (1053–4). Blood and tears both issue from the anemone when Venus plucks it and tucks it into her bosom: "She crops the stalk, and in the breach appears/Green-dropping sap, which she compares to tears" (1175–6). But not in so many words. This bit of narration occurs *before* Venus puts things into focus by apostrophizing the flower, allegorizing it, turning it into words: "'Poor flower,' quoth she, 'this was thy father's guise …'" (1177). And so it has been with the transformation itself.

129

Figure 3.17   Venus and Adonis (conjectured subject), from Lucas Kilian, *Newes Gradesca Büchlein* (Augsburg, 1607).

The metamorphosis happens *while* Venus is orating, not as a *result* of her oration. First come five stanzas of prophecy that love will henceforth be attended with sorrow; then comes the narrative detail "By this, the boy that by her side lay killed/ Was melted like a vapour from her sight" (1165). The poem may end with an act of verbal framing, but the melting of body into body and body into the world-at-hand is postponed until the last possible moment.

The seed or semen that both males and females were thought to produce in the moment of sexual climax was composed, according to Crooke and other sixteenth- and seventeenth-century physicians, of double matter: blood and spirits. Hence the double nature of seed, "one airy, spumous or frothy, another waterish and diffluent" (Crooke 1615: sig. BB1v). And hence the curiously diffuse nature of erotic perception. A fascination on the part of THWS and his readers with that melting and melding can be witnessed in Lucas Kilian's image of a kneeling female figure embracing a boy-like figure and kissing him just above his *inguen*. (See Figure 3.17.) Included in a pattern book of grotesque designs published at Augsburg in 1607, the figures are plausibly conjectured in the British Museum's catalogue to be Venus and Adonis. Another design from the same book was used by Rowland Buckett for the decorations he painted four years later on the chamber organ still to be seen at Hatfield House, Hertfordshire (Wells-Cole 1997: 30–2). No less erotic than the embracing lovers in Figure 3.17 are the metamorphoses going on around the pair, as vines become human forms (note how the hunter above the pair's heads emerges from leaves), as animals emerge from ripening fruit (note the monkey at the bottom, on the right, hunting a boar that is being attacked by a hound), as living forms of all sorts merge into abstract designs (note the arabesques, complete with grotesque faces, immediately beneath the lovers' feet). Kilian's erotic image, like WSA's *Venus and Adonis*, gestures toward a material world-at-hand that seems quite specific to the sixteenth and seventeenth centuries. Carnal knowledge of that world is located, not *in* the body or *on* the body or *outside* the body, but *between* the body and the world-at-hand. In a state of ambient swoon the seething erotic body bleeds into the world-at-hand in just the way Adonis's body bleeds into a flower.

4

Touching Moments

Two curious things happen when Lear and Gloucester are reunited after their tortures: what they say keeps separating hearing from seeing, and what they do keeps involving their hands. "I know that voice," says the blinded Gloucester when the still mad Lear bursts onto the scene (*The Tragedy of King Lear* 4.5.95). Gloucester is moved to kneel and offers to kiss the king's hand. I must wipe it first, Lear says; "it smells of mortality" (4.5.129). That touch of lips to hand—almost certainly a physical touch in performance—sets up a segue from knowing-through-hearing in Gloucester's case to knowing-through-seeing in Lear's. "Dost thou know me?" Gloucester asks. "I remember thy eyes well enough," Lear replies. "Dost thou squiny at me?/ No, do thy worst, blind Cupid, I'll not love" (4.5.131–3). And with that, Lear hands Gloucester a "challenge" to read—or at least says he is doing so—as if the two of them were dueling suitors or Lear were serving notice to his tormentors that he will be revenged. "Mark but the penning of it," Lear commands. "Were all thy letters suns," Gloucester replies, "I could not see" (4.5.135–6).

"Blind Cupid": the cruelty of the joke is continued in the excruciating literalness of Lear's puns on "case" (4.5.143) as situation, purse, and eye-sockets and in his figure of speech "you see how this world goes" (4.5.143–4). Gloucester's response introduces another pun: "I see it *feelingly*" (4.5.145, emphasis added). As with all puns, the effect here is to sever words from their usual meanings and to set up connections that don't follow the rules of logic. In this case, the connections involve visual analogies: eye-sockets : purse : emptiness. Into this visual matrix Gloucester's pun on "feelingly" insinuates touch as the one dependable medium in a world where appearances have deceived, where sight and sound have been disjoined, where words have been used as physical weapons. In such a world a piece of writing like the challenge Lear tries to hand to Gloucester is utterly useless: it is unseeable, unhearable, unreadable. Instead, the space between man and man, like the space between man and objects, is reduced to vacancy, empty of everything but air. That space can be bridged, if at all, not by speech alone, by giving voice to words, but by touch, by putting lips to hand. In Gloucester's pun the medium of touch connects outside ("feeling" as a blind man's making his way through the world with hands outstretched) to inside ("feeling" as sensation, passion, suffering).

:

People who lose their vision as adults sometimes, but not always, compensate for that loss by developing an especially acute sense of hearing. Others testify to having concentrated on keeping their "inner eye" active. Surveying this conflicting testimony, Oliver Sacks reaches a conclusion that corroborates Gloucester's sentiments. The differing responses of people who have become blind, according to Sacks, point up the individual nature of human imagination, "where there is a continual struggle for concepts and form and meaning, a calling upon all the powers of the self." In such a situation, "one can no longer say of one's mental landscapes what is visual, what is auditory, what is an image, what is language, what is intellectual, what is emotional—they are all fused together and imbued with our own individual perspectives and values" (Sacks 2005: 41). As we know from Chapter 1, Sacks does no more here than repeat what was commonsense among The Historical William Shakespeare (THWS) and his contemporaries about "the common sense." Within the fiction of *King Lear* touch supplements knowing-through-hearing on Gloucester's part and knowing-through-seeing on Lear's, even as it partly substitutes for

Figure 4.1   William Shakespeare, *The Tragedy of King Lear*, 4.5.128 ("O, let me kiss that hand!") to 145 ("I see it feelingly"), in Braille.

Gloucester's missing vision and Lear's uncomprehending listening. But the touch of hand to lips does more than that. In Gloucester's gesture, vision and audition, along with olfaction ("it smells of mortality") and implicitly at least touch and perhaps even taste ("let me kiss that hand"), are fused into the kinesthesia indicated by the adverb "feelingly." The communication of touch within the fiction of *King Lear* 4.5—within the frame of characters ↔ world-at-hand—is powerful. What about the frame of reader/sensor ↔ world-at-hand? How can the kinesthesia of this touching moment be communicated to someone *outside* the fiction? How is touch communicated in the theater? Words get us only so far.

Perhaps the most direct way to communicate the feelingness of *King Lear* 4.5 would be a Braille translation. The version of *The Tragedy of King Lear*, 4.5.128–45, shown in Figure 4.1 makes available to a

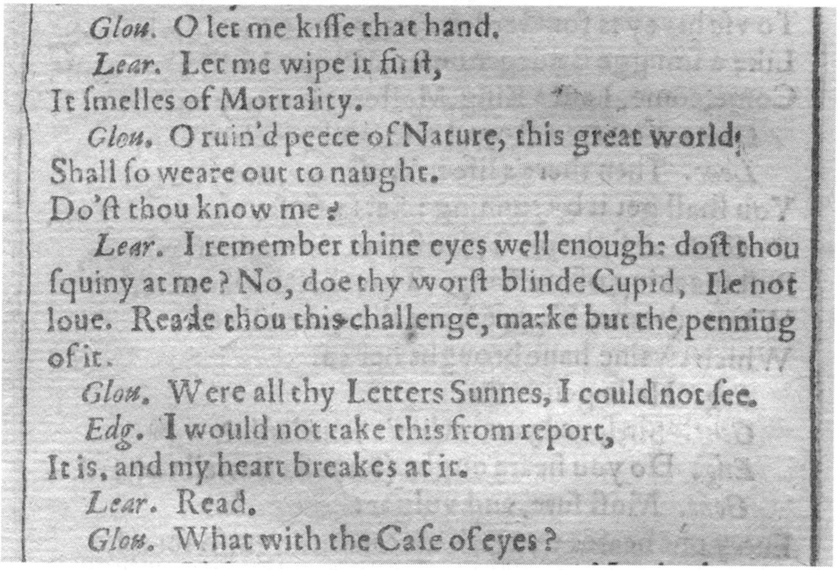

> *Glou.* O let me kiffe that hand.
> *Lear.* Let me wipe it firſt,
> It ſmelles of Mortality.
> *Glou.* O ruin'd peece of Nature, this great world'
> Shall ſo weare out to naught.
> Do'ſt thou know me ?
> *Lear.* I remember thine eyes well enough: doſt thou
> ſquiny at me ? No, doe thy worſt blinde Cupid, Ile not
> loue. Reade thou this challenge, marke but the penning
> of it.
> *Glou.* Were all thy Letters Sunnes, I could not ſee.
> *Edg.* I would not take this from report,
> It is, and my heart breakes at it.
> *Lear.* Read.
> *Glou.* What with the Cafe of eyes ?

Figure 4.2 William Shakespeare, *The Tragedy of King Lear*, sig. rr6, detail, in *Mr. William Shakespeare's Comedies, Histories, and Tragedies* (1623).

Braille-reader's own hands Gloucester's offer to kiss Lear's hand, Lear's insistence on wiping it first, Gloucester's asking if he is known by the king, Lear's quip about "blind Cupid" and his presentation of a challenge written in ink, Gloucester's lament that he cannot read it, Lear's joke "you see how this world goes," Gloucester's reply "I see it feelingly." The punches in the paper become signs of … what? Of words, yes, but of words apprehended *how*? Do the punched-out words *feel* the same as printed words? What difference does it make that readers who lack sight know words primarily through hearing? Do they experience a connection between touching and hearing that sighted readers lack? Touched with the tips of one's fingers—leadingly with the tips of one's *index* fingers—the punches function not only as *symbols* of absent sounds but as *indices* of a tactile experience, an experience that is literally *at hand*.

A similar thing happens—though often overlooked by sighted people—in letterpress, in words printed with ink on paper. (See Figure 4.2.)

The inked symbols present themselves in the first instance to the reader's eyes and thus remain distanced from the reader—by 18 inches or so, if my calculations in Chapter 3 are right. But inked signs in the books read by THWS and his contemporaries could be touched as well as seen. The printing technology that produced *Mr. William Shakespeares Comedies, Histories, and Tragedies* (1623) was a relief process in which raised type was inked, a sheet of paper was placed on top, and a heavy plate was pressed down on top of that, leaving on the paper embossed depressions of the raised type as well as the dried ink that in liquid form filled those depressions. Look closely at the portion of signature rr6 shown in Figure 4.2 and you may be able to make out with your eyes what your fingers would feel if you ran your fingers over the surface of the page. You can't do that with the book you now have in your hands, which, like most commercially produced books since the 1950s, has been printed with an offset technology, whereby the letters and images to be inked are transferred to a flat carrier (usually a rubber plate) and then imprinted on paper via a process that separates oil-based ink from blank areas coated with water. Add machine-smoothed paper, and the result is a flat page that almost never calls attention to itself and certainly does not ask to be touched.

Even the paper on which the first folio is printed has a tactile quality. Paper in the seventeenth century was made out of rags that had been pounded by hand into pulp. The resulting product retained the irregularities of the materials and the vagaries of the process. Wanting to give products of human artifice the same close observation as natural phenomena, Francis Bacon in *The New Organon* encourages his readers to look at paper as if they had never seen or touched it before. Paper: "a common enough thing," Bacon will admit, but "look at the matter carefully" and you will discover a man-made material that hardly resembles more common artifacts like woven things (silk, wool, linen) and things made out of dried liquids (bricks, glass, porcelain). Paper, in contrast to artifacts that are either flexible (woven things) or substantial (things made out of dried liquids), is both: it is "a tenacious substance which can be cut and torn;

so that it imitates and almost rivals the skin or membrane of an animal, or the foliage of a vegetable, and such natural products" (2.31 in Bacon 2000b: 151). The way Bacon makes paper "strange" is not unlike the way Husserl, as we noticed in Chapter 1, casts fresh eyes on the objects in his study. In both cases the observer performs an act of *epochē* or bracketing.

With respect to tactility, as with respect to much else, the earlier single-play edition of *Mr William Shakespeare his True Chronicle History of the Life and Death of King Lear and His Three Daughters* (1608) is a more complicated affair than the folio edition of 1623. The full title page advertises the play as being presented in lead type "As it was played before the King's Majesty at Whitehall upon St. Stephen's night in Christmas holidays, By his Majesty's servants playing usually at the Globe on the Bankside"—as if the text were a souvenir of a performance. Very few readers of the quarto are likely to have been present at Whitehall Palace on 26 December 1606, but they could (if the play remained in the King's Men's active repertory) take in a live performance at the location so conveniently provided on the title page. For someone who had seen the play, the speeches of Gloucester and Lear embossed and inked on signature I4 (see Figure 4.3) would have figured not just as symbols of sounds that might be heard anywhere anytime but as indices of sounds that had actually been heard and bodies that had actually been seen in the theater. To these aural and visual sensations the 1608 quarto would have added an even stronger, more present sense of touch than the 1623 folio would later provide. Measuring about 5 inches by 7 inches in the Huntington Library's somewhat cut-down copy, *The History of King Lear* could, like the editions of *Venus and Adonis* noticed in Chapter 3, be grasped in the reader's hands as she or he read. The folio was too big for that.

Touch is implicit in other media that communicate *King Lear* to a sensor within the third paradigm of phenomenological experience. The unsigned plates illustrating Shakespeare's collected plays in Nicholas Rowe's 1709 edition, for example, provide "cuts" in the reader's experience of the text. The first known illustration of *King*

Figure 4.3 William Shakespeare, *The History of King Lear* (1608), sigs. I3v–I4.

Figure 4.4 Unsigned cut for *King Lear* 3.4, from *The Works of Mr. William Shakespear*, ed. Nicholas Rowe (1709), detail, magnified.

Lear, a detail from which is shown much magnified in Figure 4.4, was made by incising into a brass plate hundreds of short, thin lines that received the printer's ink and left behind evidence of those incised lines on the pages—lines that could be touched in their crispness as well as seen. "Adorn'd with cuts": the running subtitle to Rowe's edition of the Collected Works of William Shakespeare (CWWS) calls attention to the tactile making of the images and raises expectations that the printed story line will periodically be interrupted by incursions from other senses, including the sense of touch. In this particular image the way Lear uses his hands to expose his flesh to the storm ("Off, off, you lendings!" [3.4.102]), as the hands of Kent and Edgar try to prevent him from doing so, invites a *feeling* response of just the sort Gloucester describes, a tactile engagement of the reader's body.

Incising of another sort has produced the grooves that carry the sound of Donald Wolfit's voice in the 1962 vinyl recording of *King Lear* shown in the first panel of Figure 4.5. One of the last actor-managers in the tradition of David Garrick, the author of an autobiography *First Interval* (1954), and the protagonist of Ronald Harwood's play *The Dresser* (1981), Wolfit appears in the second panel of Figure 4.5 in his first attempt (1942) at what became his signature role: King Lear. The 1962 recording, featuring Wolfit's wife Rosalind Iden as Cordelia and *musique concrète* by Desmond Leslie, celebrated Wolfit's reputation as the greatest Lear of his generation.[1] The transition from Wolfit's raised hand in Figure 4.5 to the hand that guides the stylus on the turntable depends on several technologies of touch. Before being incised into the vinyl disc the sound waves of Wolfit's speaking in 1961 were first converted into electrical signals and imprinted on magnetic tape via a ring-shaped recording head. In the earliest sound recordings in the late nineteenth century the transition from voice to disc was direct, as sound waves of the actor's voice were cut directly from the air into a revolving cylinder made of tinfoil or wax. The anecdote that opens Wes Folkerth's *The Sound of Shakespeare* describes the process (Folkerth 2002: 1–4). In 1898 the great actor Henry Irving was asked to speak the first eleven and a half lines of *Richard III* ("Now is the winter of our discontent …") into a large tube that concentrated the sound waves for transfer into an electrical signal that was then incised directly onto a white wax cylinder, a medium that Bacon would have classified as a dried liquid. From wax or vinyl, the transfer of sound signals through the air to the listener's ear is usually imagined as "waves," but Thomas Wright in *The Passions of the Mind* imagines sounds in a more tactile way as "a certain artificial shaking, crispling or tickling of the air" (Wright 1971: sig. M5v). Before the advent of digital recording and the CDs that carry the digits, the "crispling" could be heard in the white noise of stylus rubbing against

---

[1] Published by the Oldbourne Press as SKL 3A-4A in the "Living Shakespeare" series, the LP is a good listen if you can find it. The catalogue number in the British Library's Sound Archive is 1LP0107672; in the Library of Congress's Motion Picture, Broadcasting, and Recorded Sound Section it is r62001148.

Figure 4.5 Donald Wolfit seen as King Lear (1942), right, and heard on an LP recording (1962), left.

grooves and the pops caused by scratches. These audible touches kept the medium of transcription constantly present in the listener's ears.

Less tactile, because less forcibly present in the moment of perception, are celluloid strips like those that recorded Paul Scofield's performance in *King Lear*, directed by Peter Brook (1971). (At the time Scofield's voice was to be had in a five-disc vinyl audio edition published four years earlier. A new audio recording featuring Scofield's voice—this time a digital CD—celebrated his eightieth birthday in 2002.) Even in film, however, the tactility of the physical medium is unavoidable. Scratches and blotches from earlier showings can make the celluloid strip suddenly, distractingly present. So can pops produced by breaks in the magnetic band that carries the sound. By comparison with these media, the electrical signals that transmit to the sensor's eyes and ears the reformatted version of Scofield's Lear and Alan Webb's Gloucester on DVD (2005) aim for transparency. The sensor is invited to see through the medium into an illusion of presence in which the medium itself virtually disappears. But only virtually.

:

Each of the foregoing cases of touch involves some sort of physical medium: paper that has been punched or pressed, brass that has been cut, wax that has been incised, vinyl that has been impressed, celluloid that has been coated with chemicals. Performances in these media can be touched, but it is not the performance itself that is being touched, only a simulacrum of that performance. In live performances, too, a physical medium is present, but that medium is much harder to feel. The medium in question is, of course, air. It is molecules of nitrogen, oxygen, argon, carbon dioxide, and traces of other gases that transmit the sound waves that reach our ears and impede the light waves that reach our eyes. Except when the wind is blowing, however, or when the air is full of water drops or when the temperature is unusually cold or unusually hot, it is hard even to notice air, much less feel it. (Come to think of it, the usually cold and moist conditions in London in the winter, when Philip Henslowe's accounts register only a slight drop in attendance [Gurr 1992: 213], may have made the air more palpable to audiences in London's outdoor playhouses than it is in the air-conditioned indoor theaters where we are most likely to take in a play today.) How can touch operate in so thin a medium as air?

One solution was tried by the James Joyce Memorial Liquid Theater in the early 1970s. The name refers to the dramatic event (a "happening" was the word at the time), not the company, which was the Company Theater of Los Angeles, directed by Steven Kent. Patrons were welcomed and given a silk bag—red, yellow, or green—in which they were asked to place and leave behind shoes, coats, valuables, and other (psychological) encumbrances, and were then divided into groups according to bag color and escorted on an "odyssey" ("trip" figured prominently in the argot of the time). Clive Barnes describes what happened next in a performance in the Guggenheim Museum in New York in October 1971:

> With closed eyes you enter the maze—a maze of hands, soft voices and drifting muslin. Something may be thrust at you to eat, your hand may touch unexpected water. You move here and there, guided by blind voices and silent hands. You are embraced by abstract strangers; softly but firmly, you are delicately kissed with an asexual friendliness, that is pre-erotic in its innocence. You are asked to open your eyes. A man and a woman are embracing you—they ask you to enter the

142

other section of the play area. From here you see the maze—full of
filmy lights and Blake-like bodies, and watch the ritual passage of later
voyagers. (Barnes 1971)

A sequence of further games in "the play area" moved the voyagers
toward the one mimetic event of the evening, a ballet danced by
anthropoid apes and Adam and Eve, followed by a game in which
members of each odyssey group were invited to lie on the floor and
allow their bodies to be massaged, pummeled, passed around, or raised
in the air by other members of the group. General dancing to music
by a rock band concluded the evening in the 1970s equivalent of the
jigs that ended performances at the Globe. "When the play was over,"
Thomas Platter reports in 1599, "they danced very marvelously and
gracefully together as is their wont, two dressed as men and two as
women" (Platter 1937: 166). The dancing that is scripted to end *As
You Like It* suggests that play could segue into jig without a break. In
masques at court, as at the Guggenheim Museum in 1971, the final
turn came when the spectators joined the actors in dancing.

Extreme measures like those tried by the James Joyce Memorial
Liquid Theater were not needed by the King's Men. The actor's art, as
Joseph Roach points out, was thought by THWS and his contemporaries to depend on touch. The challenge for an actor like Richard
Burbage, playing Lear, was to cultivate in his heart, sinews, and limbs
a certain passion or combination of passions—anger, fear, pity, amazement—and to communicate those passions to the bodies of his
viewer/listeners. With respect to sound, we still share an understanding that the speaking actor uses lungs, larynx, tongue, teeth, and lips to
set up sound waves of certain frequencies in the ambient air, waves
that strike the listeners' ear drums and are decoded by the listeners'
brains as phonemes of speech. Other aspects of sound—volume, pitch,
rhythm, cadence, timbre, non-semantic sounds—register more subliminally and may not be consciously noticed at all (Smith 2009b:
168–207). In both cases, however, we recognize that sound *touches* us:
it invades our bodies and, if loud enough, reverberates in our gut.

With respect to vision, we are less tactile. If we think about it at all,
we realize that colors and shapes are the result of reflected light waves

forming an image on our retinas. Unless a light is very bright (as when we look directly at the sun), we don't think much about the light waves as having direction and force. Objects seem to stay *over there*. Vision for THWS, Burbage, their fellow actors, and their customers was a more visceral affair. In Roach's summation, the actor's passions, "irradiating the bodies of spectators through their eyes and ears, could literally transfer the contents of his heart to theirs" (Roach 1985: 27). Recall that it was spirits and humors that did the internal work of transmission. A "humor," Jonson's spokesman Asper explains in the Induction to *Every Man Out of His Humor*, is "a quality of air or water." Pour water on the floor, and it will run; blow air through a horn or trumpet, and it will leave behind a residue of moisture.

> So, in every human body,
> The choler, melancholy, phlegm, and blood,
> By reason that they flow continually,
> In some one part and are not continent,
> Receive the name of humors.

"Humor" as a psychological disposition follows "by metaphor" (Ind. 87, 96–100, 101 in Jonson 2001: 118). Instead of the King's Men the company might aptly have been called the William Shakespeare Liquid Theater.

:

Phillip Stubbes at a performance of the James Joyce Memorial Liquid Theater: now, there's a thought to brighten the mind's eye. Stubbes's fulminations in *The Anatomy of Abuses* (1583) against the eroticism of theatrical performances diverted us in Chapter 1. "Such wanton gestures, such bawdy speeches, such laughing and fleering, such kissing and bussing, such clipping and culling, such winking and glancing of wanton eyes" (Stubbes 1877–9: 22): the fundamental appeal of theater is that it makes you want to do with your own hands, arms, and mouth what you have seen the actors do with theirs—but with the addition at home of your genitals. Theater, in Stubbes's view, is a touching experience. As if to illustrate Stubbes's complaint there is John Manningham's story about how THWS intercepted an invitation to a sexual tryst that had been sent to Richard Burbage from a lady enamored of his performance as Richard III, got to the lady's house first, and sent down a message to Burbage at the door that "William the Conqueror was before Richard the Third" (Manningham 1976: 73). Whether, after a performance, everybody in the audience "brings another homeward of their way very friendly and in their secret conclaves (covertly) they play the sodomites, or worse" we have as direct evidence only Stubbes's word (Stubbes 1877–9: 22).

Be that as it may, CWWS are rife with fantasies of touch, especially when the occasion at hand is an apparition, the discovery of something behind a curtain, or a play within the play. "Is this a dagger I see before me, / The handle toward my hand?" Macbeth questions. "Come, let me clutch thee" (2.1.33–4). When Paulina in *The Winter's Tale* draws aside the curtain to reveal Hermione's statue, Leontes' first impulse is to reach out and touch it. "O, patience!" Paulina cries. "The statue is but newly fixed; the colour's/ Not dry" (5.3.46–8). Touch is postponed until the statue comes to life. Similarly in *The Tempest* Alonso reacts with astonishment when, according to the stage direction, "*Prospero discovers Ferdinand and Miranda, playing at chess*" (SD before 5.1.174). When the betrothed young lovers move into the spectators' space, Alonso touches what he has seen, encircling the vision in his arms: "Now all the blessings/ Of a glad father compass thee about" (5.1.182–3).

"The Mousetrap" in *Hamlet* touches off in Claudius the opposite reaction, an impulse to withdraw. Telling Claudius the name of the play, Hamlet has assured him "it touches us not" (3.2.230). Yet the moment of the poisoning provokes Claudius to rise, call for light, and make his way offstage. *The Mousetrap* functions as synecdoche, and the point of contact is the hand that pours the poison. "Give o'er the play," Polonius says (3.2.256), as if the play could be handed off to someone standing by or cast away from one's hands. In the 1603 first quarto the Polonius figure insinuates physical force. He says to Hamlet, "The king is moved, my lord" (sig. F5v in Shakespeare 1981: 600). What Claudius feels is, in his own words, "offence." "Have you heard the argument?" he has asked Hamlet. "Is there no offence in it?" (3.2.221–2). Having seen and heard an enactment of the murder of his brother, Claudius confesses "O, my offence is rank! It smells to heaven" (3.3.36). It is the nostrils of God that are offended in Claudius's image, but the fundamental sense of "offence" is even more tactile: a striking of one's foot against an obstacle (*OED* 1989: "offence," *n.*, †1.a), hence figuratively a transgression or sin (2.a).

The physicality of the word "offend" is registered in three quotations from Christ's Sermon on the Mount (Matthew 5:29–30, 18:9, and Mark 9:47). The earlier quotation in Matthew is the fullest: "if thy right eye offend thee, pluck it out, and cast it from thee .... And if thy right hand offend thee, cut it off, and cast it from thee." The occasion for this striking bit of advice is just such an occasion as Stubbes locates in the theater. Hearing is distinguished from seeing, even as seeing is conflated with touching. "Ye have heard that it was said by them of old, Thou shalt not commit adultery," Christ reminds his listeners in the verses just before; "But I say unto you that whosoever looketh on a woman to lust after her hath committed adultery with her already in his heart" (Bible 1967: Matthew 5:27–28). By this account imagined touching in the heart is the same as physical touching with hands.

Fantasies of touch in the theater could be indulged by those willing and able to pay for a stool on the stage or a seat in the lords' room, close enough to see the actor's bodies at first hand and hear their words as if those words were being spoken to themselves alone. Elsewhere I have suggested that stools on stage at the Globe and the Blackfriars provided an early equivalent of the green room in Restoration and eighteenth-century playhouses, a space where privileged playgoers could flirt with the performers in close quarters (Smith 2009b: 243–7). The before-the-main-event inductions supplied by WSA, Francis Beaumont, Ben Jonson, John Marston, and others register a variety of dynamics in the relationship of stool-sitters to board-stalkers—dynamics that range from a need to control in Jonson's case to gentle mockery in Beaumont's and Marston's to metatheatrical irony in WSA's. The Wife in Beaumont's *The Knight of the Burning Pestle* keeps interrupting the action of the play by yelling encouraging words to her son Ralph, who is playing the knight, but at one point she actually *hands* him encouragement: "there's some sugar candy for thee, proceed, thou shalt have another bout with him" (II.321–2 in Beaumont 1966: 38). In the induction to *The Taming of the Shrew* a piquant moment occurs when Christopher Sly, taking up the jokers' suggestion that what is happening to him is real, orders his servants to leave so that he can go to bed with "Lady Madam" (aka Bartholomew) who at close quarters is of course a male actor. Bartholomew begs off for a night or two: "I hope this reason stands for my excuse," he says (Ind. 2.121), perhaps punning on the pronunciation of /reɪsɪn/ with "raising" and gesturing toward his penis. Certainly Sly takes it that way: "Ay, it stands so that I may hardly tarry so long" (122).

But what about patrons who could *not* afford a stool?

:

The visceral responses of characters like Sly, Claudius, Leontes, and Alonso—their desire to touch an illusion and to be touched by it—are illuminated by recent experiments with virtual reality, which demonstrate how readily a subject can be induced to locate tactile sensations in a projected image of his body. Two separate series of experiments reported in the journal *Science* in 2007 reached similar conclusions. In each case subjects were asked to wear virtual-reality goggles that projected, several feet in front of them, images of their own backs as observed by cameras several feet behind them. (See Figure 4.6.) When researchers used wands to stroke the subjects' chests or backs out of camera range and simultaneously stroked the virtual figures' chests or backs *within* camera range, almost all the subjects attributed the sensation of being touched to the virtual figure in front of them rather than to their actual bodies (Ehrsson 2007, Lenggenhager, Tadi, Metzinger, and Blanke 2007). That is to say, they felt that they inhabited the projected body rather than their own.

"Proprioceptive drift" the phenomenon has been called, and it can be explained by the dominance of vision over other sensations (in this case, touch) when cues are contradictory (Lenggenhager, Tadi,

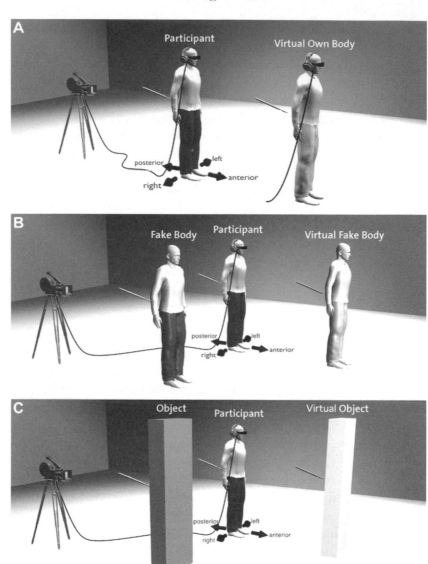

Figure 4.6 Virtual reality experiments carried out by Bigna Lenggenhager, Tej Tadi, Thomas Metzinger, and Olaf Banke (2007).

Metzinger, and Blanke 2007: 1096). Once the subjects had experienced proprioceptive drift, they were much more likely to react viscerally in their physical body to an object (in the experiment, a hammer) that seemed to threaten their virtual body (Ehrsson 2007: 1048). One group of experimenters tested the results by substituting dummies (actual and virtual) and large rectangular objects (actual and virtual) for the projected images of the subjects' bodies. Consciousness drifted toward the dummies almost as strongly as toward images of the subjects' own backs, but not at all toward the rectangular objects (Lenggenhager, Tadi, Metzinger, and Blanke 2007: 1097). Montaigne in his essay "Of Cruelty" argues that, for purposes of torture and punishment at least, corpses might serve as well as living bodies.[2] Montaigne instances the execution of a notorious highway thief that he witnessed at Rome. Mutilation of the malefactor's corpse worked a more visceral effect on the spectators than the act of killing had done: "at his strangling no man of the company seemed to be moved to any ruth; but when he came to be quartered, the executioner gave no blow that was not accompanied with a piteous voice, and hearty exclamation, as if every man had had a feeling of sympathy or lent his senses to the poor mangled wretch" (2.11 in Montaigne 1613: sig. X8). Lacan in his lecture on "The Mirror Stage as Formative of the *I* Function" makes a similar point: fear of bodily disintegration is frequently registered in dreams as disconnected limbs or exoscopic organs in the manner of Hieronymus Bosch's paintings, while "*I* formation" takes shape as a fortified camp or even a stadium (Lacan 2006: 78).[3] Scenes of torture in *The Unfortunate Traveler* and *King Lear* replicate these anxieties, permitting reader/spectators to confront painful spectacles of mutilation and dismemberment from the comfortably distant position of a nameless face in Nashe's fictional mob or an anonymous spectator within the Globe's wooden O.

Having tried out virtual reality myself in the Institute for Creative Technologies at the University of Southern California, I can report that the illusion, while powerful, is never complete. That figure over

---

[2] For this reference I am grateful to Penelope Geng.
[3] For making this connection between Montaigne and Lacan, I am grateful to Will West.

there both is and is not me. How often do I see myself from behind? Even with the three angled mirrors in a clothing store it is tricky to position myself just right to get a backside view. (And I would rather not contemplate my baldness anyway.) Furthermore, it is not *my* hands that are causing the sensation but another person's hands. I am aware of that control and am more sensitive as a result. No less important in the production of the illusion are the goggles. In effect, they induce the *epochē*, the act of framing that sets up the illusion and that primes me for the experience of being touched. The proscenium arch, the boundaries of the playing platform, the edges of the screen perform the same function in theater and film.

Finally, I could not help but notice that some areas of my body were more sensitive than others. What you see in Figure 4.7 are areas of the cerebral cortex that receive and process tactile sensations from various parts of the body. The diagram is called the "Penfield Homunculus," after Wilder Penfield, MD, whose experiments using electrodes to stimulate various parts of the brain during open-skull surgery in the 1930s and 1940s resulted in this map drawn by Mrs. H. P. Cantlie—a map that still serves, despite criticism and additional findings, as a reference for clinicians and scientists (Penfield and Rasmussen 1950: 21–65, Griggs 1988: 105–6, Feinsod 2005: 524–5, Colapinto 2009: 80–1). Shown here is the rear portion of the left hemisphere, with dotted lines of various lengths and body parts of various sizes to indicate relative areas of surface tissue devoted to particular sensitivities. (Note that hands and feet are located on the top, the face and mouth toward the bottom.) Also shown in the diagram is the proximity of those specialized tissues to each other. Not only do the face and the hands occupy comparatively large areas; those areas are next to each other.

Recent clinical studies indicate that if a limb is removed, the tissue devoted to sensation in that limb in some cases redirects itself to body parts that are adjacent in the brain even if they are quite remote on the body itself. Thus, a patient who had lost the lower half of his left arm could be made to feel his phantom thumb when his face was stroked, his phantom index finger when his lips were touched, his phantom little finger when his lower jaw was touched

(Colapinto 2009: 81). The proximity of the genitalia to the feet (specifically the toes) is remarkable. One might suppose that in the theater as in the laboratory the erogenous zones of mouth, face, and hands would be the most suggestible.[4] The evidence of *King Lear*, along with *The Taming of the Shrew, Hamlet, The Winter's Tale*, and *The Tempest*, proves that hunch to be right. In addition to all the cues to hands, lips, and tongue, one notes the connection between the size of the foot in "Penfield's Homunculus" and the fundamental sense of Claudius's "offence" as a foot striking an obstacle. One notes, too, Stubbes's fixation on the interconnections among roving hands, kissing lips, lascivious tongue, dancing feet, and rampant genitals.

The virtual-reality experiments suggest how startlingly easy it is to expand the boundaries of consciousness to include another body when the sense of touch is cued by vision. The operational principle here seems to be analogy, not identification. It is my sense of touch that allows me to project what I can feel with my body *here* onto his body *there* and, reversing direction, to take what I see happening to his body *there* and feel it with my body *here*. Those exchanges are the stock-in-trade of theater. Indeed, they constitute theater's first law of physics. In Bert O. States's words, gesture is not "the kinetic imprint" of speech on an actor's body nor even the impetus for speech (as Vygotsky, for example, imagines) but something that happens in space and time: "Gesture is the *process* of revelation of the actor's presence … and this presence, as the organ that feeds on the dramatic text, is the governing center of what is possible in the theater" (States 1987: 138, emphasis original). The mechanism that makes such exchanges possible is "mirror neurons." The version of "Penfield's Homunculus" in Figure 4.8 shows comparative sizes and locations of areas devoted to motor control, again in the left hemisphere but this time in the front half. As you can see, the proportions and the proximities are remarkably close to those for sensation shown in Figure 4.7. Feet, hands, and vocal apparatus loom large; hands and face are adjacent. If you took Figure 4.8 (the

---

[4] For raising the question about relative sensitivities in different parts of the body and for making me remember Cantlie's homunculus, which I first encountered in R. L. Gregory's *Eye and Brain*, I thank Brandon Som.

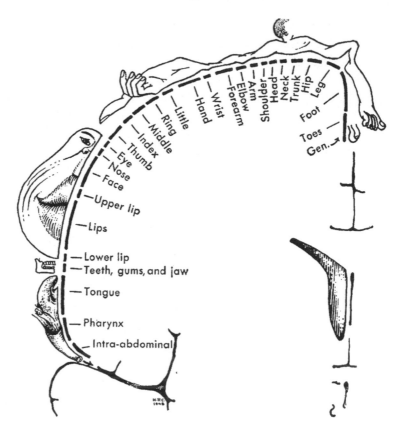

Figure 4.7   The Penfield homunculus, sensory view, drawn by Mrs. H. P. Cantlie (1948).

front of the left hemisphere) and flipped Figure 4.7 (the rear of the left hemisphere) and placed it behind Figure 4.8, so that the curves line up, you could see that the sensory face is contiguous with the motor face, the sensory hand with the motor hand, the sensory tongue with the motor tongue, etc.—suggesting close connections between feeling (in the rear of the left hemisphere) and doing (in the front). On a smaller scale, experiments in neuroscience have demonstrated that the same neurons fire when a particular action is being perceived as when that action is being performed by oneself—only they fire in the reverse direction. These "mirror neurons" may provide the physiological

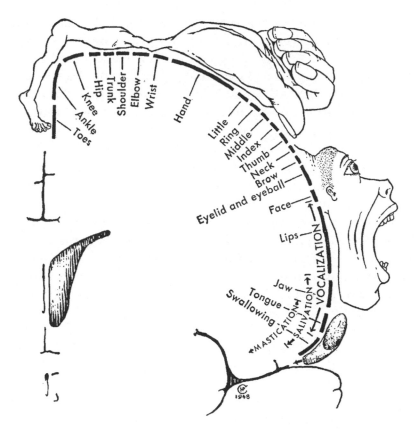

Figure 4.8   The Penfield homunculus, motor view, drawn by Mrs. H. P. Cantlie (1948).

grounding for empathy in interpersonal relations (Gallese, Eagle, and Migone 2007: 131–76, Colapinto 2009: 85–7).[5] I believe they also help to explain why trans-body relations in theater are experienced so intensely.

Verbal cues to "proprioceptive drift" can be found throughout Shakespeare's scripts, particularly in moments of cruelty. When Gloucester cries out, just before being blinded, "I am tied to th'stake, and I must stand the course" (3.7.52), he is putting himself into the

---

[5]   For this explanation and for the reference to Gallese, Eagle, and Migone I am grateful to Richard M. Waugaman, MD.

position of a bear being baited by dogs or a criminal being tortured by his executioners or perhaps both. Macbeth seizes on the same image when the prophecy of his destruction comes true and Birnam Wood begins advancing on Dunsinane: "They have tied me to a stake. I cannot fly/ But bear-like I must fight the course" (5.7.1–2). Macbeth's speech in particular sets up two subject positions, "they" and "me," opening up the possibility of the spectator/listener's feeling one of two things: the punisher's ardor and the victim's suffering.

Two episodes in Thomas Nashe's prose fiction *The Unfortunate Traveler* (1594) confirm Montaigne's curious double experience at the execution in Rome: indifference to or tacit approval of the punisher's ardor followed by anguish at the punished person's suffering. Nashe's episodes suggest that it was possible to take both subject positions, and in just the order Montaigne suggests: first the punisher, then the punished. Modern sensibilities are likely to tend toward the victim's subject position—his fears, his pains, his death—but Nashe makes it clear that a viewer might shift back and forth, now entertaining the tormentors' subject position, now the victim's. The status of the victim seems less important in Nashe than the exhilaration of experiencing such violence from multiple points of view. Nashe's first episode is the rout of Jan van Leiden and his Anabaptist army at Münster in northern Germany in 1535. To the narrator's eyes, van Leiden and his followers are religious extremists thoroughly deserving of rough treatment. In the pitch of battle, however, the narrator suddenly changes his mind:

> To see even a bear, which is the most cruelest of beasts, too too bloodily overmatched and deformedly rent in pieces by an unconscionable number of curs, it would move compassion against kind, and make those that, beholding him at the stake yet uncoped with, wished him a suitable death to his ugly shape, now to recall their hard-hearted wishes and moan him suffering as a mild beast, in comparison of the foul-mouthed mastiffs, his butchers. (Nashe 1972: 285)

Even more remarkable is the narrator's double mind at the execution of a nefarious Jew in Rome. Nashe describes the tortures in detail: the Jew's body pitched up the ass on an iron stake, the flesh roasted, the skin basted with alum and mercury, the back whipped with red-hot wire, the head baptized with pitch and set on fire, the penis and testicles tied with exploding fireworks, the skin on the shoulders flayed with red-hot pinchers, the breast and belly grated with rough seal skins, the finger-nails half plucked off and propped up with pricks, the fingers broken back to the wrist, the toes broken off by the roots, the body burnt from the feet upwards with a small oil fire "till his heart was consumed, and then he died" (359). The point of view here—if "view" is the right word—might seem to be exclusively the torturers'. Implements of torture are catalogued (the iron stake, alum and mercury, red-hot wire, red-hot pinchers, rough seal skins, pricks), body parts are anatomized (ass, flesh, skin, back, breast, belly, finger-nails, fingers, toes). But the implied pain that those particular implements inflict on those particular body parts involves a shift, if only a partial shift, to the victim's point of view, or rather point of touch. The punishments are catalogued with fetishistic delight—but so are the pains. Gloucester's blinding, I believe, shapes up in the theater as just such an occasion.

It was in the eighteenth century, during the cult of sensibility, when "the man of mode" was giving way to "the man of feeling," that *King Lear* acquired its reputation as Shakespeare's cruelest play. In his notes on the play Samuel Johnson cites his friend Thomas Wharton's opinion that "the instances of cruelty are too savage and shocking"— "savage" being a property of the action, "shock" a property of the spectators (Shakespeare 2008: 171). And the cruelest scene in Shakespeare's cruelest play? Johnson does not hesitate to name it: "the extrusion of Gloucester's eyes, which seems an act too horrid to be endured in dramatic exhibition, and such as must always compel the mind to relieve its distress by incredulity" (171). The blinding of Gloucester touches the spectator in what to Johnson, as a man of sensibility, are overwhelming, unendurably painful ways.

Lear's cruel hailing of Gloucester as "blind Cupid" in 4.5 is a reprise of the shifting subject positions in 3.4: he inflicts the pain all over again, this time in words. "Blind Cupid": the pain in Lear's greeting is kinesthetic. We *see* something that usually we only *hear* about: Gloucester is not just *figuratively* blind but *actually* blind (at least within the fiction).

155

Furthermore, in the verbal reprise of the scene of torture we hear about something we have actually seen: the gruesome physicality of Gloucester's blinding has been witnessed by the play's spectators in 3.7. "Upon these eyes of thine I'll set my foot" (3.7.66), Cornwall snarls, but the Servant's attempted intervention—"Hold your hand, my lord" (3.7.70)—suggests that Gloucester's eyes are pulled out by hand and only then, perhaps, crushed under foot. It may be Gloucester himself who has unwittingly suggested the blinding when he tells Regan that he has sent Lear to Dover "Because I would not see thy cruel nails/ Pluck out his poor old eyes, nor thy fierce sister/ In his anointed flesh stick boarish fangs" (3.7.54–6). Certainly the pains are articulated—"O cruel! O you gods!" (3.7.68), "All dark and comfortless" (3.7.83)—but so are the details of punishment: the cruel nails, the boarish fangs, the chair, the foot, the hands, the tongues. Confronted with that scene of cruelty, the spectator can move between the out-flowing of passion in the inflicting of torture and the inner-ebbing of passion in the experience of pain. The result of these transactions is a kinesthetic experience: neither sight nor hearing but a crawling in the flesh. If one is touched *here* by what is being represented *there*, it is because the air between here and there has been activated by two sorts of movement: light rays reflected from the actors' moving bodies and sound waves set in motion by the actors' moving tongues. Between the sixteenth century and now there may be different explanations of light rays and sound waves (most of us do not believe that our eyes send out light rays, even though that feels right) and of the biochemicals that transmit sensations and impulses within the human body (for us "humor" is only a metaphor), but the basic psychophysics of the transaction remain the same: movement across space. And so do the media: air or ether, nerves or "sinews."

:

Let us begin with light waves and moving bodies. The findings in the virtual-reality experiments and the mappings of neuroscience suggest that John Bulwer was on to something in the 1640s with his two treatises on gesture *Chirologia* and *Chironomia* as well as *Pathomyotamia or a Dissection of the Significative Muscles of the Affections of the Mind* and *Philocophus or The Deaf and Dumb Man's Friend*. In the first of these four treatises, *Chirologia*, as we had occasion to consider in Chapter 2, hand gestures are presented as a kind of natural language. Motions of the hands are often swifter than speech, Bulwer observes; "nor in their senses remote from the true nature of the things that are implied" (Bulwer 1974: 16). The true nature of things, in Bulwer's account of communication, is not oral reason but bodily passions. The medium for passions is not just the tongue but arms, hands, torso, legs, and feet. Theater historians like J. L. Styan and analysts of movement like P. A. Skantze have demonstrated how Shakespeare's 1,300-square-foot stage at the Globe required actors to be in almost constant movement as they spoke their lines (Styan 1967: 53–80, Skantze 2003: 21–58). It was not just their feet that moved but their entire bodies. Lear's exchanges with Gloucester in 4.5 need to be viewed, listened to, and understood in this light, as motions of the mind that are signified not only in words but in externalizations of passion made with movements of arms and hands and changes in posture and position.

If we attempt to transfer Bulwer's gestures, laid out as cells on the page in *Chirologia* and *Chironomia*, to the stage, we are apt to imagine those gestures as photographic stills or, in terms of film, as freeze-frames that momentarily fix meaning while speech goes on its voluble way. (See Figure 4.9.) The fragmentary, chaotic quality of Lear's speeches in 4.5 seems to encourage such a cubist view of his passions. First comes anger ("No, they cannot touch me for crying. I am the King himself" [4.5.83–4]), then fear ("Look, look, a mouse! Peace, peace, this piece of toasted cheese will do it" [4.5.88–9]), then self-pity and grief ("When the rain came to wet me once, and the wind to make me chatter; when the thunder would not peace at my bidding, there I found 'em, there I smelt 'em out ....They told me I was everything; 'tis a lie, I am not ague-proof" [4.5.100–5]), then anger again ("Down from the waist/ They're centaurs, though women all above" [4.5.121–2]), and finally compassion ("If thou wilt weep my fortunes, take my eyes" [4.5.172]).

Figure 4.9 John Bulwer, *Chirologia* (1644), chirograms for anger, fear, grief, and compassion arranged as a sequence.

Anger, fear, grief, compassion: for each of these affects Bulwer specifies a discrete gesture. A bent fist is one gesture for anger. (See *Minor*, "I threaten," in Figure 4.9.) A second is provided in *Chironomia*, Bulwer's treatise on how to take such natural gestures and put them to rhetorical use: "The forehead stricken with the hand, is an action of dolor, shame, and admiration." It may be over-emphatic except when used "by such who are of a more hot complexion, and are apt to boil over with a sudden motion, whose choler in the seething, bubbles into action" (Bulwer 1974: 183). (This particular gesture from *Chironomia* is not illustrated, but see an approximation from *Chirologia* in *Impatientiam prodo*, "I show impatience," in Figure 4.9.) Earlier in *The Tragedy of King Lear* there has been an explicit call for such a gesture when Lear responds to Goneril's perversity by exclaiming, "O Lear, Lear, Lear!/ Beat at this gate that let thy folly in/ And thy dear judgment out" (1.4.249–51).

Fear has its own motions of the hands. "The smiting of the hand upon the thigh," according to Bulwer, is irresistible among men who are "angry and enraged with grief," but "this gesture of the hand is significant also in fear, admiration and amazement" (Bulwer 1974: 76–7). (See *Indignatione timeo*, "I fear indignantly," in Figure 4.9.) The self-pity and grief that Lear articulates when he remembers his sufferings in the storm would call for the clasped hands that we noticed in Chapter 2 in connection with "I all alone beweep my outcast state" in sonnet 29. (See *Ploro*, "I beweep," in Figure 4.9.) Anger returns as Lear thinks about cruelty and injustice in the world at large. Hands figure prominently in his imagination. See the justice railing against the thief? "Change places, and handy-dandy, which is the justice, which is the thief?" (4.5.149–40). References contemporary with Shakespeare suggest that "handy-dandy" was a children's game in which one player shifted an object from hand to hand and the other player had to guess which closed hand finally held the object (Shakespeare 1908: 282).

A segue from Lear's rant against injustice to his recognition of Gloucester as his faithful courtier is provided by one those strings of repeated words in *King Lear* that empty out semantic meaning: "Now, now, now, now!" (4.5.168). Do these exclamations conclude Lear's rant against injustice, or do they lead to Lear's order to Gloucester, "Pull off my boots. Harder, harder! So" (4.5.169)? Either way, Lear's hotly felt rage at the arm of the law—"Thou rascal beadle, hold that bloody hand./ Why dost thou lash that whore? Strip thy own back" (4.5.156–7)—gives way to a touching moment that restages the power dynamics of the proffered lips and wiped hand—but with a difference. This time, the offer comes from Lear's side, and the touch ends in mutuality. "If thou wilt weep my fortune," Lear says to the sometime blind Cupid, "take my eyes./ I know thee well enough: thy name is Gloucester" (4.5.172–3). Here, in almost Aristotelian terms, is the *anagnorisis*, the recognition we have been hoping for. Lear's reaching out here may be physical as well as verbal. If so, Bulwer provides the gesture. "To extend and offer out the right hand unto any," Bulwer notes in *Chirologia*, "is an expression of pity, and of an intention to afford comfort and relief" (58). (See *Auxilium fero*, "I bring aid," in Figure 4.9.)

That gesture of openness undoes the closed quality of Lear's earlier cruelty. No specific gesture of cruelty is catalogued in Bulwer's *Chirologia* or *Chironomia*, but the rhetorical gesture of prayer—hands raised and clasped or raised and spread outward—gives Bulwer occasion to suggest the closed-fist quality of cruelty. "Can we think to receive ease from God with that hand that oppresses another? mercy from God with that hand that exercises cruelty upon another? or bounty from God with that hand that withholds right from another?" Bulwer asks. "How can we expect God should open with his hands of benediction, who shut up our hands, and that which is due to another, in them? How much more then, if we strike with those hands by oppression, or (as Isaiah) we lift up the bloody hands of cruelty"

(Bulwer 1974: 31). The tightness and fixity of cruel hands is extended to neck and head in Bulwer's *Pathomyotamia* (1649). "This rigid form of fierce audacity, looks like a cramp or crick in the neck," Bulwer observes, "and makes the muscles to remain so stretched out, that the head and neck seem indeed immoveable." Bulwer calls this muscular rigidity "the voluntary rick of stiff-necked Cruelty" (Bulwer 1649: 79–80). The softening that we witness in the reunion of Lear and Gloucester is thus, in physical as well as verbal terms, a relaxation. The touch of cruelty is hard and closed; the touch of pity, soft and open.

Lear's passions, parsed into a sequence, and Bulwer's gestures, snipped out of the charts in *Chirologia* and placed in a row as in Figure 4.9, look disconcertingly like a comic strip or a passage in a graphic novel. Theatrical performance, in 1606 as now, was not like that. Lear's passions—and the movements that display them—don't make up a linear sequence; they are various and overlapping. Instead of a linear sequence of passions, we need to imagine, as in Figure 4.10, a *layering* of passions that are simultaneously present. Anger may supply the through-bass, but there are passages of fear, grief, shame, and admiration, in solo and in consort. Consider Lear's beating his head with his hands. According to Bulwer, this gesture expresses not just one passion, anger, but multiple, indeed *contradictory* passions: anger, shame, sorrow, admiration, fear, grief, wonder, strangeness, amazement. So what do we see in Lear's beating himself on the head? Dolor? Shame? Amazement? Choler? Or all four together? The gesture supplies more possibilities than Lear's 18 words, laid out in a row, can specify. There are more feelings in those words than "folly" at one extreme and "judgment" at the other. Similarly, the smiting of hands upon thighs may indicate enraged grief, but it also indicates fear.

Certainly a layered schema like the one in Figure 4.10 helps to explain Bacon's explanations of the signs and causes of the passions in Experiments 904–11 of *Silva Silvarum*. Anger and fear, the first two passions Lear expresses in 4.5, are closely related according to Bacon. "Anger causeth palenesse in some, and the going and coming of the color in others: also trembling in some, swelling; foaming at the mouth; stamping; bending of the fist. Paleness, and going, and coming of the color, are caused by the burning of the spirits about the heart"

(Bacon 1627: sig. AA4). If, however, paleness alone prevails, without a return of color, the anger "is commonly joined with some fear" (sig. AA4). Another sign of anger joined with fear, says Bacon, is trembling. The gestures for anger and fear in Bulwer's *Chirologia* are likewise continuous, not discrete, as with striking one's hand on the thighs. Just as the passions themselves are fluid and continuous, just as the large stage of the Globe required the actors to be in constant motion, so must we imagine the gestures in Bulwer's schema.

Shakespeare's original audience would have witnessed in Lear's gestures, not a series of freeze-frames, but a continuous movement from bent fist to hand or hands striking the head to hand or hands striking the thighs to clasped hands to bent fist to hand or hands striking the head to an outstretched hand. Of course there would have been seconds, even whole minutes, when arms and hands were not moving in such large sweeping ways, and there was no necessity of translating every single word into a visual sign, but the overall effect would have been not unlike Chris Garcia's signing of sonnet 29, described in Chapter 2. The necessity of moving about with legs and feet on the Globe's vast stage, combined with gestures made with arms and hands, would have made Richard Burbage's original performance of Lear much more extrovert than the self-contained inwardness encouraged by method acting or the limited body movement imposed by the motion-picture camera's obsessive focus on the head. Some contemporary actors—I am thinking especially of David Tennant as Hamlet in the Royal Shakespeare Company's 2008 production—manage to capture the kinetic effect implied by Bulwer and Bacon, Styan and Skantze. Production stills like the one in Figure 4.5, showing Wolfit with his

Figure 4.10
John Bulwer, *Chirologia* (1644), chirograms for grief, fear, and anger arranged as layers beneath compassion.

raised hand, cannot capture this effect of movement from inside the actor's body into ambient space. Gloucester's kissing of Lear's hand stands out as a touching moment, but it is the culmination of bodily movements that have begun in the play's first scene.

:

After the play's overt physical cruelties, the reunion of Gloucester and Lear in 4.5 presents a moment of *verbal* cruelty. In its brute physicality Lear's greeting of Gloucester as "blind Cupid" is like the heart on a dagger that Giovanni brandishes at the end of John Ford's *'Tis Pity She's a Whore* (acted 1629–33). In both cases we confront a startling visualization of what usually remains a figure of speech. For the astonished courtiers Giovanni provides a verbal caption to what they are seeing: "'Tis a heart,/ A heart, my lords, in which is mine entombed" (5.6.26–7 in Ford 2003: 115). The impaled heart is that of Giovanni's lover—and sister—Annabella. The verbal images startle us when they become things we can actually see. *The Tragedy of King Lear* is replete with moments in which words become physical presences.

The static quality of the play's beginning, in which words dictate actions, is deceptive. First Kent and Gloucester speak with Edmund in what amounts to an extended aside, then Lear takes command of the stage and with his words choreographs every move of the characters who share the stage with him. In the context, Cordelia's verbal asides (1.1.62, 76–8) are daring acts, defiances of the controlling power of language. "Give me the map there" (1.1.37): Lear reduces all possible actions to a proposition in geometry. His "there" likely comes with a gesture, an indication of a static physical place where things heard will take shape as things seen and Lear will do the pointing out. Despite Lear's determination, the subsequent play undoes all attempts to put words and actions into separate categories and keep them there. *King Lear* is full of verbally threatened cruelties that become physical realities. Lear himself begins the series with a verbal threat ("Peace, Kent./ Come not between the dragon and his wrath"

[1.1.121–2]) that soon becomes a physical deed in Oswald's report that Lear has struck Goneril's gentleman-servant for chiding the Fool (1.3.1–3). The pace of physical cruelties quickens in 1.4, as Lear strikes Oswald (1.4.83) and Kent trips him (1.4.85), amid numerous threats that speakers of unwelcome truths will be whipped (1.4.109, 146–7, 162, 164–6). Cornwall's condemning of Kent to the stocks in 2.2—"cruel garters!" the Fool exclaims (2.2.190)—and Lear's sufferings during the storm scenes (2.2, 3.2, 3.4, 3.6) reach a climax in 3.7 in the blinding of Gloucester by Cornwall and Regan. When Cornwall's hand plucks out one of Gloucester's eyes, a name for the deed is voiced in Gloucester's cry "O cruel! O you gods!" (3.7.68). The tactility of the word "cruel"—hard, crude, crunching, like teeth biting into *crudités*, raw vegetables—comes across in the word Gloucester gives to the deed.

Often enough in *King Lear* words themselves become assault weapons. Lear's curse of Goneril in 1.4 ("Hear, nature; hear, dear goddess, hear" [1.4.254]) comes with a sharp edge. Lear's words knife through his daughter's body and anatomize her organs: "Into her womb convey sterility./ Dry up in her the organs of increase" (1.4.257–8). Among the many cruelties of *King Lear* tongues, arms, and fists frequently work in consort. At the end of his curse of Goneril in 1.4 Lear's bent fist opens, as it were, to seize on the word "feel" and throw that word at his daughter in a visual image of biting, of flesh being ripped by teeth:

> Turn all her mother's pains and benefits
> To laughter and contempt, that she may feel—
> That she may feel—
> How sharper than a serpent's tooth it is
> To have a thankless child. Away, away!
> $(1.4.265–9)$

The /ʃ/ and the iterations of /s/ in "sharper than a serpent's tooth" provide a climax to hisses heard throughout the curse ("suspend," "sterility," "increase," "spring," "spleen," "stamp," "tears," "cheeks").

The explosion of sound denoted by "laughter" recapitulates the loud frontal vowels (the /i/ in "creature," "increase," "teem," "spleen," the /e/ in "convey," "babe," "create," "tears," "pains"). In "contempt" and in "tooth" we hear again the spitting dentals of "dry," "derogate," "teem," "disnatured torment," "cadent tears." Above all, the /r/ in "sharper" and "serpent's" maintains to the end the low roar heard throughout the curse in "nature," "purpose," "creature," "sterility," "increase," "derogate," "spring," "create," "a thwart disnatured torment to her," "wrinkles in her brow," "tears fret channels," "turn." These sounds, whether consciously attended to or not, have their effect on epidermis and nerves. In modern productions, the actor playing Goneril often recoils under the force of Lear's words: she bends over and wraps her arms and hands around her body.

The serpent's tongue that concludes Lear's curse darts out again in 2.2, when Regan suggests that Lear and his train return to Goneril. "Never, Regan," Lear replies. "She hath abated me of half my train,/ Looked black upon me, struck me with her tongue/ Most serpent-like upon the very heart" (2.2.331–4). Especially in this repetition of the image, Goneril's verbal cruelty takes on the same physicality as "blind Cupid" in 4.5. The word "tongue" is literalized in the same startling way that Gloucester's blindness literalizes the description of Cupid. The dental /t/ thrusts the speaker's tongue against his teeth, while the /θ/ in "hath" and "with" lets the spectators actually see Goneril's heart-ripping weapon—and Lear's—in action. That weapon is the tongue. As a result, the words seem all the more horrible, all the more cruel.

What the 2007 experiments on virtual reality failed to investigate is how sound might cue the sensations that subjects experience when confronted with visual projections of their own bodies. Indeed, most people would assume that *virtual* reality is a specifically *visual* reality. The shock of the experiments was to reveal that virtual reality extends to touch. How might sound mediate the analogy between "me *here*" and "him *there*"? If I recoil at photographs of mutilated bodies (of victims of automobile accidents, say, or victims of torture), if the sight produces a shiver in my groin, it is because, at the moment of looking *that* body becomes *my* body. The power, we tell ourselves, is in the seeing. But hearing a friend's story of how a knife slipped in his hand and sliced his finger can work the same effect. How can that be? An easy explanation would have two parts: (1) my friend's words cue visual images and (2) those visual images make my flesh crawl. Novels seem to work that way. We read, silently usually, verbal cues on the page that conjure up richly stocked visual worlds in our imagination. The sequence of events shapes up as verbal cue → visual image → tactile image → shudder. But when the friend tells me his story, it is not a knife of such-and-such shape, such-and-such size, such-and-such color that I imagine but the feel of my flesh being sliced. Ockham's razor fits the situation perfectly. The sequence does indeed have three parts, but a detour through vision is not required. What we have instead is verbal cue → *tactile* image → shudder. The sensations that provide raw material to imagination in Aristotelian psychology and Galenic physiology are not just visual images but *imagines* produced by all the sensing organs, including the sense of touch. These *imagines* are fused in "the common sense," the synthetic sense "common" to all the sensing organs, and in that fused form are delivered to the heart. Visual images *may* be combined with images of touch, but not necessarily. Just as touch may be combined with vision, so may touch be combined with sound.

The workings of speech throughout *King Lear* are, then, no less tactile than the moving of arms and hands, no less assaultive than brandished fists, no less suasive than hands outstretched to raise another up. Tongue and lips are treated in Bulwer's *Pathomyotamia* as muscles particularly sensitive to moving of the spirits:

> if speech be made by motion, and signify the affections of the mind, which are motions without all question, the moving of the instruments must be answerable to the movings of the mind but, since nothing is swifter than the mind, deservedly therefore the movings of the tongue and lips are very swift, as those which are to follow the motions of the mind. (Bulwer 1649: 238–9)

Tongue and lips are moved by other muscles, Bulwer argues, but they are also muscles in their own right. "*Musculi Rationationis & orationis*"

Bulwer styles them: "the muscles of discourse and oral reason" (239). Linguistics as defined by Saussure and redeployed in deconstruction is not, in Bulwer's phrase, "answerable to the movings of the mind," particularly when words are combined with gestures in theatrical performance. What is needed is a linguistics that takes into account touch as well as speech, seeing as well as hearing, feeling as well as decoding.

:

The prominence of "tongue" and "tongues" in *King Lear*—not only in seven explicit verbal references but in attention drawn to the physicality of speaking—never lets an audience forget that words are more than signifiers. The very term "linguistics" (from Latin *lingua*, tongue) forces attention to the slippage—the *literal* slippage—between "tongue" as a muscular piece of flesh and "tongue" as the language shaped by that piece of flesh. *The Tragedy of King Lear* forces recognition of such slippage from the play's first moments, when Cordelia contrasts the unseen passions of her heart with the all-too-obvious flickings of her sisters' tongues. Cordelia's own tongue takes on physical presence when she says in an aside, "I am sure my love's/ More ponderous than my tongue" (1.1.77–8), with its exquisite pun on "ponderous" as heavy (*OED* 1989: "ponderous," *adj.*, 1.a), deliberate (3.b), and given to pondering or deliberation (4). (In the earlier and more verbose *History of King Lear* the word is "richer" [scene 1, line 73], not "more ponderous.") Toward the end of the play, Edmund, ever the glib shaper of words, endows his unknown vanquisher's tongue with the same physicality as his vanquisher's visage: "In wisdom I should ask thy name,/ But since thy outside looks so fair and war-like,/ And that thy tongue some say of breeding breathes,/ What safely and nicely I might well demand/ By rule of knighthood I disdain and spurn" (5.3.132–6). *Breathes?* In acts of synecdoche like Cordelia's and Edmund's, the tongue refuses to remain just a word and takes on physical presence.

Literalizations of the tongue as the organ of speech have the same disorienting effect as Lear's literalization of "Blind Cupid" as a man

Figure 4.11   Jacques Callot, Zanni or Scapino (1618–20).

who lacks the organs of vision. If Jacques Callot's print of Zanni is
any indication, sticking out the tongue was part of the wily servant's
irreverent behavior in *commedia dell'arte*. (See Figure 4.11.) Lear's
Fool may not always go around with his tongue hanging out, but it
is his tongue that offends Goneril the most. "Yes, forsooth," the
Fool tells her, "I will hold my tongue; so your face bids me, though
you may say nothing" (1.4.176–8). Zanni's placement of his hands
on his crotch in Callot's print (not to mention his very long sword)
may raise suspicions that a pun on "no *thing*" lurks in the Fool's
retort to Goneril—suspicions that are confirmed when the Fool
winds up the next scene by turning to the spectators and saying,
"She that's a maid now, and laughs at my departure,/ Shall not be a
maid long, unless *things* be cut shorter" (1.5.49–50, emphasis added).
An analogy between tongue and penis is given serious consideration

167

in Bulwer's *Pathomyotamia*. "The action in kissing, which some beastly lechers use when their veins are inflate with lust would induce one to think," Bulwer observes, "that there were some analogy between the extension of these two unruly members" (1649: 231). True to a degree. However, the virile member increases in length, thickness, and compass, while the tongue increases in length only. No less remarkable is the power of the tongue in showing contempt: "In derision, scoffing[,] insultation and contumelious despite men are seen sometimes to lill out their tongue at those they scoff and deride" (228).

As he suffers the wounds of his daughters' serpent-like tongues Lear reenacts a scene from the Passion of Christ. Matthew's account is the most circumstantial. After Christ had been interrogated, the soldiers took him into the Praetorium or common hall, stripped him, and decked him with mock-regal props similar to those which Lear comes bearing in 4.5: "And when they had platted a crown of thorns, they put it upon his head, and a reed in his right hand; and they bowed the knee before him, and mocked him, saying, Hail, King of the Jews! And they spit upon him, and took the reed, and smote him on the head" (Bible 1967: Matthew 27:29–30). In medieval and Renaissance visualizations of this episode the spitting is turned into a thrusting out of tongues, as in Hieronymus Wierix's 1619 version from a suite of prints illustrating the Passion of Christ. (See Figure 4.12.) Something like that physical assault with tongues attends the cruelties visited upon Lear by Goneril and Regan—and the cruelty Lear visits upon Gloucester in 4.5. In most versions of "The Scourging of Christ," as the subject is known to art historians, the face of Christ is placed near the center of the composition, giving a viewer an implicit point of entry or subject position. Wierix's print is unusual in showing Christ blindfolded and his head being turned by one of the mockers' hands. The subject position in this case, despite Christ's halo, seems to be that of the mockers. *Both* subject positions, however—that of the mockers and that of the mocked—are implied by all versions of the subject. In that respect, the Passion of Christ is recapitulated in the Passion of Gloucester and Lear.

Figure 4.12 Hieronymus Wierix, *The Scourging of Christ* (detail), from a suite of prints of Christ's Passion (1619).

And the passion of both is experienced by the audience via a palimpsest of analogies aural, visual, and tactile.

⋮

Giovanni with Annabella's heart on his dagger is seized upon by Antonin Artaud in the "Theater of Cruelty" as a signal instance of theater's power to exteriorize "perverse possibilities of the mind" (Artaud 1958: 30). A long-standing habit of regarding theater as a diversion, Artaud argues, "has made us forget the idea of a serious theater, which, overturning all our perceptions, inspires us with the fiery magnetism of its images and acts upon us like a spiritual therapeutics whose *touch* can never be forgotten" (84–5, emphasis added). Plague is one of Artaud's explanations for how touch operates in the

theater; cruelty is another. The contagion of plague spreads via physical touch; revelation of cruelty, by virtual touch. Artaud speaks of
the theater of cruelty as delivering *"analogical* disturbances" (109,
emphasis added).

Ordinarily we think of analogies as verbal or mathematical propositions, as statements like "A is like B" or as formulas like 1:2::4:8. But
A, B, 1, 2, 4, and 8 exist quite apart from the phrase "is like" or the
symbols /:/ and /::/. The entities being analogized—A, B, 1, 2, 4,
8—don't have to be words or numbers. They can be anything in a
series. So in Artaud's theater the analogical disturbances involve not
just words but gesture and movement. "If we are clearly so incapable
today of giving an idea of Aeschylus, Sophocles, Shakespeare that is
worthy of them," Artaud argues in one of his letters on language, "it is
probably because we have lost the sense of their theater's *physics*" (108,
emphasis added). The physics of performance certainly includes verbal
language—after all, words are formed by movements of lungs, larynx,
tongue, and lips—but Artaud shares Vygotsky's conviction that thought
begins with something deeper. Artaud's "language of nature" (110) is
something akin to Vygotsky's "inner speech," a language with a lexi-
con and syntax that are different from external speech. "The grammar
of this new language is still to be found," Artaud says. "Gesture is its
material and its wits; and, if you will, its alpha and omega. It springs
from the NECESSITY of speech more than from speech already
formed" (110, emphasis original).

This is, quite literally, a *deeper* idea of language than the repeated
markings of difference assumed in deconstruction, Lacanian psychoanalytical theory, and other critical practices based on Saussure's *Course
in General Linguistics*. Verbal language, according to Saussure and his
disciples, operates through repetitions of the formula $s \mid S$, where s is
the signified and S is the signifier. But the relation of s to S is arbitrary,
so that (tragically or joyously, depending on your point of view) $s \neq S$.
That may be true with respect to words, but Artaud holds onto the
analogizing impulse that gives rise to words in the first place, and so
do I. If spoken language operates through repetitions of $s \mid S$, theatrical language operates through repetitions of $A : A^1$, where A stands for
Actor and A^1 for Audience. *Analogia* in ancient Greek designated a

ratio or a proportion between two things. Analogy brings reasoning or accounting (*logos*) "up to" (*ana*) two things (*OED* 1989: "analogon," etymology). Analogy doesn't claim to explain those two things in their entirety. It doesn't pretend to completeness about either entity. Rather, it attends to the *relationship* between the two things. The equivalence (or, more exactly, the lack thereof) that has so preoccupied Saussure and his post–modern followers is not an issue with analogies. A colon is not an equal sign. In the case of theater, the Actor is quite obviously not the Audience. Rather, the Actor is *like* the Audience in certain ways, and the Audience in certain ways (but not in *all* ways) is *like* the Actor. Not *the same as*, but *like*.

Analogy is the structural principle that governs Shakespeare's theater no less than Aeschylus' and Sophocles'. Analogies may be physical or verbal or visual or aural or some combination of the above, but all those analogies involve a body *over there* (A) and a body *in here* (A¹). Cruelty, because it engages the human body in such visceral ways, heightens an effect that is always present in dramatic performance. In the theater of cruelty analogical disturbances are set off by touch. This situation demands a mode of analysis that is neither verbal nor visual but a combination of the two, a "linguistics of touch" that can attend to the fit between the physical and the verbal. Analogy as a structural principle asks to be investigated on two fronts: first in terms of the Actor, then in terms of the Audience. Even more worthy of attention are the two dots that mark the zone of contact, the space of merging, the place where A touches A¹.

Actor and Audience, A and A¹, are patently *there* as objects of study. They can be approached from any number of critical directions: theater history, social history, psychoanalytical theory, cognitive theory, even deconstruction. They stay in place. By comparison, the two dots in A : A¹ are elusive. How to account for "is like" or "is to" or "fits with"? Those are relationships, not things. And relationships are precisely what phenomenology tries to address. The relationship to be investigated in this case is indicated by /:/. Shakespeare and his contemporaries knew that particular punctuation mark in palpably physical terms as a puncture, as "two pricks" or jabs of the pen, which sometimes produced two small holes in the surface of the paper, not unlike the pricks used to produce Braille transcriptions. Those jabs or holes could be thought about in the seventeenth century, and still today, in terms of body, space, time, and sound. As it happens, body, space, time, and sound are the four basic elements present in every dramatic performance.

What is in the /:/? A body, or rather a member of a body. Our own term "colon," which was just beginning to supplant the term "pricks," more usually referred not to the marks themselves but to what was being separated by the marks. Since the ancient rhetoricians, a colon had been understood in bodily terms, as a limb or member (*OED* 1989: "colon²," etymology). Bulwer's treatises keep that sense of /:/ alive, with particular respect to hands, arms, and facial muscles. It is space as well as the speaker's body that John Hart has in mind as he sets the rules of punctuation in *An Orthography* (1569). For Hart, a colon is an "*artus membrorum* or *internodium*, which is the space, or the bone, flesh and skin betwixt two joints" (Hart 1955–63: 1:200). A colon was like the joint between arm and hand or the space between two bones in a finger.

What is in the /:/? Time is Ben Jonson's criterion in *The English Grammar*, when he distinguishes "two pricks" from other punctuation marks according to the longer pause for breath that they cue: "For, whereas our breath is by nature so short, that we cannot continue without a stay to speak long together; it was thought necessary, as well for the speaker's ease, as for the plainer deliverance of the things spoken, to invent this means, whereby men pausing a pretty while, the whole speech might never the worse be understood" (Jonson 1947: 8:551).

What is in the /:/? With regard to space, somewhere between 5 feet and 50 feet. In the 1599 Globe a groundling standing below the edge of the platform might find himself 5 feet or so from an actor who had stepped right to the edge. According to calculations by Styan and other theater historians, most members of the audience in the Globe were never more than 50 feet from the actors (Styan 1967: 14–16). With regard to space/time, the /:/ marks 0.02 seconds, the lapse of time between the production of a sound and the reception of that sound in a space of 243,028 cubic feet like the Globe (Smith 1999:

210, 213). The transmission of light across 50 feet happens, of course, much more rapidly, in about 50 nanoseconds. But those calculations of space and time are missing the point. What really interests us is the bodies involved in the theatrical transaction. So many feet in space and so many fractional seconds in time don't put those bodies in touch. For that we must turn to analogy, to the ways in which A^1 is proportional to A, to the fit between A^1 and A.

What is in the /:/? A language: sounds that begin as movements within a body, extend in space, open out in time. Like Artaud, writers on gesture like David F. Armstrong, William C. Stokoe, and Sherman E. Wilcox, along with David McNeill, understand the term "language" in more capacious terms than Saussure's linguistics. Where Saussure and his followers locate meaning-making in synchronic up-and-down space where "this" *is marked off* from "that," McNeill and his cohorts locate meaning-making in a diachronic side-to-side space inhabited by the constantly moving human body, a space where "this" *merges with* "that." As Armstrong, Stokoe, and Wilcox put it, "Language is not essentially formal; rather, the essence of language is richly *intermodal*—it is motoric, perceptual, and kinesthetic" (1995: 42, emphasis added). Saussure's static "forms" become Armstrong, Stokoe, and Wilcox's moving "modes." An intermodal language, made up of actions as well as words. The primary site where actions and words meet, where A touches A^1 most forcefully and continuously, is indicated in Gloucester's spoken gesture "O, let me kiss that hand!" (4.5.128). In that moment tongue and gesture merge in a language that is not early modern English or modern English, much less a dialect of computer language, but the language of theater.

::

Jonson may have criticized Shakespeare's prolixity—he never blotted a line, Jonson laments, when he should have blotted a thousand—but *King Lear* in both the quarto and folio versions ends in radical understatement. After Lear's death, the survivors Edgar, Kent, and Albany can manage, at first only half lines, then two lines, then three, then four—but no more than that. Lear dies with bodily gestures on his lips: "Do you see this? Look on her. Look, her lips. / Look there, look there" (5.3.286–7). What ensues after his last breath is more gestural speech, particularly on the part of Edgar. "My lord, my lord!" Edgar cries out to the dead king, almost certainly bending his body toward Lear and reaching out with suppliant arms. As for Kent, his gesture is reminiscent of Edgar's response to the reunion of Lear and Gloucester ("my heart breaks at it" [4.5.138]) and Edgar's report of Gloucester's death ("his flawed heart ... / Burst smilingly" [5.3.188–91]). "Break, heart, I prithee break" (5.3.288), Kent says. This verbal gesture to the heart apparently involves a lowering of Kent's head if not a move-ment of his hand toward his heart, since Edgar completes Kent's line with one last upward gesture: "Look up, my lord" (5.3.288). (I advance this reading despite the Oxford text's directing both speeches "*to Lear*" in editorial additions to the script.) In this terse context, the script's final speech, two rhymed couplets, could be heard as downright expansive:

> The weight of this sad time we must obey,
> Speak what we feel, not what we ought to say.
> The oldest hath borne most. We that are young
> Shall never see so much, nor live so long.
> (5.3.299–302)

Critical response to these final lines has not always been sympathetic. Charles Jennen's complaint in the late eighteenth century is perhaps the most egregious: "The two last lines, as they stand, are silly and false; and are only inserted that any one may alter them for the better if they can" (Shakespeare 1908: 350). What Jennen wants is words adequate to the occasion, even if those words have to be extemporized by an actor. Twentieth-century critics, their minds opened and emptied by existentialism, have been more accepting of the ending's understate-ment. Peter Brook, for example, celebrates the fact that *King Lear* "refuses all moralizing" and considers the play, not a narrative, but "a vast, complex, coherent poem designed to study the power and the emptiness of nothing" (Shakespeare 2008: 181). To my own eyes and ears, the key contrast in the final speech is *feeling* versus *saying*.

"Speak what we feel, not what we ought to say": what this phrase means very much depends on who actually says it. If Albany speaks the two quatrains, as he is scripted to do in the quarto text, we have here a continuation of the glib verbalization that Albany has been trying to muster all along. If Edgar speaks the lines, as directed in the folio text, we have something much more complex. Albany's personal and political sympathies may shift during the play, but he maintains to the end a belief that words can do the job at hand. Edgar, by contrast, has been a linguistic shifter. He has spoken multiple languages in multiple registers: the cultivated speech of an aristocratic son, the ramblings of Tom o'Bedlam, the plain-speaking of the yeoman who leads Gloucester to the cliff, the cautious speech of a survivor of cruelty. Through it all, Edgar has pointed up disjunctions not only between appearance and reality (as he does in the cliff scene) but between word and deed. Tom o'Bedlam's language, radically centrifugal, is always teetering on the edge of nonsense. The speech of Lear's Fool, by contrast, is radically centripetal. The Fool trades in puns, but his verbal squibs are always aimed at a patent truth. The Fool may be silenced, but Edgar lives to speak again the rational speech with which he began the play—but this time with a difference. From his time as Tom and the yeoman, Edgar knows the power of gestures when words fail. His final four lines, if they are indeed his, occupy a middle ground between gesture and words, between feeling and saying. To speak what we feel involves not a deconstruction of language but an attempt to align language with feeling, in the double sense that Gloucester implies when he tells Lear that he sees the world "feelingly." Like Gloucester before him, Edgar suffers the passions of cruelty and loss even as he makes his way in the dim world through reaching out as well as speaking. Among the many touching moments in *The Tragedy of King Lear*, Edgar's final speech may be the most layered, the most intense.

Moving toward the conclusion of his treatise "On the Soul," Aristotle finds occasion to observe that "the soul is analogous to the hand; for as the hand is a tool of tools, so thought is the form of forms and sense the form of sensible things" (432a1 in Aristotle 1984: 1:686). An analogy: the entity-that-thinks is like a hand. We can accept that. But shortly beforehand Aristotle has made the startling claim, noticed in the Prologue to this book, that it is not just language that distinguishes humankind from other animals but an exquisite sense of touch. "While in respect of all the other senses we fall below many species of animals," Aristotle observes,

> in respect of touch we far excel all other species in exactness of discrimination. That is why man is the most intelligent of animals. This is confirmed by the fact that it is to differences in the organ of touch and to nothing else that the differences between man and man in respect of natural endowment are due; men whose flesh is hard are ill-endowed with intellect, men whose flesh is soft, well-endowed. (421a20–5)

It is perhaps instructed by Aristotle that Lear strips to the skin and bares himself to the storm in 3.4. (See Figure 4.4.) In this gesture of fingers undoing buttons and limbs throwing off garments we have been encouraged to see a fall down the great chain of being, as Lear exposes his skin to feel what lesser creatures feel. "Unaccommodated man," he tells Edgar in the guise of Tom, "is no more but such a poor, bare, forked animal as thou art" (3.4.100–2). Tom's filthy skin, let it be remembered, is stuck with "Pins, wooden pricks, nails, sprigs of rosemary" (2.2.179). If Aristotle is right, Lear in baring his flesh is discovering, not an underlying animality, but his full humanity. Duke Senior, in the happier circumstances of a comedy, can say of the winter wind's assaults, "These are counselors/ That feelingly persuade me what I am" (*As You Like It*, 2.1.10–11).

Epilogue:
What Shakespeare Proves

It may not have been the fashion in The Historical William Shakespeare's time for the lady to speak the epilogue, but it is certainly the fashion in our own time for books like this one to end with some version of *Q.E.D.* Remember that anagram from plane geometry? You finish the problem and then write the abbreviation for "*Quod erat demonstrandum*" ("which was to be demonstrated"). The practice can be traced back to Euclid, who invented geometry as a strategy of deductive thinking. You establish a few axioms that seem intuitively right ("Let us assume that ..."), you set up something you want to *do* in the form of a problem or something you want to *demonstrate* in the form of a theorem ("Suppose that ..., it is required that ..."), you use the agreed axioms to do it or to demonstrate it ("If *x*, then *y* ..."), you write the conclusion ("*Q.E.D.*")—and you feel very proud of yourself ("Oh, what a good boy am I").

Doing something versus demonstrating something: that is the fundamental distinction between problems and theorems in Euclid's *Elements of Geometry.* "A Problem," Euclid says in Henry Billingsley's 1570 translation, "is a proposition which requireth some action, or doing," like making a figure, dividing a figure, applying one figure to another, adding a figure, subtracting a figure, etc. The action is made with the mind, but in plane geometry a hand is implied, and a straight-edge, a compass, and a pen or a pencil is usually within reach. Only the mind is involved in a theorem, defined by Euclid as "a proposition, which requireth the searching out and demonstration of some property or passion of some figure: Wherein is only speculation and

177

contemplation of mind, without doing or working of any thing" (Euclid 1570: sig. C3v). *Passion?* Can a figure have a passion? It could in early modern English. What Billingsley has in mind is an innate quality of a figure, but a quality that is determined passively, by "a way in which a thing is or may be affected by external agency" (*OED* 1989: "passion," *n.*, †III.11.b, with citation of another passage from Billingsley's translation of Euclid). Until the early eighteenth century (the *OED*'s last citation is dated 1707) figures could suffer passions just as the human body could. At the end of a problem, after the demonstration, you are supposed to write, in Billingsley's English, "*Which is the thing, which was required to be done*"; at the end of a theorem, "*Which thing was required to be demonstrated or proved*" (sig. C3v, emphases original). "Done," "demonstrated," "proved": the three verbs in Billingsley's formulations are different (we shall take up the differences between "demonstrate" and "prove" shortly), but the practical result in all three cases is the same. The conclusion, in Billingsley's succinct phrase, "is ever the proposition" (sig. C4). You must end where you began. You have exercised your mind within a closed system.

Most criticism of Shakespeare is like that. A domain or field of discourse is established, often in the subtitle of the book or article in question: philology, bibliography, aesthetics, psychology, biography, theater history, political history, social history, Marxism/cultural materialism, cultural anthropology, structuralist linguistics, deconstruction, gender studies, sexuality studies, post-colonial studies, Queer theory, race and ethnicity studies, religious history, eco-criticism (to list some of the more prominent domains in roughly chronological order). Within each domain certain axioms are assumed, sometimes explicitly (as in Norman Holland's *Psychoanalysis and Shakespeare* or Michael Bristol's *Big-Time Shakespeare* or Catherine Belsey's *The Subject of Tragedy*), more often tacitly. Certain theorems are proposed with respect to a text or texts from the Collected Works of William Shakespeare (CWWS). Demonstration follows in the form of external pressure brought to bear on the texts, so that certain passions of those texts are exposed. And WSCI, William Shakespeare as Cultural Icon, if not THWS, The Historical William Shakespeare, is claimed for this or that cause.

Demonstration, as Euclid points out, can take three forms. In *a priori* demonstration, or "composition," we start with first principles, then "pass descending continually, till after many reasons made, we come at the length to conclude that, which we first chiefly intend" (sig. D1). Deduction pure and simple. *A posteriori* demonstration, or "resolution," works in the other direction: "we pass from the last conclusion made by the premises, and by the premises of the premises, continually ascending, till we come to the first principles and grounds, which are indemonstrable, and for their simplicity can suffer no farther resolution" (sig. D1). This is induction of a sort, but induction severely restricted by the number of axioms assumed in the beginning. Both of these strategies, familiar to us all, are positive ways of proceeding. Each has its advantages, as I know from firsthand experience with *Shakespeare and Masculinity* (*a priori* demonstration) and "The Curtain between the Theatre and the Globe" in *The Key of Green* (*a posteriori* demonstration). But there is also a negative strategy, demonstration by leading the argument to impossibilities, "when it concludeth directly against any principle, or against any proposition before proved by principles, or propositions before proved" (sig. D1). A certain conclusion cannot be entertained because it contradicts the axioms with which you started.

According to Hobbes, Locke, and many cognitive scientists, the human mind works that way: sense impressions produce ideas about sense impressions, which produce verbal propositions about how things are (axioms), which produce higher-order reasoning (demonstration). Locke in his *Essay concerning Human Understanding* is just sorry that ethical reasoning doesn't proceed as efficiently as Euclid's geometry: "Confident I am, that if men would in the same method, and with the same indifferency search after moral as they do mathematical truths, they would find them to have a stronger connection one with another, and a more necessary consequence from our clear and distinct ideas, and to come nearer perfect demonstration, than is commonly imagined" (4.3.20 in Locke 1690: 275–6).[1] The problem

---

[1] For pointing out the connection between Euclid's geometry and Locke's ethical program I am grateful to my USC colleague Angus Fletcher.

with such faith in the logic of human understanding emerges from a search for "*Q.E.D.*" in Early English Books Online's Text Creation Partnership. Aside from geometry, the domain in which "*Q.E.D.*" occurs most often is religious controversy, especially during the very years Locke was thinking and writing. Two years before *An Essay concerning Human Understanding*, for example, Samuel Johnson (no relation to the one you're thinking) published *The Absolute Impossibility of Transubstantiation Demonstrated*, in which seven propositions are considered one by one. Before the case is clinched in the seventh proposition, the first six are concluded with a triumphant "*Q.E.D.*" The proposition that the body of Christ can be in heaven and on earth at the same time, for example, is subjected to demonstration of the third sort: "So that this pretended Supernatural manner of Existence, is full of Contradictions, that is to say, it is Impossible. Which was to be Demonstrated" (Johnson 1688: 7). As a closed system, Protestant dogma is smaller than Euclid's geometry. Or is it?

A priori demonstration, *a posteriori* demonstration, demonstration via logical impossibilities: phenomenology distrusts all three courses. Phenomenology begins by setting aside all axioms but one: you cannot know anything apart from the way in which you come to know it. And phenomenology doesn't demonstrate. It *proves*. A distinction between these two seeming synonyms drives Iago's seduction of Othello. Terms of logic and argumentation dominate the exchanges that follow Iago's report that Cassio cried out "Sweet Desdemona" in his sleep, kissed Iago hard on the lips, and threw his leg over Iago's thigh:

> OTHELLO   O, monstrous, monstrous!
> IAGO   Nay, but this was but his dream.
> OTHELLO   But this denoted a foregone conclusion.
> IAGO   'Tis a shrewd doubt, though it be but a dream,
>   And this may help thicken other proofs
>   That do demonstrate thinly.
> OTHELLO   I'll tear her to pieces.
>
>   (3.3.430–6)

Iago's reply to Othello's "foregone conclusion" combines "doubt," "proof," and "demonstrate" in ways that add to Othello's epistemological confusion. The doubt that Iago inserts might be "shrewd" for any number of reasons: because it is fraught with evil (*OED*, "shrewd," *a.*, †4) or hard to take (8) or very likely (†10) or damaging as a piece of evidence (11). In the context of "proofs" that the doubt may help to "thicken"—proofs that as yet "demonstrate thinly"—one can also feel in "shrewd" the keen edge of a knife or sword (†2). Just as keen is Iago's deft distinction between "proofs" and "demonstrate." By privileging the word "demonstrate" Iago picks up on Othello's first reaction to the story of Cassio's dream: "O, monstrous, monstrous!" Othello's reaction gives Iago his cue. "Monstrous" shares an etymological root with "demonstrate" as *de+monstrare*, literally to point at, point out, point to (*OED* 1989: "demonstrate," *v.*, etymology). Cassio's dream is "monstrous" not just because it is horrific for Othello to hear and imagine but because it *indicates* a horrific fact and makes the reality of that fact undeniable. In *Othello*, as in Euclid's geometry, what gets demonstrated is something that is presumed to be *already there*, something waiting to be searched out—or so Iago hopes to demonstrate to the Moor. "Proof," as Iago implies, is less certain.

In a court of law things can be proved or disproved, proofs can be offered for or against a proposition, evidence can be probed, cases for and against can be improved, reproofs can be delivered, opinions can be approved, judgments can receive approbation, defendants can receive probationary sentences. Beginning in the seventeenth century, many of the same determinations could be made in a scientific laboratory. And yet "prove" stubbornly keeps its subjective quality. It leads a double life. On the one hand, to prove is to demonstrate or establish a truth (*OED* 1989: "prove," *v.*, I); on the other, to try or to test (II), originally to *taste* (II.6.a). (In Alsace the signs outside vineyards read "*Dégustation de vins*," "*Weinprobe*," "Wine Tasting.") Again and again, but especially in the sonnets, and especially in quasi-legal contexts, Shakespeare plays on the ambiguity. "Let me not to the marriage of true minds/ Admit impediments": the words that launch sonnet 116, the words that have launched a thousand weddings (my own included, literally as icing on the cake), in fact establish a legal scene that continues in the next sonnet ("Accuse me thus ..."). Legal exactitude dissolves, however, in the couplet: "If this be error and upon me proved,/ I never writ, nor no man ever loved" (116.1–2, 13–14).

"Proved" here carries the double meaning of demonstration by evidence or argument (*OED* 1989:"prove," *v.*, I.1) and knowing through firsthand experience (II.7)—which is just the point. Sonnet 117 renews the legal conceit ("Book both my wilfulness and errors down,/ And on just proof surmise accumulate"), only to dispel it once again in the couplet ("Since my appeal says I did strive to prove/ The constancy and virtue of your love") (117.9–10, 13–14). The legal proof that the beloved insists on in line 10 is countered by the having-found-out-by-experience (*OED* 1989: "prove," *v.*, II.7) that the poet-lover brings forward in the couplet. To judge from the narrative context implied by Thomas Thorpe's 1609 quarto, neither the lover nor the beloved is in a good position to insist on legal proof. "Most true it is that I have looked on truth/ Askance and strangely," the lover has confessed in sonnet 110. "And worse essays proved thee my best of love" (110.5–6, 8). The emphasis here, as in other similar sonnets, falls on "essays" as testings, as tryings-out.[2] The fact that so many of these plays on proof-as-evidence and proof-as-experience occur at the very end, in the sonnets' couplets, points to a fascination on Shakespeare's part with the subjective aspect of what purports to be objective truth, especially in matters of the heart.

Other valences of "prove" and "proof" come to the fore in *Venus and Adonis*. "But if the first heir of my invention prove deformed ...": the conceit of poem-as-offspring sired by two males in William Shakespeare as Author's dedication to Southampton turns on a now obsolete sense of prove as come to be, become, grow to be (I.3.†e), a sense that figures in the advice to marry in sonnet 8 ("thou single wilt prove none" [14]) as well as in Adonis's defense of his unripeness ("If springing things be

---

[2]   See also sonnets 26 ("Then may I dare to boast how I do love thee;/ Till then, not show my head where thou mayst prove me" [13–14]); 32 ("But since he died, and poets better prove,/ Theirs for their style I'll read, his for his love" [13–14]); 72 ("After my death, dear love, forget me quite;/ For you in me can nothing worthy prove" [3–4]); 88 ("Upon thy side against myself I'll fight,/ And prove thee virtuous though thou art forsworn" [3–4]); 129 ("A bliss in proof and proved, a very woe" [11]; 136 ("In things of great receipt with ease we prove/ Among a number one is reckoned none" [7–8]); and 151 ("Then, gentle cheater, urge not my amiss,/ Lest guilty of my faults thy sweet self prove" [3–4]).

any jot diminished,/ They wither in their prime, prove nothing worth"
[417–18])—a curious triple echo. All three instances fuse what can be
seen from the outside with what can be felt through one's body, one's
sexual body. That subjective aspect colors Venus's aggressiveness ("To
tie the rider she begins to prove" [40, in the sense of *OED* 1989:
II.†8.a, to try, endeavor, attempt]) as well as her frustration ("All is
imaginary she doth prove" [597]). The outside/inside dichotomy shows
up also in the adjectival sense of "proof" as possessing a tested power of
resistance, originally said of armor (*OED* 1989: "proof," *adj.*, A.1.a).
Thus Venus warns Adonis that the boar's brawny sides "Are better
proof than thy spear's point can enter" (626). The same cannot be said
of Adonis's thin skin *vis-à-vis* the boar's tusks.

King Lear, like Othello, is obsessed with demonstration, with reveal-
ing something that is presumed already *to be there*. Lear's mistake, like
Othello's, is to confuse outsides with insides, words with feelings, observable objects with subjective states. "Did your letters pierce the Queen to
any demonstration of grief," Kent asks the gentlemen who has just
returned from Cordelia and the invading French army in scene 17 of
The History of King Lear. The letter contained news of Lear's cruel treatment at the hands of Cordelia's sisters. "Ay, sir," the gentleman replies.

> She took them, read them in my presence,
> And now and then an ample tear trilled down
> Her delicate cheek. It seemed she was a queen
> Over her passion who, most rebel-like,
> Sought to be king o'er her.
>
> (sc. 17.10–16)

In her tears Cordelia is true to character: the passion of grief was there
for the reading to those with eyes to read bodies and deeds, just as
Cordelia's passion of love was there for the reading in the trial of "Which
of you shall we say doth love us most" in the play's first scene (*Tragedy*
1.1.51). But no, Lear wants a demonstration that can be measured,
first in number of words and then in figures on a chart. Goneril's
62-word testimony of her love for Lear is turned into so many square
miles: "Of all these bounds even from this line to this,/ ... / We make

thee lady" (1.1.63–66). In effect, Lear sees his daughters' feelings as a problem in plane geometry, with the map of the kingdom supplying the figures. *Their* passions become, in Henry Billingsley's terms, the *figures'* passions. The speaking daughters and the figures on the chart are subject to the external agency of Lear the geometer—radically so in the case of Cordelia. "Nothing will come of nothing" (*Tragedy* 1.1.90): Cordelia is eliminated from the theorem through demonstration of impossibility. *Q.E.D.*

"Proof" to Lear is the armor that protects inside from outside. That sense of proof, indicative of Lear's character all along, is made verbally explicit in 4.5 of *The Tragedy of King Lear* when the mad Lear challenges Tom o'Bedlam "There's my gauntlet. I'll prove it on a giant" (4.5.90), confesses to Gloucester "They told me I was everything; 'tis a lie, I am not ague-proof" (4.5.104–5), and declares that he will shoe horses with felt and "put't in proof,/ And when I have stol'n upon these son-in-laws,/ Then kill, kill, kill, kill, kill!" (4.5.181–3). Wiser heads than Lear's know that proof is not all on the outside. Edgar in particular understands "prove" and "proof" in the double sense of the sonnets, as evidence that entails experience. When triumphant Edmond is challenged in 5.3 of *The Tragedy of King Lear*, the terms at first echo Lear's own belief that "proof" is a property of armor. "If none appear to *prove* upon thy person/ Thy heinous, manifest, and many treasons," Albany proclaims, "There is my pledge" (5.3.84–6, emphasis added). He throws down his glove. "I'll make it on thy heart,/ Ere I taste bread, thou art in nothing less/ Than I have here proclaimed thee" (5.3.86–8). In the earlier printed *History of King Lear* Albany pledges to "prove it on thy heart"—not "make it"—as well as on Edmond's person (sc. 24.90). In the later published and probably revised *Tragedy of King Lear* action on the heart is left to Edgar: "This sword, this arm, and my best spirits are bent/ To prove upon thy heart, *whereto I speak,/* Thou liest" (5.3.130–2, emphasis added). Albany speaks to Edmond's person, Edgar to his heart.

In this wresting of proof from outside to inside Edgar echoes the double-sided observation he made when he first took on the disguise of Tom o'Bedlam: "The country gives me proof and precedent/ Of Bedlam beggars" (2.2.176–7). "Proof and precedent"

Epilogue

belongs to the rhetoric of the crown's proclamations against vagrants. As Edgar's words and deeds suggest, however, "proof" also comes with a subjective sense of the beggars' suffering. Edgar responds to the world's anguish in *The History of King Lear*, scene 13, no less feelingly than Gloucester does later. "How light and portable my pain seems now," Edgar confides to the audience, "When that which makes me bend, makes the King bow" (*History* sc.13.101–2). Putting his abject disguise back on, Edgar comforts himself with anticipation of the day "When false opinion, whose wrong thoughts defile thee,/ In thy just proof repeals and reconciles thee" (sc. 13.105–6). "Just proof" at the end of the play entails, for Lear no less than for Edgar, "the action or fact of experiencing or having experience of something" (*OED* 1989: "proof," *n.*, II.†6) as well as "evidence or argument establishing a fact or the truth of anything" (I.1.a). Historical phenomenology embraces "proof" in the first sense, in the belief that it can establish "proof" in the second sense.

To say that phenomenology starts by setting aside all axioms but one—that you cannot know anything apart from the way in which you come to know it—is not to say that phenomenology does away with other axioms altogether. It is just careful about how and when axioms get formulated and acted upon. Three primal scenes of observation (see Figures 1.1, 1.2, and 1.3) were described in Chapter 1:

- Francis Bacon's, in which the visible world shakes hands with the intellectual world
- René Descartes', in which the cogitating subject is separated from the real-world object via geometrical figures
- Edmund Husserl's, in which the experiencing subject sits at the center of a teeming ambient world that must be experienced with the senses before it can be thought.

Phenomenology as a school of philosophy may have started in Husserl's study, but it is Bacon's imagined world that provides the most habitable space for historical phenomenology as a way of encountering sixteenth- and seventeenth-century plays and poems. Obviously Bacon's scene of observation has period specificity to recommend it—THWS and his

185

Epilogue

original readers and audiences would, to varying degrees, have found
Bacon's scene of observation familiar—but it also invites an inductive way
of proceeding that maintains firmer footing and leads to broader prospects
than the deductive methods of most criticism since the linguistic turn.

The "idols of the theater" that Bacon attacks in his *New Organon*
are produced "*ex fabulis theoriorum, & perversis legibus demonstrationum*"
("on the basis of fairytale theories and mistaken rules of proof," in the
most recent translation) (1.61 in Bacon 1620: sig. H1, trans. Bacon
2000b: 49), axioms that create closed systems of thought and fail to
stay in touch with the experiences that stimulated those thoughts in
the first place. What Bacon proposes instead is step-by-step induction
that proceeds from particulars to universals by degrees—*four* degrees
to be precise:

> one may expect anything from the sciences when the ascent is made
> on a genuine ladder, by regular steps, without gaps and breaks, from
> particulars to lesser axioms and then to intermediate axioms, one above
> the other, and only at the end to the most general. For the lowest axi-
> oms are not far from bare experience. And the highest axioms (as now
> conceived) are conceptual and abstract, and have no solidity. It is the
> intermediate axioms which are the true, sound, living axioms on which
> human affairs and human fortunes rest; and also the axioms above them,
> the most general axioms themselves, are not abstract but are given
> boundaries by these intermediate axioms. (1.104 in Bacon 2000b: 83)

It is those lowest axioms, those axioms "not far from bare experience,"
that have been allowed to drop since the 1970s. That is not to say that
higher axioms are false or useless. But it *is* to say that intermediate
axioms, those "true, sound, living axioms" in between sense experience
at the bottom of Bacon's ladder and abstract propositions at the top,
offer the best purchase on plays and poems. Only with that secure footing can one venture higher. Historical phenomenology by no means
refuses "high theory," but it heeds Bacon's advice: "we do not need to
give men's understanding wings, but rather lead and weights, to check
every leap and flight" (1.104 in Bacon 2000b: 83). Look up, look
around, but stay grounded.

Works Cited

Adams, Thomas 1619. *The Happiness of the Church*. London: John Grismond.

Aristotle 1984. *On the Soul*, trans. J. A. Smith. In *The Complete Works of Aristotle*, ed. Jonathan Barnes. Vol. 1. Princeton: Princeton University Press.

Armstrong, David F., William C. Stokoe, and Sherman E. Wilcox 1995. *Gesture and the Nature of Language*. Cambridge: Cambridge University Press.

Artaud, Antonin 1958. *The Theater and Its Double*, trans. Mary Caroline Richards. New York: Grove Press.

Bacon, Francis 1620. *Instauratio Magna*. London: Bonham Norton and John Bill.

Bacon, Francis 1627. *Silva Silvarum or A Natural History*, ed. William Rawley. London: W. Lee.

Bacon, Francis 1987. *The Essays or Counsels, Civil and Moral*, ed. Michael Kiernan. Oxford: Clarendon Press

Bacon, Francis 2000a. *The Advancement of Learning*, ed. Michael Kiernan. Oxford: Clarendon Press.

Bacon, Francis 2000b. *The New Organon*, ed. Lisa Jardine and Michael Silverthorne. Cambridge: Cambridge University Press.

Barnes, Clive 1971. "Stage: Joining the Odyssey of the Liquid Theater." *New York Times*, 12 October. www.nytimes.com. Accessed March 2, 2009.

Bartlet, John 1606. *A Book of Airs, with a Triplicity of Music*. London: John Windet.

Beaumont, Francis 1602. *Salmacis and Hermaphroditus*. London: John Hodgets.

Beaumont, Francis 1966. *The Knight of the Burning Pestle*, ed. Cyrus Hoy. In *The Dramatic Works in the Beaumont and Fletcher Canon*. Gen. ed., Fredson Bowers. Vol. 1. Cambridge: Cambridge University Press.

Belsey, Catherine 1985. *The Subject of Tragedy: Identity and Difference in Renaissance Drama*. London: Methuen.

Benveniste, Emile 1971. *Problems in General Linguistics*, trans. Mary Elizabeth Meek. Coral Gables, FL: University of Miami Press.

Bergeron, David M. 1999. *King James and Letters of Homoerotic Desire*. Iowa City: University of Iowa Press.

Bible 1967. *Holy Bible: Authorized King James Version*, ed. C. I. Scofield. New York: Oxford University Press.

Bleich, David 1978. *Subjective Criticism*. Baltimore: Johns Hopkins University Press.

Blundeville, Thomas 1617. *The Art of Logic*. London: William Stansby.

Boorsch, Suzanne 1985. *The Engravings of Giorgio Ghisi*. New York: Metropolitan Museum of Art.

Booty, John E., ed. 1976. *The Book of Common Prayer 1559*. Charlottesville: University of Virginia Press.

Boys, John 1610. *An Exposition of All the Principal Scriptures Used in Our English Liturgy*. London: Felix Kingston.

Brinsley, John 1615. *The Posing of the Parts*. London: Thomas Man.

Bristol, Michael 1996. *Big-Time Shakespeare*. London: Routledge.

Buchstaller, Isabelle 2001. "*He goes* and *I'm like*: The New Quotatives Revisited." www.ling.ed.ac.uk/~pgc/archive/2002/proco2/buchstaller02. pdf. Accessed January 4, 2007.

Buchstaller, Isabelle 2003. "The Co-Occurrence of Quotatives with Mimetic Performance." *Edinburgh Working Papers in Applied Linguistics* 12: 1–9.

Bullough, Geoffrey, ed. 1958. *Literary and Dramatic Sources of Shakespeare*. Vol. 2. New York: Columbia University Press.

Bulwer, John 1649. *Pathomyotamia or a Dissection of the Significative Muscles of the Affections of the Mind*. London: Humphrey Moseley.

Bulwer, John 1974. *Chirologia: or the Natural Language of the Hand* and *Chironomia: or the Art of Manual Rhetoric*, ed. James W. Cleary. Carbondale: Southern Illinois University Press.

Butler, Judith 1990. *Gender Trouble: Feminism and the Subversion of Identity*. London: Routledge.

Callaghan, Dympna 2003. "(Un)natural Loving: Swine, Pets and Flowers in *Venus and Adonis*." In *Textures of Renaissance Knowledge*, ed. Philippa Berry and Margaret Tudeau-Clayton. Manchester: Manchester University Press.

Chodzko, Dana 2001. "Spatial Relations." Printed statement in connection with "Spatial Relations Alphabet" installation. Andrea Schwartz Gallery, San Francisco.

Clabburn, Pamela 1988. *The National Trust Book of Furnishing Textiles*. London: Viking.

Clough, Patricia Ticineto 2007. *The Affective Turn: Theorizing the Social*. Durham, NC: Duke University Press.

Cockburn, J. S. 1975–85. *Calendar of Assize Records*. 11 vols. London: Her Majesty's Stationery Office.

Coke, Edward 1614. *A Book of Entries: Containing Perfect and Approved Precedents*. London: Society of Stationers.

Coke, Edward 1642. *The Second Part of the Institutes of the Laws of England*. London: M. Flesher and R. Young.

Coke, Edward 1644. *The Third Part of the Institutes of the Laws of England*. London: M. Flesher for W. Lee and D. Pakeman.

Colapinto, John 2009. "Brain Games: The Marco Polo of Neuroscience." *The New Yorker*, 11 May: 76–87.

Cornwallis, William 1600. *Essays*. London: Edmund Mattes.

Craik, Katharine A. 2007. *Reading Sensations in Early Modern England*. Basingstoke, UK: Palgrave Macmillan.

Crooke, Helkiah 1615. *Microcosmographia, or A Description of the Body of Man*. London: William Jaggard.

Damasio, Antonio R. 1999. *The Feeling of What Happens: Body and Emotion in the Making of Consciousness*. New York: Harcourt.

Daston, Lorraine and Galison, Peter 2007. *Objectivity*. New York: Zone Books.

Derrida, Jacques 1973. *Speech and Phenomena, and Other Essays on Husserl's Theory of Signs*, trans. David B. Allison. Evanston, IL: Northwestern University Press.

Derrida, Jacques 1997. *Of Grammatology*, trans. Gayatri Chakravorty Spivak. Corrected edn. Baltimore: Johns Hopkins University Press.

Descartes, René 1988. *Selected Philosophical Writings*, trans. John Cottingham, Robert Stoothoff, and Dugald Murdoch. Cambridge: Cambridge University Press.

Donne, John 1959. *Collected Sermons*. Vol. 5, ed. George R. Potter and Evelyn M. Simpson. Berkeley: University of California Press.

Donne, John 1978. *The Epithalamions, Anniversaries, and Epicedes*, ed. W. Milgate. Oxford: Clarendon Press.

Ehrsson, H. Henrik 2007. "The Experimental Induction of Out-of-Body Experiences." *Science* 317 (August 24): 1048.

Euclid 1570. *Elements of Geometry*, trans. Henry Billingsley. London: John Day.

Featley, Daniel 1638. *Transubstantiation Exploded*. London: G. Miller.

Feinsod, Moshe 2005. "Kershman's Sad Reflections on the Homunculus." *Neurology* 64: 524–5.

Floyd-Wilson, Mary and Garrett A. Sullivan, Jr., eds. 2007. *Environment and Embodiment in Early Modern England*. Basingstoke, UK: Palgrave Macmillan.

Foakes, R. A. 2002. *Henslowe's Diary*. 2nd edn. Cambridge: Cambridge University Press.

Fodor, Jerry A. 1975. *The Language of Thought*. Ithaca, NY: Cornell University Press.

Folkerth, Wes 2002. *The Sound of Shakespeare*. London: Routledge.

Ford, John 2003. *'Tis Pity She's a Whore*, ed. Martin Wiggins. 2nd edn. The New Mermaids. London: A&C Black, New York: Norton.

Gallese, V., M. N. Eagle, and P. Migone 2007. "Intentional Attunement: Mirror Neurons and the Neural Underpinnings of Interpersonal Relations." *Journal of the American Psychoanalytical Association* 55: 131–76.

Girouard, Mark 1978. *Life in the English Country House: A Social and Architectural History*. New Haven, CT: Yale University Press.

Goldberg, Jonathan 1992. *Sodometries: Renaissance Texts, Modern Sexualities*. Palo Alto, CA: Stanford University Press.

Greene, Robert 1615. *Thieves Falling Out, True Men Come by Their Goods*. London: T. Gubbin.

Gregory, R. L. 1997. *Eye and Brain: The Psychology of Seeing*. 5th edn. Princeton: Princeton University Press.

Griffiths, Anthony 1998. *The Print in Stuart Britain, 1603–1689*. London: British Museum.

Griggs, Richard A. 1988. "Who Is Mrs. Cantlie and Why Are They Doing These Terrible Things to Her Homunculi?" *Teaching of Psychology* 15.2: 105–6.

Gurr, Andrew 1992. *The Shakespearean Stage*. 3rd edn. Cambridge: Cambridge University Press.

Harrington, D. O. 1971. *The Visual Fields*. St. Louis, MO: C.V. Mosby.

Hart, John 1955–63. *John Hart's Works on English Orthography and Pronunciation, 1551, 1569, 1570*, ed. Bror Danielsson. 2 vols. Stockholm: Almqvist & Wiksell.

Harvey, Elizabeth, ed. 2003. *Sensible Flesh: On Touch in Early Modern Culture*. Philadelphia: University of Pennsylvania Press.

Heller-Roazen, Daniel 2007. *The Inner Touch: Archeology of a Sensation*. New York: Zone Books.

Holland, Norman 1966. *Psychoanalysis and Shakespeare*. New York: McGraw-Hill.

Howard, Skiles 1998. *The Politics of Courtly Dancing in Early Modern England*. Amherst: University of Massachusetts Press.

Husserl, Edmund 1950. *Ideen zu Einer Reinen Phänomenologie und Phänomenologischen Philosophie*, ed. Walter Biemel. In *Hussleriana: Gesammelte Werke.*Vol. 3.The Hague: Martinus Nijhoff.

Husserl, Edmund 1982. *Ideas Pertaining to a Pure Phenomenology and to a Phenomenological Philosophy*, trans. F. Kersten. In *Collected Works.*Vol. 2. The Hague: Martinus Nijhoff.

Ingleby, C. M., L.Toulmin Smith, and F. J. Furnivall, eds. 1909. *The Shakespere Allusion-Book*. 2 vols. London: Chatto & Windus.

Iser, Wolfgang 1978. *The Act of Reading: A Theory of Aesthetic Response*. Baltimore: Johns Hopkins University Press.

James,William 1890. *The Principles of Psychology*. London: Macmillan.

Johnson, Samuel 1688. *The Absolute Impossibility of Transubstantiation Demonstrated*. London:William Rogers.

Jonson, Ben 1947. *The English Grammar*. In *Ben Jonson*, ed. C. H. Herford, Percy Simpson, and Evelyn Simpson. Vol. 8. Oxford: Clarendon Press.

Jonson, Ben 2001. *Every Man Out of His Humor*, ed. Helen Ostovich. The Revels Plays. Manchester: Manchester University Press.

Lacan, Jacques 2006. *Écrits*, trans. Bruce Fink. New York: Norton.

Laqueur, Thomas 1990. *Making Sex: Body and Gender from the Greeks to Freud*. Cambridge, MA: Harvard University Press.

Lambin, Georges 1962. *Voyages de Shakespeare en France et en Italie*. Geneva: E. Droz.

Lawner, Lynne, ed. 1988. *I Modi: The Sixteen Pleasures*. Evanston, IL: Northwestern University Press.

Lenggenhager, Bigna, Tej Tadi, Thomas Metzinger, and Olaf Blanke 2007. "Video Ergo Sum: Manipulating Bodily Self-Consciousness." *Science* 317 (24 August): 1096–9.

Lewis, Charlton S. 1879. *A Latin Dictionary*. Oxford: Clarendon Press.

Lily, William 1543. *An Introduction of the Eight Parts of Speech*. London: Thomas Berthelet.

Locke, John 1690. *An Essay concerning Human Understanding*. London: Thomas Bassett.

Luhmann, Niklas 1989. *Ecological Communication*, trans. John Bednarz, Jr. Chicago: University of Chicago Press.

191

Luther, Martin 1963. *Works*. Vol. 26, ed. Jaroslav Pelikan and Walter A. Hansen. St. Louis, MO: Concordia.

Lyotard, Jean François 1991. *Phenomenology*, trans. Brian Beakley. Albany: State University Press of New York.

Manningham, John 1976. *The Diary of John Manningham of the Middle Temple 1602–1603*, ed. Robert Parker Sorlien. Hanover, NH: University Press of New England.

Marlowe, Christopher 1981. *Complete Works*, ed. Fredson Bowers. 2nd edn. 2 vols. Cambridge: Cambridge University Press.

Marrapodi, Michele 2007. *Italian Culture in the Drama of Shakespeare and His Contemporaries: Rewriting, Remaking, Refashioning*. Aldershot, UK: Ashgate.

Marston, John and John Webster 1604. *The Malcontent*. London: Valentine Simmes.

Massumi, Brian 2002. *Parables for the Virtual: Movement, Affect, Sensation*. Durham, NC: Duke University Press.

Mazzio, Carla and David Hillman 1997. *The Body in Parts: Fantasies of Corporeality in Early Modern Europe*. London: Routledge.

McNeill, David 2005. *Gesture and Thought*. Chicago: University of Chicago Press.

Merleau-Ponty, Maurice 1962. *Phenomenology of Perception*, trans. Colin Smith. London: Routledge.

Milton, John 1998. *Paradise Lost*. In *The Riverside Milton*, ed. Roy Flannagan. Boston: Houghton Mifflin.

Montaigne, Michel 1613. *Essays*, trans. John Florio. 2nd edn. London: Edward Blount and William Barret.

Morton, Timothy 2007. *Ecology without Nature: Rethinking Environmental Aesthetics*. Cambridge, MA: Harvard University Press.

Nashe, Thomas 1965. *Summer's Last Will and Testament*. In *Selected Writings*, ed. Stanley Wells. Cambridge, MA: Harvard University Press.

Nashe, Thomas 1972. *The Unfortunate Traveler and Other Works*, ed. J. B. Steane. London: Penguin.

Novak, Peter 2008a. ASL Shakespeare Project. www.aslshakespeare.com. Accessed May 23, 2008.

Novak, Peter 2008b. "'Where Lies Your Text?': *Twelfth Night* in American Sign Language Translation." *Shakespeare Studies* 61: 74–90.

OED 1989. *Oxford English Dictionary Online*. http://dictionary.oed.com. Accessed at various times 2005–9.

Orlin, Lena Cowen 2007. *Locating Privacy in Tudor London*. Oxford: Oxford University Press.

Works Cited

Ovid 1567. *The XV Books of P. Ovidius Naso Entitled Metamorphoses*, trans. Arthur Golding. London: William Serres.

Ovid 1959. *Fasti*, trans. James Frazer. Loeb Classical Library. Cambridge, MA: Harvard University Press.

Owen, G. E. L. 1975. "*Tithenai ta phainomena.*" In *Articles on Aristotle*, ed. Jonathan Barnes, Malcolm Schofield, and Richard Sorabji. Vol. 1. London: Duckworth.

Park, Katherine 1988a. "The Concept of Psychology." In *The Cambridge History of Renaissance Philosophy*. Gen. ed., Charles B. Schmitt. Cambridge: Cambridge University Press.

Park, Katherine 1988b. "The Organic Soul." In *The Cambridge History of Renaissance Philosophy*. Gen. ed., Charles B. Schmitt. Cambridge: Cambridge University Press.

Partridge, Eric 2001. *Shakespeare's Bawdy*. London: Routledge.

Paster, Gail Kern 2004. *Humoring the Body: Emotions and the Shakespearean Stage*. Chicago: University of Chicago Press.

Penfield, Wilder and Theodore Rasmussen 1950. *The Cerebral Cortex of Man: A Clinical Study of Localization of Function*. New York: Macmillan.

Plato 1997. *Complete Works*, ed. John M. Cooper. Indianapolis: Hackett.

Platter, Thomas 1937. *Thomas Platter's Travels in England 1599*, trans. Clare Williams. London: Jonathan Cape.

Praz, Mario 1963. *Shakespeare e l'Italia*. Florence: Le Monnier.

Quintilianus, Marcus Fabricus. 1921. *Institutio Oratoria*, trans. H. E. Butler. 4 vols. Loeb Library. London: Heinemann.

Raven, James, Helen Small, and Naomi Tadmor, eds. 1996. *The Practice and Representation of Reading in England*. Cambridge: Cambridge University Press.

Rayner, Alice 2006. *Ghosts: Death's Double and the Phenomena of Theatre*. Minneapolis: University of Minnesota Press.

Reynolds, Edward 1971. *A Treatise of the Passions and the Faculties of the Soul of Man*, ed. Margaret Lee Wiley. Gainesville, FL: Scholars' Facsimiles and Reprints.

Richardson, Caroline 2006. *Domestic Life and Domestic Tragedy in Early Modern England: The Material Life of the Household*. Manchester: Manchester University Press.

Roach, Joseph R. 1985. *The Player's Passion: Studies in the Science of Acting*. Newark: University of Delaware Press.

Sacks, Oliver 2005. "The Mind's Eye: What the Blind See." In *Empire of the Senses: The Sensual Culture Reader*, ed. David Howes. Oxford: Berg.

193

Works Cited

Sander, Nicholas 1566. *The Supper of Our Lord Set Forth According to the Truth of the Gospel and Catholic Faith.* Louvain: Johannes Foulerus.

Saussure, Ferdinand de 1959. *Course in General Linguistics*, ed. Charles Bally and Albert Sechehaye, trans. Wade Baskin. New York: Philosophical Library.

Schoenbaum, Samuel 1987. *William Shakespeare: A Compact Documentary Life.* Rev. edn. Oxford: Oxford University Press.

Schoenfeldt, Michael C. 1999. *Bodies and Selves in Early Modern England: Physiology and Inwardness in Spenser, Shakespeare, Herbert, and Milton.* Cambridge: Cambridge University Press.

Sedgwick, Eve Kosofsky 1985. *Between Men: English Literature and Male Homosocial Desire.* New York: Columbia University Press.

Serres, Michel 1995. *Angels: A Modern Myth*, trans. Francis Cowper. Paris: Flammarion.

Serres, Michel 1997. *The Troubadour of Knowledge*, trans. Sheila Faria Glaser. Ann Arbor: University of Michigan Press.

Shakespeare, William 1609. *Shake-speares Sonnets. Never before Imprinted.* London: Thomas Thorpe.

Shakespeare, William 1625–40. "How oft, when thou, my music, music play'st." MS Rawlinson Poetic 152, Bodleian Library, Oxford.

Shakespeare, William 1908. *King Lear*, ed. Howard Horace Furness. New Variorum Edition. 10th edn. Philadelphia: Lippincott.

Shakespeare, William 1913. *Gulielmi Shakespeare Carmina quae Sonnets nuncupantur Latine reddita ab Alvredo Barton*, ed. James Harrower. London: Riccardi Press.

Shakespeare, William 1968. *The First Folio of Shakespeare*, ed. Charlton Hinman. New York: Norton.

Shakespeare, William 1981. *The Tragical History of Hamlet Prince of Denmark* (1603). In *Shakespeare's Plays in Quarto*, ed. Michael J. B. Allen and Kenneth Muir. Berkeley: University of California Press.

Shakespeare, William 1997. *Shakespeare's Sonnets*, ed. Katherine Duncan-Jones. Arden Edition, series three. London: Thomas Nelson.

Shakespeare, William 2000. *Shakespeare's Sonnets*, ed. Stephen Booth. New Haven: Yale University Press.

Shakespeare, William 2005. *The Complete Works*. 2nd edn. Gen. eds., Stanley Wells and Gary Taylor. Oxford: Clarendon Press.

Shakespeare, William 2008. *King Lear*, ed. Grace Ioppolo. Norton Critical Edition. New York: Norton.

Works Cited

Skantze, P. A. 2003. *Stillness and Motion in the Seventeenth-Century Theatre*. London: Routledge.

Smith, Bruce R. 1998. "I, You, He, She, and We: On the Sexual Politics of Shakespeare's Sonnets." In *Shakespeare's Sonnets: Critical Essays*, ed. James Schiffer. New York: Garland. Rpt. London: Routledge, 2000.

Smith, Bruce R. 1999. *The Acoustic World of Early Modern England: Attending to the O-Factor*. Chicago: University of Chicago Press.

Smith, Bruce R. 2000. *Shakespeare and Masculinity*. Oxford: Oxford University Press.

Smith, Bruce R. 2009a. "How Should One Read a Shakespeare Sonnet?" *Early Modern Literary Studies* special issue 19. http://purl.org/emls/si-19/smitsonn.htm.

Smith, Bruce R. 2009b. *The Key of Green: Passion and Perception in Renaissance Culture*. Chicago: University of Chicago Press.

Smith, Bruce R. 2010. "Dot Dot or Dash: A Strange SOS from Prospero's Island." In *Shakespeare without Boundaries*, ed. Christa Jansohn, Lena Cowen Orlin, and Stanley Wells. Newark: University of Delaware Press.

Spenser, Edmund 1989. "Epithalamion." In *The Yale Edition of the Shorter Poems of Edmund Spenser*, ed. William A. Oram, Einar Bjorvand, Ronald Bond, Thomas H. Cain, Alexander Dunlop, and Richard Schell. New Haven, CT: Yale University Press.

Spivey, Michael 2007. *The Continuity of Mind*. Oxford: Oxford University Press.

Spurgeon, Caroline 1935. *Shakespeare's Imagery, and What It Tells Us*. New York: Macmillan.

States, Bert O. 1987. *Great Reckonings in Little Rooms: On the Phenomenology of Theater*. Berkeley: University of California Press.

States, Bert O. 1992. *Hamlet and the Concept of Character*. Baltimore: Johns Hopkins University Press.

Stubbes, Phillip 1877–9. *The Anatomy of Abuses in Ailgna*, ed. F. J. Furnivall. London: New Shakespeare Society.

Styan, J. L. 1967. *Shakespeare's Stagecraft*. Cambridge: Cambridge University Press.

Taylor, Charles 1992. *Sources of the Self: The Making of Modern Identity*. Cambridge, MA: Harvard University Press.

Time 1967. "Men without Women." *Time*, 13 October. www.time.com. Accessed September 17, 2008.

Veldman, Ilja M. 2001. *Profit and Pleasure: Print Books by Crispijn de Passe*, trans. Michael Hoyle. Rotterdam: Sound & Vision Publishers.

Vendler, Helen 1997. *The Art of Shakespeare's Sonnets*. Cambridge, MA: Harvard University Press.

Victoria and Albert Museum 1904. Textiles Section, acquisition file T.10475/04.

Vygotsky, Lev S. 1987. *Problems of General Psychology*. Vol. 1 in *The Collected Works*, ed. Robert W. Rieber and Aaron S. Carton, trans. Norris Minick. New York: Plenum Press.

Walker, Obadiah 1659. *Some Instructions concerning the Art of Oratory*. London: John Grismond.

Watson, Robert N. 2006. *Back to Nature: The Green and the Real in the Late Renaissance*. Philadelphia: University of Pennsylvania Press.

Wells-Cole, Anthony 1997. *Art and Decoration in Elizabethan and Jacobean England: The Influence of Continental Prints, 1558–1625*. New Haven: Yale University Press.

Wordsworth, William 1982. *The Poetical Works*, ed. Paul D. Sheats. New York: Houghton Mifflin.

Wright, Thomas 1971. *The Passions of the Mind in General*, ed. Thomas O. Sloan. Urbana: University of Illinois Press.

Picture Credits

The author and publisher gratefully acknowledge the permission granted to reproduce the copyright material in this book:

American Association for the Advancement of Science: 4.6

Bodleian Library, Oxford: 2.4

British Museum, London, Department of Prints and Drawings, © Trustees of the British Museum: 3.5, 3.7, 3.9, 3.10, 3.17, 4.11

Dana Chodzko, Abiquiu, New Mexico: 2.17, 2.18

University of Chicago Press: 2.7

Culture and Sport Glasgow (Museums), The Burrell Collection: 3.13

Gordon Davis, Los Angeles, California: frontispiece (tattoo by Calicousa for the Folger Shakespeare Library, hands of Ana Karen Campos, Los Angeles, California), 4.1, 4.5 (panel one)

Derek Johns Ltd., London: 3.8

Fine Arts Museums of San Francisco: 4.12 (Gift of Mr. Julius Landauer, 1974, 1974.13.346)

Crescenciano Garcia, Long Beach, California: 2.1, 2.8, 2.9, 2.10, 2.11

Folger Shakespeare Library, Washington, DC: 1.1, 3.1, 3.2, 4.2

Getty Images, Hulton Archive: 4.5 (panel two)

The Huntington Library, San Marino, California: 1.2, 2.12, 2.13, 2.14, 2.15, 2.16, 3.12, 4.3, 4.4, 4.9, 4.10

Director of the Husserl-Archief, Katholike Universiteit, Leuven, Belgium: 1.3

© The Metropolitan Museum of Art, New York: 3.6 (Harris Brisbane Dick Fund, 1953, 53.601.20[63])

St. Albans Museums: 3.11

V&A Images, Victoria and Albert Museum, London: 3.3, 3.4, 3.14, 3.15, 3.16

Every effort has been made to trace copyright holders and to obtain their permission for the use of copyright material. The publisher apologizes for any errors or omissions in the above list and would be grateful if notified of any corrections that should be incorporated in future reprints or editions of this book.

Index

Aeschylus   170–1

affect   *see* feeling(s)

analogue(s)   *see* analogy

analogy   11, 59, 151, 164, 167–8, 170–1, 173, 175

Aretino, Pietro   94

Aristotle   xvii, 30, 34, 48, 54, 123, 157, 175–6, 187*ref*

Armstrong, David F.   173, 187*ref*

Artaud, Antonin   xv, 169–70, 173, 187*ref*

assize courts   *see* law(s)

audition   xii, xvi, ix, 1–3, 5, 10, 13, 17, 19, 24, 28, 33–6, 43–7, 49, 50*fig*, 53, 62, 80, 82, 112, 119, 123–4, 132–3, 135, 137, 140–3, 140*n*, 141*fig*, 145–6, 155–6, 162–6, 172–3, 175, 181, 190*ref*, 195*ref*

Augustine   122

Bacon, Francis   xii–xvi, 5, 11–13, 14*fig*, 16, 20, 28–31, 64–5, 107, 136–7, 140, 160–1, 185–6

  The Advancement of Learning   xii–xiv, 5, 11–13, 14–15*fig*, 16, 64, 187*ref*

  Essays   29, 187*ref*

  The New Organon   xiii, 11, 136–7, 186, 187*ref*

  Silva Silvarum   13, 16, 30–1, 64–5, 160–1, 187*ref*

Barnes, Clive   142–3, 187*ref*

Barthes, Roland   xi*n*

Bartlet, John   109–13, 110–11*fig*

Barton, Alfred Thomas   72, 194*ref*

Beaumont, Francis   84–5, 92, 122, 146–7

  The Knight of the Burning Pestle   146–7, 187*ref*

  Salmacis and Hermaphroditus   84–5, 92, 105, 126, 187*ref*

bed   87, 92, 95, 99, 103–4, 113–19, 113*fig*, 114*fig*, 115*fig*, 116*fig*, 121–8, 147

bed hangings   *see* bed

bedroom   *see* bed

Belsey, Catherine   178, 188*ref*

Benveniste, Emile   65, 188*ref*

bestiality   xvi, 82–5, 121, 125, 128

Billingsley, Henry   177–8, 189*ref*

Bleich, David   32, 188*ref*

Blundeville, Thomas   71, 188*ref*

body   ix, xvi–xviii, 3–4, 10, 16–17, 23, 25–26, 28, 32, 34–5, 44–49, 52, 54–7, 59, 62, 64–8, 73–5, 80, 84, 86–7, 90, 92, 94–5, 97, 103, 105, 109, 117–22, 124–5, 127–9, 131, 137, 139, 143–7, 149–51, 153–7,

199

body (*Cont'd*)   161–4, 171–4, 178, 180, 183, 189*ref*, 190*ref*, 191*ref*, 192*ref*, 193*ref*, 194*ref*

book   xv–xvii, xi–xii, 3, 12–13, 14–15*fig*, 21*fig*, 26–7, 29, 31–4, 36, 38, 43–5, 47, 49, 61–2, 75, 83, 85–92, 88*fig*, 89*fig*, 90*fig*, 91*fig*, 97, 101–3, 109, 110–11*fig*, 112, 119, 123, 131, 136, 138*fig*, 176–8, 180, 182

Booth, Stephen   79–80, 194*ref*

Bosch, Hieronymus   149

bracketing   20, 22, 26–7, 28, 33, 36, 39, 50, 82, 117, 137, 150

Braille   134–5, 134*fig*, 172

brain   34–5, 41, 44, 53–4, 65, 123, 143, 150–1, 152*fig*, 153*fig*, 189*ref*, 190*ref*

Brinsley, John   70–1, 188*ref*

Bristol, Michael   178, 188*ref*

Brook, Peter   141, 174

Buchstaller, Isabelle   2–3, 188*ref*

Buckett, Rowland   131

Buckingham, Duke of   *see* Villiers, George

buggery   *see* bestiality; sodomy

Bulwer, John   61–9, 74, 156–61, 165–6, 168, 172

   Chirologia   61–8, 63*fig*, 65*fig*, 68*fig*, 156–61, 158*fig*, 161*fig*, 188*ref*

   Chironomia   61–2, 66*fig*, 66–9, 69*fig*, 156–9, 188*ref*

   Pathomyotamia   156–7, 160, 165, 168, 188*ref*

   Philocophus   157

Burbage, Richard   143–5, 161

Butler, Judith   125, 188*ref*

Callaghan, Dympna   121, 188*ref*

Callot, Jacques   167, 167*fig*

Cantlie, H. P., Mrs.   150, 151*n*, 152–3*fig*

Chapman, George   84, 92, 122

Chodzko, Dana   75–8, 76*fig*, 77*fig*, 188*ref*

Christ   *see* Jesus Christ

Cicero   30, 68*fig*, 71

cinema   *see* film

Cock, Hieronymus   97

codex   *see* book

cognition   32, 36–7, 53–54, 171, 179

cognitive science   *see* cognition

cognitive theory   *see* cognition

Coke, Edward   82–7, 102, 123, 129

   A Book of Entries   83, 189*ref*

   Institutes of the Laws of England, Part Three   82–3, 85, 189*ref*

common sense   35, 54, 62, 133

consciousness   2, 7, 20, 23–4, 34, 50–1, 51*fig*, 54, 67, 122–3, 143, 149, 151, 164, 189*ref*, 191*ref*

Cornwallis, William   29, 189*ref*

Craik, Katharine A.   32, 189*ref*

Crooke, Helkiah   48, 131, 189*ref*

Damasio, Antonio   64, 189*ref*

dance   4–6, 143, 151, 191*ref*

Daston, Lorraine   xii*n*, 13, 189*ref*

Davent, Léon   97*n*

Davies, John   84

de Passe, Crispijn   97–8, 98*fig*, 101, 196*ref*

de Passe, Simon   12

de Saussure, Ferdinand   6–7, 19, 27, 49–51, 54, 56, 62, 71, 86, 166, 170–1, 173, 194*ref*

Deane, John   43

Delaune, Étienne   97*n*

della Bella, Stephano   105, 107*fig*

Derrida, Jacques   17, 26–8, 26*n*, 30, 52–3, 55, 62, 189*ref*

   Of Grammatology   26*n*, 53, 62, 189*ref*

   Speech and Phenomena   26–8, 189*ref*

Descartes, René   6, 11, 16–20, 28,
    35, 185
  Discourse on Method   17–19
  Meditations on First Philosophy
    16–17, 19–20, 189*ref*
  Optics   17
  The Passions of the Soul of Man   6,
    189*ref*
  Principles of Philosophy   17, 189*ref*
Donne, John   xiii, 118, 129, 189*ref*
Dowland, John   41–2
Duncan-Jones, Katherine   80, 194*ref*

ecology   86, 191*ref*
Elizabeth I   70, 82–3, 121
Elizabeth Stuart, Countess Palatine   6,
    118, 129
embodiment   *see* body
emotion   *see* feeling(s)
Engels, Friedrich   xv
epochē   *see* bracketing
Erasmus, Desiderius   43, 70–1, 74
Euclid   53, 177–81, 179*n*, 189*ref*
experience   xii–xvi, 11–13, 20, 25–6,
    28–31, 33–5, 47, 51, 68, 76–7,
    86–7, 92–4, 123, 128–9, 135,
    137, 145, 149–50, 153–4, 156,
    164, 169, 179, 182, 184–6,
    189*ref*

fancy   *see* fantasy
fantasy   35, 42, 54, 62, 128
Fantuzzi, Antonio   97*n*
Featley, Daniel   74, 190*ref*
feeling(s)   xviii, 2, 6–8, 13, 16–17, 23,
    28, 34–5, 41, 48, 51, 54, 61–2,
    64–7, 80, 102–3, 109, 112, 120,
    122–3, 125, 128, 132–5, 139–40,
    143–4, 149, 152, 154–8, 160–1,
    165–6, 168–9, 174–76, 178,
    183–5, 188*ref*, 189*ref*, 192*ref*,
    193*ref*

film   4–5, 92, 141, 143, 150, 157, 161
Fineman, Joel   55
Fiorentino, Rosso   97*n*
Floyd-Wilson, Mary   35, 190*ref*
Fodor, Jerry   43, 190*ref*
Folkerth, Wes   140, 190*ref*
Ford, John   162, 190*ref*
Foucault, Michel   xi*n*
framing   *see* bracketing
Freud, Sigmund   7

Galen   34, 54, 125, 165
Galenic physiology   *see* Galen
Galison, Peter   13, 189*ref*
Galle, Philips   96–7, 96*fig*, 98*n*,
    101, 116
Garcia, Crescenciano   39, 39*fig*, 43–6,
    48–9, 56–7, 58*fig*, 58–61, 59*fig*,
    61*fig*, 71–2, 74–5, 78–9, 161
Garrick, David   140
Geng, Penelope   149
geometry   xii, 11, 18*fig*, 19–20, 26, 43,
    53, 88, 162, 177, 179–82, 184–5,
    189*ref*
gesture   xvi–xvii, 2, 4–5, 28, 45, 48–9,
    52, 55–9, 61–2, 64–8, 74–5, 80,
    99, 102, 131, 134, 144, 151,
    156–62, 166, 170, 173–6, 187*ref*,
    192*ref*
Ghisi, Giorgio   96*n*
Goldberg, Jonathan   125, 190*ref*
Golding, Arthur   103, 119, 126, 193*ref*
Greene, Robert   104, 190*ref*
Gregory, R. L.   151*n*, 190*ref*
Griffiths, Anthony   98, 190*ref*

hand   xiii, xv, xvii, 4–5, 7, 12–13, 14*fig*,
    16, 20, 22–4, 26–9, 31–4, 36,
    38–9, 39*fig*, 41–9, 53, 57–62,
    58*fig*, 59*fig*, 61*fig*, 63*fig*, 64–7,
    65*fig*, 66*fig*, 68*fig*, 69*fig*, 71, 73,
    85–9, 88*fig*, 92, 95, 101–3, 105,

hand (*Cont'd*)   112, 131–7, 134*fig*,
    138*fig*, 139, 139*fig*, 140*fig*,
    141*fig*, 142, 144–7, 150–2,
    152–3*fig*, 156–65, 158*fig*,
    161*fig*, 167–8, 172–5, 177,
    183, 185, 188*ref*
Haraway, Donna   xv
Harrington, D. O.   91*n*, 190*ref*
Hart, John   172, 190*ref*
Harvey, William   35
Harwood, Ronald   140
hearing   *see* audition
Hegel, Georg Wilhelm Friedrich   6
Heidegger, Martin   22, 31, 36
Heller-Roazen, Daniel   xvii–xviii,
    190*ref*
Henslowe, Philip   27, 142
Hobbes, Thomas   20, 179
Holland, Norman   178, 191*ref*
homunculus   150–3, 152–3*fig*
Hume, David   6
humors   29, 35, 144, 156
Hunt, Simon   70
Husserl, Edmund   11, 20–4, 26–8, 26*n*,
    31, 33, 36, 137, 185
    Ideas   11, 20–4, 26–7, 191*ref*
    Origin of Geometry   26

Iden, Rosalind   140
imagination(s)   xiii–xiv, xvi, 2,
    4, 12, 16, 23, 35, 51, 54, 60–2,
    108, 113, 118, 124–5, 128, 133,
    140, 146, 151, 157–8, 160–1,
    165, 179, 181, 185
imagines   *see* imagination(s)
indictments   *see* law(s)
Irving, Henry   140
Iser, Wolfgang   32, 191*ref*

James I   6, 82, 99, 101, 104, 117
James Joyce Memorial Liquid
    Theater   142–4

James, William   xvi, 50–3, 51*fig*, 60,
    191*ref*
Jameson, Fredric   7
Jennen, Charles   174
Jesus Christ   73, 96, 96*fig*, 122, 146,
    168–9, 169*fig*, 180
Johnson, Samuel (1688)   180, 191*ref*
Johnson, Samuel (1765)   155
Jonson, Ben   47, 72–4, 144, 146,
    172–4
    "Drink to me, only, with thine
       eyes"   47, 191*ref*
    An English Grammar   72, 172–4,
       191*ref*
    Everyman Out of His Humour
       144, 191*ref*

Kent, Steven   142
Kilian, Lucas   130*fig*, 131
kinesthesia   xvi, 35, 43, 109, 112, 129,
    134, 155–6, 173
    see also synesthesia

Lacan, Jacques   6–7, 23–6, 28, 113,
    149, 149*n*, 170, 191*ref*
language(s)   xvi–xvii, 2, 6, 23–7, 45,
    48–54, 50*n*, 56, 59, 61–2, 64–8,
    70, 133, 157, 162, 166, 170, 173,
    175–6, 187*ref*, 188*ref*, 190*ref*
    American Sign Language (ASL)
       39, 44–8, 59–61, 64, 192*ref*
    aural (spoken) English   44, 59–60, 70
    computer   173
    Early Modern English   xii, xiv,
       25–6, 58, 60, 66, 70–2, 121, 173,
       178, 192*ref*
    Flemish   71
    French   29, 50–1
    German   10, 22
    gesture as language   45
    Latin   xiii, 3, 11–12, 16, 62, 64–8,
       70–5, 80, 101, 166, 191*ref*

Modern English   10, 26, 56, 72, 77, 173, 192*ref*
    natural   61, 64, 68, 157, 188*ref*
    Old English   10
    "posited" (Bulwer)   64, 66, 68
    Russian   51
    Spanish   59
Laqueur, Thomas   125, 191*ref*
law(s)   xvi–xvii, 13, 22, 29, 82–6, 122, 151, 159, 181–2, 189*ref*
Leech, Clifford   70
legal proceedings   *see* law(s)
legal writing   *see* law(s)
Leslie, Desmond   140
Lewis, Wyndham   xv
Lily, William   70–1, 74, 191*ref*
Livy   119
Locke, John   6, 17, 179–80, 179*n*, 191*ref*
Lodge, Thomas   7–9
Luhmann, Niklas   86, 191*ref*
Luther, Martin   73, 192*ref*
Lyotard, Jean François   24, 28, 36, 192*ref*

Manners, Katherine   98–101, 100*fig*
Manningham, John   145, 192*ref*
Marlowe, Christopher   101, 117, 122
    All Ovid's Elegies   101, 192*ref*
    Hero and Leander   117, 126, 192*ref*
Marrapodi, Michele   32, 192*ref*
Marshall, William   12, 14–15*fig*, 67, 68–9*fig*
Marston, John   115, 146, 192*ref*
Marx, Karl   xv, 7, 178
Matham, Jacob   94, 95*fig*, 101, 113
McNeill, David   52–4, 52*fig*, 59, 173, 192*ref*
memor(ies)   12, 23, 30, 33, 35, 40, 46, 54–5, 62, 69, 93, 99, 128, 132, 158, 176
Meres, Francis   33, 41, 46–7, 85

Merleau-Ponty, Maurice   xvii–xviii, 22, 36, 86, 121, 192*ref*
middle voice verbs   65–6, 81, 99
Mignon, Jean   97*n*
Millot, Philippe   105, 106*fig*
Milton, John   129, 192*ref*
mirror neurons   151–2, 190*ref*
Montaigne, Michel   29–30, 149, 149*n*, 154, 192*ref*
Morrison, Fynes   104
Morton, Timothy   86, 192*ref*
motion pictures   *see* film
muscle(s)   45–6, 48, 153*fig*, 165–6, 157, 160, 172, 188*ref*

Nashe, Thomas   68, 149, 154
    Summer's Last Will and Testament   68, 192*ref*
    The Unfortunate Traveler   154, 192*ref*
Novak, Peter   44, 192*ref*

Ovid   84–5, 87, 92–5, 97, 98*fig*, 101, 103, 105, 107, 107*fig*, 109, 117–21, 126–8
    Amores   101
    Fasti   119, 193*ref*
    Metamorphoses   97, 103, 121, 126, 193*ref*

paper   16, 36, 39, 44–5, 47, 77*fig*, 87, 134*fig*, 135*fig*, 135–7, 141, 171
Park, Katherine   34, 193*ref*
passion   *see* feeling(s)
Paster, Gail Kern   35, 193*ref*
Paul (apostle)   121–2
Penfield, Wilder   150–3, 152*fig*, 153*fig*, 193*ref*
Penni, Luca   96*n*, 97*n*
perceiving   *see* perception(s)
perception(s)   4, 10, 17, 18*fig*, 22–3, 25, 28, 31, 34, 36, 62, 152
phantasmata   *see* fantasy

phenomenal   *see* phenomenon/
    phenomena
phenomenology   1, 7, 11, 22, 25–7,
    31–2, 36, 171, 180, 185–6
  historical   xvi–xvii, 26–8, 32, 34,
    36–7, 185–6
phenomenon/phenomena   xi, xi*n*,
    xii–xv, xviii, 3, 5–6, 11, 13, 16,
    31, 41, 52, 85, 87, 103, 118,
    127–8, 136, 147
Plato   85, 123, 193*ref*
Platter, Thomas   105, 108, 143, 193*ref*
pronouns   3–4, 19, 28, 38–9, 55–7,
    66–8, 70–5, 78–81
proprioception   48, 78, 147,
    149, 153
proprioceptive drift
    see proprioception
proof(s)   xiv–xv, xvii, 8, 13, 83, 85, 122,
    127–8, 130, 151 157, 178–86
proving   *see* proof(s)
putting-in-parentheses   *see* bracketing

Quintilian   48, 193*ref*
quotatives   2, 188*ref*

Raimondi, Marcantonio   94
rape   82–3, 85, 93, 118, 127
rationality   *see* reason(s)
Rayner, Alice   32, 193*ref*
readers   *see* reading
reading   xi–xviii, xi*n*, 3, 8, 12–13,
    23–6, 29, 31–6, 38–9, 41, 43,
    45–8, 79–88, 90–5, 101–3, 105,
    107, 115, 118–20, 122–4, 126,
    128–9, 131–7, 134*fig*, 139, 149,
    165, 174, 181, 182*n*, 183, 186,
    189*ref*, 191*ref*, 193*ref*
reason(s)   xiii–xiv, xviii, 12–13, 29–30,
    54, 62, 65, 82, 144, 147, 157,
    166, 171, 179
reduction   *see* bracketing

remembering   *see* memor(ies)
Roach, Joseph   44*n*, 138*fig*, 143–4,
    193*ref*
Romano, Giulio   94
Rowe, Katherine   xvii
Rowe, Nicholas   137, 139, 139*fig*
Rowley, William   12
Royden, Matthew   84

Sacks, Oliver   133, 193*ref*
Sander, Nicholas   73–4, 194*ref*
Schoenfeldt, Michael   35, 194*ref*
Scofield, Paul   141
seeing   *see* vision
sensation   *see* sense(s)
sense(s)   xv–xvii, 7, 17, 10–12, 16–17,
    22, 25–7, 30–7, 42, 47–8, 52, 54,
    62, 64, 67, 80, 84, 102–3, 105,
    108, 121, 126–7, 133, 137, 139,
    146–7, 149–51, 152*fig*, 156–7,
    164–5, 170, 172, 175–6, 179,
    182–6, 189*ref*, 190*ref*, 192*ref*,
    193*ref*
sensing   *see* sense(s)
Serres, Michel   75, 194*ref*
Shakespeare, John   xi
Shakespeare, William   xi, xiv–xviii, 1*n*,
    33, 41, 46, 81, 84, 85, 137, 140*n*,
    144, 153, 155, 157, 159, 161,
    170–1, 173, 177, 178, 181, 182,
    194*ref*
  Collected Works of William
    Shakespeare (CWWS)   xi, 120,
    139, 178
  The Historical William Shakespeare
    (THWS)   xi, 2, 41, 85, 133,
    177, 178,
  William Shakespeare as Author
    (WSA)   xi, 7, 38, 84, 182
  William Shakespeare as Cultural Icon
    (WSCI)   xi, 38, 178
  All's Well That Ends Well   xiv

Index

Antony and Cleopatra   xiv
As You Like It   1–7, 9–11, 25, 28–9, 125–6, 143, 176
Cymbeline   102
Hamlet   3, 52, 64, 145–6, 151, 161, 194*ref*
Henry IV, Part One   46, 109
Henry V   xiv
King Lear   xii, xiv, xvii, 132–5, 137–41, 139*fig*, 141*fig*, 143, 149, 151, 154–68, 170, 173–6, 183–5, 194*ref*
Love's Labour's Lost   124
Macbeth   xiv, 145, 154
Measure for Measure   xiv–xv
The Merry Wives of Windsor   69–70
A Midsummer Night's Dream   105
Othello   122, 180–1, 183
The Passionate Pilgrim   120
The Rape of Lucrece   85, 93
sonnets   xvi, 1*n*, 33–4, 38, 41, 46–7, 55–6, 79–81, 85, 101, 125, 181–2, 184, 194*ref*, 195*ref*
   number 8   182
   number 20   120, 125
   number 23   33–4
   number 26   182*n*
   number 29   39*fig*, 39–41, 43–4, 46–7, 49, 55–61, 58*fig*, 59*fig*, 61*fig*, 64, 66, 72, 75, 78–80, 158, 161
   number 110   182
   number 116   181
   number 117   181–2
   number 128   41–2, 42*fig*
The Taming of the Shrew   xiv, 147, 151
The Tempest   xiv, 12, 102–3, 145, 151
Twelfth Night   44, 83, 192*ref*
The Two Gentlemen of Verona   102

Venus and Adonis   xvi, 84–93, 88*fig*, 89*fig*, 90*fig*, 91*fig*, 99, 101, 103, 113, 116–18, 120–1, 125, 127–9, 131, 137, 182
The Winter's Tale   103, 145, 151
Shelley, Percy   6
sight(s)   *see* vision
Skantze, P. A.   157, 161, 195*ref*
smell(s)   17, 132, 134, 146
smelling   *see* smell(s)
sodomite   *see* sodomy
sodomy   4, 23, 82–3, 85, 121, 145, 190*ref*
Sophocles   170–1
sound   *see* hearing
Southampton, Earl of   *see* Wriothesley, Henry
speaking   *see* speech(es)
speech(es)   xvi, 2–5, 7–10, 13, 23–8, 31–2, 34, 42, 44, 48–54, 52*fig*, 56–60, 62, 65–7, 70, 72, 74–5, 79–80, 93–4, 99, 101–2, 112, 121–4, 132–3, 137, 143–4, 151, 154, 157, 162, 165–6, 170, 172, 174–5, 177, 184
Spenser, Edmund   117, 125, 128
   "Epithalamion"   117, 128, 195*ref*
   The Shepheardes Calender   125
Spivey, Michael   36, 53–4, 195*ref*
Spurgeon, Caroline   31–2, 195*ref*
States, Bert O.   32, 151, 195*ref*
Stokoe, William C.   173, 187*ref*
Stubbes, Phillip   4, 144–6, 151, 195*ref*
Styan, J. L.   157, 161, 172, 195*ref*
Sullivan, Garrett A.   35, 190*ref*
synesthesia   34, 36, 54
   see also kinesthesia

taste(s)   xvi, 17, 47, 101, 105, 108, 129, 134, 181, 184
tasting   *see* taste(s)
Tennant, David   161

thinking   *see* thought(s)
thought(s)   xi, xi*n*, xiii–xviii, 2, 4–6,
        11, 13, 16–17, 19–20, 21*fig*, 22,
        24, 26, 28, 33, 38, 40–2, 48–55,
        52*fig*, 57–62, 64, 67, 69–70,
        73–4, 79, 80, 83, 86, 93, 105,
        115, 119, 124, 128, 131, 142–4,
        158–9, 161, 168, 170, 172, 175,
        177, 180, 185–6, 190*ref*, 192*ref*
Titian   94, 96*n*
tongue   43, 46, 59, 62, 85, 102, 115,
        124, 143, 151–2, 152–3*fig*,
        156–7, 163–68, 170, 173
touch   xvii–xviii, 13, 16–17, 30–2, 35,
        46–8, 64, 96, 102, 108, 112, 119,
        129, 132–7, 139–43, 145–7,
        150–1, 155–7, 159–60, 162,
        164–6, 169–71, 173, 175–6, 186,
        190*ref*
trials   *see* law(s)

van Blocklandt, Anthonis   96*fig*,
        97, 97*n*
Van Dyck, Anthony   98–101, 100*fig*
van Leiden, Jan   154
Vendler, Helen   80, 196*ref*
Villiers, George, Duke of
        Buckingham   98 101, 100*fig*,
        104, 117
Virgil   87, 119, 125

virtual reality   *see* virtuality
virtuality   141, 147–49, 148*fig*, 151,
        156, 164, 170, 192*ref*
vision   ix–x, xiii–xiv, xviii, 3, 5–6, 13,
        17, 18*fig*, 20, 23, 25–9, 31, 33–6,
        39, 44, 46–7, 51–3, 56, 61–2, 67,
        75, 90–3, 90*fig*, 91*fig*, 91*n*,
        91–95, 97, 99, 101–2, 112,
        115–16, 118–24, 127, 129,
        131–7, 139, 141, 143–6, 147,
        150–2, 154–6, 160–9, 171,
        174–6, 190*ref*
Vygotsky, Lev   51–4, 56, 59–60, 62, 67,
        70, 151, 170, 196*ref*

Walker, Obediah   49, 196*ref*
Webb, Alan   141
Webster, John   115, 192*ref*
West, Will   149
Wharton, Thomas   155
Wierix, Hieronymus   168, 169*fig*
Wilcox, Elizabeth   33
Wilcox, Sherman E.   173, 187*ref*
Williams, Thomas   84
Wolfit, Donald   140–1, 141*fig*, 161
Wordsworth, William   25, 25*n*, 55,
        196*ref*
Wright, Thomas   34–5, 53, 140, 196*ref*
Wriothesley, Henry, Earl of
        Southampton   84, 182